NU HERMETICA

NU
HERMETICA

INITIATION
AND
METAPHYSICAL REALITY

OLIVER ST. JOHN

Nu Hermetica—Initiation and Metaphysical Reality

© Oliver St. John 2021

All Rights Reserved. No part of this publication may be reproduced, distributed, or transmitted in any form or by any means, including photocopying, recording, or other electronic or mechanical methods, without the prior written permission of the publisher, except in the case of brief quotations embodied in critical reviews and certain other non-commercial uses permitted by copyright law.

ISBN 978-1-7391549-8-1

Cover design and graphics © Oliver St. John 2021

Second Edition 2024

Paperback Edition 2025

ORDO ASTRI IMPRIMATUR

www.ordoastri.org

My prophet is a fool with his one, one, one...

AIWASS

CONTENTS

Concerning Metaphysics	i
Preface	iii
Aspiration and Materialism	1
Until the Stars be Numbered	6
Every Number is Infinite	10
The Masque of the Beast	14
Schiller and Self-Love	16
Thelema Beyond Self-Love	19
Cosmic Cycles	23
Metaphysical Basis of Love and Will	28
Ra Hoor Khuit: Cosmology of Thelema	31
The Nephilim and Sons of Anak	37
The Company of Heaven	42
Initiation	47
Three Grades of Love and Will	55
Three Ways of Initiation	58
The Magi	63
King Scorpion and the Royal Way	68
Recollection and Spiritual Realisation	70
Psychism and Subversion	73
The Star of the Order	77
The Kiss of Nuit	82
The Way and the Way Forward	86
The Return to the Holy City	88
Gates of the Sun	93
The Whole World	98
Enochian Keys to the Apocalypse	103
The Prophecy of Hermes	112
Oracle of Isis	120
Oracle of Shenut	121

The Holy Guardian Angel	122
Hekate Soteira: Fire of Mind	126
Powers of the Soul	131
Solar and Lunar Phases	138
Karma and Sin	142
Oracle of Sekhet	144
Unicorn of the Stars	145
Dragons and Serpents	149
The Sorrows of Isis	155
Nu and the Number 11	158
The Rejection of Religion	166
The Sons of Gods	169
The Ass of God	181
Monas Hieroglyphica	187
The Honeybee	192
The House of the Net	197
The End is with the Beginning	202

Appendices

i Schiller and Self-Love	211
ii Gold Tablet Orphic Inscription	212
iii Biblical References to the Nephilim	214
iv Notes on the Khabs Hieroglyphs	216
Bibliography	217
Other Books by Oliver St. John	—

Illustrations

Metaphysical Cross	29, 30
Ra Hoor Khuit (falcon form)	33
The Bulaq 'Stele of Revealing'	34
The *swt* parasol	39
Orion	41
The stele of Hru-het-djet	67
The Hand of Orion (five-fingered star)	77

The Khabs as Da'ath	79
Triple Precinct of the Druids	88
Precinct as Truncated Pyramid	90
Manvantara	92
Thread of Ain Soph Aur	96
The Whore of Babylon from Revelation, Durer	102
Mount Hermon	107
Hekate (wood engraving)	128
Knot of Isis	140
The Egyptian God Sokar	146
Egyptian 'flame' hieroglyph	147
Ouroboros	153
Yantra or 'womb' with *bindu*	175
IAI (Egyptian Tarot)	180
IAI (name and acrostic)	185
Seal of Jupiter	186
Monas Hieroglyphica (of John Dee)	188
Celestial Egg (of John Dee)	188
Pyramid of 66 or (1—11)	191
Chi-Rho	193
Three-dimensional cross	193
Yod	195
Neïth (name)	197
Khebit (bee)	198
Cross hieroglyph	199
Shrines hieroglyph	199
Crossed Arrows (Neïth)	200
House of the Net	201
Khabs (various spellings)	216

Concerning Metaphysics

Before metaphysics can be explained by discursive means, the terms used must be redefined. Metaphysics is meant here in the etymological sense of the word, which is to say, 'beyond the physical', and so nothing to do with the chemical state of the body or brain, or the psychological domain. Metaphysics refers to the infinite, unlimited universal doctrine that can only be known metaphysically. As it depends from a supra-human source, it can never be a branch of philosophy or some other science. Indeed, philosophy and the other modern theoretical sciences were originally derived from metaphysics and not vice versa.

Symbolism is the only way to convey metaphysical reality without direct knowledge; language itself comprises a set of symbols. Ancient languages, with all their subtlety of etymology, roots of words and phonetics, are nonetheless well equipped to symbolise metaphysics, which is solely concerned with principles that amount to pure knowledge. Such principial knowledge is most adequately set down in the Hindu Vedas and Vedanta. Such knowledge is not in any way derived from an individual author, as is the case with all Western philosophical theories. With the Vedanta, the goal is always that of pure knowledge: untransmissible, infinite and absolute reality. That is what we mean by 'metaphysics'.

This knowledge is not then in any way apprehended by reason or argument as it is derived from a supra-human source. All dialectics of the ancient sciences, including Hermeticism for example—something that in itself has been confused with profane science—form only an outward veil of that which is truly esoteric, which is inevitable. The ordinary meaning of the term 'dialectic', derived from Greek (διαλεκτικη), means 'a discussion', and that word derives from analysis, which is necessarily confined to the domain of reason. The limitation imposed by this is such that the conventional modern dictionary definition, 'enquiry into metaphysical contradictions and their solutions', is confused in its very nature and rests on total misunderstanding of the word's meaning. Such an enquiry removes the enquirer from anything metaphysical, even in the etymological sense. There can be no contradiction in metaphysical or principial reality, which is infinite and contains all possibilities within Itself without any disharmony entering therein. The dictionary will even inform us that metaphysics is concerned with 'abstraction' that has 'no basis in reality'! This owes to the fact that modern science imagines 'concrete existence' to be the only reality.

Some scholars have even attempted to reduce the meaning of metaphysics to the level of the utterly inane, until it becomes no more than 'in addition to' or 'after', as with the appendices of a book![1]

Inevitably, some Sanskrit terms must be used when expressing a metaphysical idea, for there are no words in modern languages to describe Atma or Brahma, for example, let alone the vast array of other technical terms and their different contextual uses. Sanskrit has the vocabulary of a complete science of consciousness itself; this is better understood if the universe is considered as ontological and not material; unfortunately even that completely escapes the grasp of ordinary rational comprehension and is only truly conveyed by direct knowledge. The means of acquiring such knowledge is the subject of the *Yoga-Sutras*, for example, but few are prepared to make the intense and prolonged effort that is needed.

We must then rely on symbolism and language, whatever its shortcomings, if we are to communicate anything at all. That limits our scope to a few that are prepared to work diligently towards an understanding, putting aside any preconceived notions they might hold. It is these few persons that we are addressing, for the rest are as in a deep sleep, lacking the strength or will to awaken. In fact, these sleepers are even the enemies of the knowledge that is our subject and our ultimate goal, which means they will never acquire it. As it is put very succinctly in the alchemical text *Aurora Consurgens*,

> Fools despise this glorious Science of God, and the Doctrine of the Secrets, and the Secret of the Philosophers, and the Medicine of the Physicians, because they do not know what she really is. ... And nor is this kind of wisdom suited to the ignorant because everyone who is ignorant of her is her enemy, and not without cause, as the Observer of All Things says. ... Nor will the spirit of this Wisdom enter into a coarse body, and nor can a fool ever grasp it, due to the poverty of his reasoning, because the wise have not spoken to the foolish, for he who speaks to a fool speaks to someone who is asleep.[2]

---

[1] We refer to S.M. Cohen, 'Aristotle's Metaphysics' [Stanford Encyclopaedia of Philosophy, California].
[2] Book I: III.

Preface

Sophia is our Guiding Light.

It should first be noted that the title of this book, *Nu Hermetica*, is not in any way meant to imply something 'new', as though we were borrowing the term advertisers use to delude the public. Spiritual realisation will not be conveyed directly through words or symbols but in so far as knowledge can be spiritual then there can be nothing new about it, even if what is written about it is not the copy or reproduction of some earlier text. 'Nu' is an ancient Egyptian name afforded the sky or heaven. It symbolises the principle of 'reach' or 'circumference', of which the two horizons denote the prime principle in dual manifestation. This automatically forms the triad, which is the most perfect expression of the inexpressible or the eternal. However, to call the book by the literal meaning of the title, which would approximate 'Knowledge of the Eternal Principle', would not be descriptive for such cannot be conveyed by discursive thought or dialectic. No symbol can convey this directly but it can act as a means, as for example with the symbolism of sacred rites. The same principle that we are speaking of here is conveyed with *Iunet*, the ancient Egyptian name of the *nome* centre or 'terrestrial location' of the Temple of Hathoor, north of Waset (Thebes) in Upper Egypt. Iunet refers to Hathoor, the principle's personification, as the 'sky' and also the 'pillar' or 'divine pillar'. The pillar is the axis, at the head of which is the principial centre, geometrically symbolised by the metaphysical point at the centre of a circle. The axis links heaven with earth, the primordial font with manifested life. It is the purpose of all true initiation to re-establish this link, or to put it another way, to bring about conditions so that conscious realisation of this is possible. René Guénon has put this very clearly:

> Assuredly, from the metaphysical point of view one could if need be confine oneself to the principial aspect only and as it were neglect all the rest; but the properly initiatic point of view, on the contrary, must start from conditions that are those of manifested beings here and now, and more precisely, of human individuals as such, the very conditions, that is, from which it would have them liberate themselves...[3]

---

[3] *Initiation and Spiritual Realisation*, pp. 26–27 [Sophia Perennis].

Having said something about the purpose of this book, we must begin with some observations on the terrestrial conditions we now find ourselves in. This will be occasionally referred to in some of the chapters that follow. The Way has not changed but the conditions we work under certainly have. We have arrived at a time when laws, news, facts and even history are updated, deleted, replaced and rewritten on a daily basis. The need to pass on traditional knowledge to those few that are willing and able to receive it has become very pressing.

The world has changed, and very quickly, since we completed the writing of *Babalon Unveiled* towards the end of 2018. The historic repression of the Gnosis by exoteric world religions was well noted there and was necessary in the context of the book. It must be said, though, particularly in view of recent events around the world, that religion, especially Christianity, is an easy target. Christianity has for centuries been the subject of prolonged and vigorous attacks, for political and financial reasons, apart from the sinister subversion of all spiritual knowledge that has been in progress throughout modern times. That campaign reached its apotheosis in the last few decades with the rise of information technology and its soft interface of digital media and fabricated news, all of which requires continuous updates. This was followed by a general and eventually totalitarian demand for submission to the translation of everything, including the data of individuals or 'identities', into measureable digital information and product.

The speed, blanket coverage and hypnotic power of modern communications means it is now possible to disseminate outright lies, misinformation and governmental or corporate propaganda on a scale previously undreamed of. Corporate politics are merged with social policy—and there is no real or meaningful difference between leaders of government or heads of state and industrial bosses, financial speculators, trade unionists and all the rest. The so called 'alternative' movements operate according to the same profane and anti-spiritual notions; in any case these have been totally infiltrated and subverted by the same forces that operate the general trend towards destruction of the human soul. Almost two years after the most abrupt change to world politics in history, one might say that religions have lost all power in the world today and have become uprooted from the traditions that kept them alive. We should not rejoice in this defeat in the face of what is going on now. The evil that was perpetrated in the name of religion long ago to control and dominate human lives is being done all over again, this time on a far greater and more destructive scale, in the name of 'science'.

The evil done in the past had nothing to do with religion as such, for that was merely used as an excuse. Likewise, the evil done today has nothing to do with science in any meaningful sense of that word—science has been subverted as religion was previously. In the technological age, truth is seen as relative, so that for the great majority of people there is effectively no truth, only necessity. The natural consequence of this philosophy, that by now holds the world in the grip of its claw, is that truth is destroyed. Human beings are turned into unthinking automatons, the obedient slaves of faceless and frequently masked corporations. The technological new world order matches and even surpasses the worst scenarios described from the imagination of visionaries. The success of the enforced 'lock-step' strategy of 2020, funded and directed by the wealthiest men and corporations in the world, owes to unprecedented technical means. Yet there are historical antecedents. Following publication of the fictitious *Malleus Maleficarum*, 'Hammer of the Witches', most people from the fifteenth century onward believed in 'witchcraft', and that witchcraft was responsible for spreading sickness and death. The printed book was then the latest technology. The book, the written word, was held as sacred; belief in it was beyond question—the only book most people had seen was the Bible. The printing press was soon put to use to disseminate lies and propaganda. Then as now, 'scientific evidence' was produced to support the fictional but compelling narrative. Then, as now, dissenters wisely kept silence rather than antagonise the mob.

How then is initiation even possible after the intervention of the new, financially based Surveillance Capitalism, which has the sole purpose of controlling and modifying human behaviour and even the human organism itself? We deal with some of the difficulties faced by the individual in 'Aspiration and Materialism'. Personal identity is pivotal in the technological coup d'état that has taken place across the whole of civilisation. Individuals are fed lies and misinformation. By means more or less brutal they are forced or coerced to become spiritually, psychically and emotionally nullified until they offer no resistance to accepting the new conditions, where they are no longer individuals but homogenised, predictable data streams. Even the 'intelligent' or in some ways gifted person becomes a willing slave to the machine. This can now happen very quickly, not over generations but in a matter of years or even months.

Whereas the industrial modern world was, by its very nature, a force of anti-initiation, the technological revolution will wipe out all possibilities of spiritual realisation for future generations. This, then, is where individualism, the product of the modern age, has led us in the technological age, as was accurately foretold by Guénon from an initiatic perspective.[4]

The next chapters deal with the problem of the 'universe made of numbers', for the analogy of the 'one' as principial point, as with so much else, has been reversed or inverted in its meaning in modern times until it is thought of as some sort of homogeneity. Postmodern occultists have even managed to posit the 'Self', or the Atma as it is more precisely termed in Sanskrit, as something more or less corresponding to the ego self, along with its insatiable desire for 'self-actualisation'—which is an oxymoron.

After an introduction to the primordial tradition, essential to understanding the Great Work, we continue with an examination of what initiation is and what it is not. The 1947 essay by René Guénon, *Perspectives on Initiation*, has been most helpful in this respect. The way having been prepared, we can move on to the core of *Nu Hermetica*. Our main subject, initiation and metaphysical reality, is developed and expanded from varying perspectives, including that of the Orphic mysteries. The importance of the Vedic Manvantara cycle in the present times, where we are nearing the end of a Great Age, is such that we have given much space to this, again, from different perspectives including the ancient 'Prophecy of Hermes'.

Nu Hermetica includes some directly received knowledge: Oracle of Isis, Oracle of Shenut and Oracle of Sekhet. By 'received', we refer to the technical use of the term and not the modern corruption that typically reverses and reduces this to mean commonplace opinion.[5] Although it should not be necessary to justify the inclusion of such material here, there are those who react against any such thing with scepticism if not outright hostility. This owes to a confusion, which rests on the obsession of our times with 'authorship', 'authority' and 'historicity'. Consequently, it is not uncommon to find among those who hold a doctorate in philosophy the opinion that Shankhya was a historic personage, and that he 'invented' a Hindu school of thought.

---

[4] *Crisis of the Modern World* and other works [Sophia Perennis].
[5] The Sanskrit term *shruti* supplies what is lacking in the English language to describe this. It means 'hearing' or 'heard', which pertains to the higher intuition, the direct knowledge as opposed to *smriti*, which is 'reflected' or recollected.

Shankhya is one of the six *darshanas* of the Hindu doctrines and has nothing to do whatsoever with any individual personage. It is the doctrine that retains authority, not the individual that sets it forth as a point of view. According to Guénon:[6]

> ... only those who know the integral *Veda* are qualified to compose authentic traditional scriptures, the authority of which is a participation in the authority of the primordial tradition whence it is derived and on which alone it is founded, without the individuality of the author playing the smallest part...

Although it will not be necessary to remind our regular readers of the fact, Guénon, for reasons we shall not go into fully here as it would require a lengthy digression, would say very little indeed about the Egyptian tradition, confining himself for the most part to a few hints here and there. Mainly, this was because the Egyptian tradition is (or was) a 'lost tradition' that disappeared completely, along with the Egyptian spoken language, almost two thousand years ago. However, the voices of the Egyptian *neteru* are as loud and clear today as they were in ancient history for those who are still able to hear them amidst the noise and tumult of a civilisation that has lost all heart.

Sophia be-with-us forever.

Oliver St. John,

Revised for the Second Edition Sol in ♌ Luna in ♌ 2024

---

[6] René Guénon, *Introduction to the Study of the Hindu Doctrines*, p. 193 [Sophia Perennis].

Aspiration and Materialism

Aspiration was effectively abolished many centuries ago. Those who seek initiation must relearn what aspiration means. That will not be easy for them to do. All the modern conventions that most of us have regarded as 'positive', such as individualism, personal expression, democracy, rights, even liberty, were based on rational and humanistic ideals that were also founded on an anti-traditional and (as a consequence) anti-initiatic prejudice. It is only now, perhaps, that we can see where all this has led us—which is to the very opposite of what those ideals were supposed to be about.

Tradition has it that we have to be careful what we ask the Gods for because we might get it. When Zeus appeared to Olympia, she was burnt to a cinder. Zeus had to appear; it was her wish. We may, for example, confuse aspiration through unknowing acceptance of materialism, which is the dominant force in the world today. Materialism prefers to substitute 'personal development' for spiritual aspiration, because that places the focus on the satisfaction of base needs and desires. Personal development is a subversive notion, especially when it is thought to be cognate with spiritual aspiration. If we think we can find a True Will through personal development, we are making that will-force subject to layers of subversive reasoning that fragment the truth until it becomes a mere collection of unrelated figures formed from the latent wish-desire.

Let us suppose how the ancient Egyptians might have dealt with someone in search of personal development in relation to seeking admission to a mystery temple. First of all, the person is stripped naked, splashed with holy water and fumigated with perfumes. Then they are directed to a small door that opens into a courtyard surrounded by high walls. In the centre of the courtyard is a shrine in an enclosure built of stone, with an open doorway. They are told that in the shrine they will learn how to realise all their goals and fulfil their every wish and desire. The shrine is surrounded by a circular lake. On the other side is a large, hungry crocodile.

There is no love in self-isolating fragmentation, which is the end result of skewed reason. Without love there can be no truth—for the metaphysical Monad is easily misconstrued or otherwise deliberately inverted until it becomes the Self-Alone-God, a mere projection of ignorance.

Monadism, to coin a term, is such a persuasive notion that it undoubtedly paved the way for the invasion of the East by Western materialism. By that time, the Western world was conditioned by centuries of humanism. Humanism, essentially atheist, places the self before all else, automatically excluding the possibility of anything beyond it. Aspiration is then strictly limited to personal goals.

This raises the question of the will. Psychologists have assumed that there must be an 'unconscious' will. If the person thinks and acts against that will, then neurosis comes about. That is the theory. The psychological theory of the unconscious reduces everything to a kind of instinctive level or worse—for the word 'unconcious' itself refers to a *sub-infra* level that is inferior even to reason. Furthermore, we will then assume that we (or other people) are unconscious of the will. We can take neurosis as particular to the human, but does it arise from unconsciousness of the will? Is it not more the case that from birth we learn to work out reasonable but lying strategies about everything, because that is the way of the (human) world? Through the double-thinking power of reason we learn that truth is adaptable according to circumstances, that it is 'all relative'.[7] This notion has long existed but Descartes is known for putting it forward as a 'truth' in itself. This is a convenient truth for anyone whose primary wish is to dominate the will of others through power of reasoning. Reason does not require intellect in any real sense. 'Facts' are selected and arranged to support the argument, however ignorant. Those who wish to control the minds and bodies of others do not want them to think, they want them to believe and obey.

---

[7] 'Double-think' was a term coined by George Orwell in his novel, *1984*, based on the world situation of 1948. The novel has been misunderstood and misrepresented ever since. It was not a dystopian fantasy but a disguised factual narrative based on Orwell's experience of working for the BBC propaganda department. In the novel, he called this the Ministry of Truth; the department's sole purpose was to disseminate misinformation. 'Truth' changed on a daily basis. That situation has not changed, in fact it has got worse, for it is greatly facilitated by new technologies.

There is a notion that the True Will or even True Self is ultimately a force of Chaos. As a force of Chaos, it is unknowing of any truth.[8] It is all about impulse, action, doing and is no different really from what psychologists call the 'unconscious', to which is relegated all instinctive behaviour.[9] This notion is false; it comes from a condition of mind that will know of no truth, only relativity. No one is 'unconscious' of the will-force, unless they are simply ignorant of the true state of affairs, but atheism and other humanistic absurdities have increased common ignorance, through the propaganda that now passes for 'education'.

Part of this campaign against real knowledge is to convey a sense that things are 'too complex' to really understand or to know for certain. The complexity, which owes to relativism, ultimately tends towards confusion, chaos and madness. We see this in the present world picture, where totalitarianism has been brought about in the name of 'democracy', which is by now a purely theatrical, staged proceeding. Corporate and governmental systems that implement totalitarian strategies owe to chaotic and thoughtless economics and science based on machines and data; and yet those who accept and even promote these strategies sincerely imagine they have 'freedom' and 'choice'.

Candidates for initiation are called 'aspirants'. It is necessary, and always has been, for spiritual aspirants to seek truth above all else and to seek that truth as wholly outside of and beyond the person, the self. To do that they must first rid themselves of all social and political attachments. We must define our terms. What is aspiration? A modern dictionary is no use here as the first definition will be something like 'ambition of achieving something', which is the purely materialist explanation of the word. Typically it removes all sense of any spiritual meaning that could be applied.

---

[8] Chaos is derived from the Greek for 'vast chasm, void' (καος). We use the word here in the conventional sense that Crowley intended. The conventional useage, and that used in physics, is a modern corruption, however. Originally, chaos did not mean 'random or disorganised force' and was the name of a god (Egyptian *neter*, 'principle').

[9] Crowley called this Chaos the 'Beast', and self-identified with it. However, the beast of St. John's Revelation, from where he took the term, is the anti-spiritual force in man. While Crowley was undoubtedly very clever, he succeeded in becoming no more than a dupe or puppet for that force, to the extent he became a sort of popular caricature of the 'Satanist', even in his own writings.

Ambition throws the whole matter straight back on to the self, the ordinary needs and desires of every profane person. The Latin root, *aspirare*, suits our purpose much better, for it means 'to breathe'. This may refer to both inhalation and exhalation, so we first must examine what kind of air we breathe. The 'breath of Ra' is not only the air that sustains life but is also 'light' that forms and sustains the intellect. The intellect, understood in the real sense, is far more than the reason that is common to all or most persons. By analogy, the air we breathe can therefore include language. Language shapes thought, and thought shapes our world.[10] The very language of modernity is corrupt, for it rests on the ignorant assumption that nothing exists beyond that which is evident to the senses. Such information, which is no more than hypnosis through repetition of a single idea, carries an insidious message that is wholly opposed to any spiritual truth.

Personal development is often now applied by corporations in the workplace, for the so-called 'wellbeing' of employees. Increasingly, these psychological terms are also used now as though they were something 'spiritual' in themselves. Traditional forms, such as yoga, have been subverted so they indicate only physical health and no more. It can even be harmful to the being to persist in such practices, for the latter will naturally carry a residue of what they carried when they were part of genuine initiated tradition; yet the person will have no means of protecting themselves against the negative inversion of such forces that will come about as a consequence.

The present generations were born into the darkest of dark ages. They have been hypnotised from the day they were born. Materialism is the air they breathe, food they eat, and water they drink. They indoctrinate others without even knowing it. The very thoughts they have, which they imagine to be their own, are the product of social engineering—which means that generations are now born that have no *logos*, no possibility of intellect in the real sense of what that means.[11]

---

[10] Schopenhauer proposed that thought shapes reality (*The World as Will and Representation*, 1818). It does not, but it cannot be argued that thought shapes the human mind and therefore the human world—which is not the same thing as *the* world. Of that, the real world, man can do nothing at all.
[11] The relentless social engineering agenda that has been in operation for many years has resulted in the spiritual vacuum of the modern age.

So-called education systems suppress all independence of thought and expression yet they pretend to develop the individual. These systems are perpetuated because they are a reliable form of brainwashing that is rigorously applied to every young person and continued through to so-called higher education. The sole aim is to produce obedient and efficient units of productivity. None of these systems encourage thought in any real sense.

Humanities, which were once called liberal sciences, are taught with a rational humanistic bias, hence the name given. Nothing is considered to be of value unless it is seen to be of benefit to man. Everything of value is thus seen to be that which is the product of man. Man is then isolated from everything that could teach him to reach beyond himself, to aspire. The consequence of individualism is that everyone must conform to a lowest common denominator, formed by the base needs and desires of the majority. All true individuality is thereby suppressed. This is the general and persistent trend of the world today. At the present time we now see an unprecedented movement to bring about the desocialisation and dehumanisation of the race across the entire globe.

Our world discourages contemplation, ruthlessly suppressing it. The machine-world of humans does not require that people think, only that they do as they are told, as obedient slaves. The most frequent complaint from our students is that they simply do not have enough time. And yet time is not a commodity, it is not even a thing in itself! What they really mean is that they are the slaves of a machine that controls every aspect of what they vainly think of as their 'life', from the moment they are born to the moment they die. Much that is commonly termed 'occultism' is no more than ordinary hypnotism. Such hypnotism is now the work of advertising agencies, media barons, governments and corporations. That kind of 'black magic' is by now a perfectly ordinary thing.

If aspiration is to satisfy the needs and wishes of the person, then it is a force of anti-initiation dressed up as something spiritual or holy. It is the worst kind of fraud. When ordinary life is separated from spiritual principles it falls into meaningless confusion. There is now, then, a pressing and urgent need for a Great Work and a return to more traditional knowledge and practices, at least for the few that are still capable of reaching beyond the sensorial domain.

Until the Stars be Numbered

Numbers only obtain, in any quantitative sense, below the Abyss marking the threshold of human reason. No number, whether Monad, Dyad or Trinity can truly say anything about the Intelligible—to use the Greek term for that which cannot be comprehended by ordinary reason or the physical senses, as opposed to the Sensible or corporeal world. Numbers are the fruits of mind, not Mind itself—they are the fruits of the Tree of Knowledge or Death. Numbers, seductive and fascinating, exist only within the sphere of abysmal human consciousness. They arise upon the surface of the Abyss as alluring phantoms, enticing men with visions of power and knowledge. If Pythagoras knew this, he certainly could not and did not speak of it. The rationalist development of Plato's *Timaeus* eventually led from 'the universe as made of numbers' to the notion that even the Cosmic Soul was made of numbers.

> The fact that the *Timaeus* situated in the Soul the basic mathematical and musical proportions, by means of which the Cosmos was ordered and organised, led to the theory that the Soul itself was composed of Number, or of all numbers.[12]

According to Aiwass, (Egyptian) Book of the Law, I: 48,

> *My prophet is a fool with his one, one, one; are not they the Ox, and none by the Book?*

The 'one' is easily prone to some foolish misunderstanding. However, according to René Guénon,

> This number 111 represents unity expressed in the three worlds, which is a perfectly apt way to characterise the very function of the Pole.[13]

The Pole symbolising the primordial, from which depends the axis of the universe, is expressed by the letter *aleph*, 'ox'. Aleph has the value of one but is the letter of the Tarot Fool, which is unnumbered. In Arabic, the word *sifre* means 'number' as well as 'zero' (compare with *sephira*). The ox is oft supposed to indicate the ploughing of a straight line or furrow, and is then further related to the principle of labour. In fact the swastika of *aleph* (א) symbolises the revolution about the Pole, traditionally figured by a horned beast. The ox goes around and around, as do the circumpolar stars. The beast thus typifies both primordial centre and circumference or radiance: ☉

---

[12] Sarah Iles Johnston, p. 17 *Hekate Soteira* [Scholar's Press, 1990].
[13] *Symbols of Sacred Science*, pp. 108–109 [Sophia Perennis].

While one or unity (which is the better term) may be used as an analogy for the infinite and primordial, the Monad may easily be the false crown of the Abyss—the crown worn by man as the tyrannical usurper of truth, beauty and natural law. It is wrong of those who have attempted to decipher the Book of the Law to assume from the interventions of Crowley (I: 27–28) that Nuit is 'none' and therefore equal to zero, or 'zero and two'. There is no more truth in zero than there is in one, so long as these are regarded as a numerical measure of quantity. The metaphysical confusion owes to a time when Egypt was dominated by the populist cult of Osiris. The Initiates kept very strict silence, through necessity. Outsiders who could not even read the hieroglyphs or speak the native language then made a rational superimposition upon the symbolism of knowledge.[14] Plato posited—or seemed to—that the soul was 'put together' by the Father Monad from remnants left over from creation of the Cosmic Soul.[15] The soul must then return to the Greek Pleroma (Πληρωμα), 'fullness' or divine body, to attain liberation from the perpetuation of corporeal manifestation.[16] According to René Guénon, who used 'unity' as an analogy,

> Finally, if Being is one, the Supreme Principle is 'without duality', as we shall see in what follows: Unity is indeed the first of all determinations, but it is already a determination, and, as such, it cannot properly be applied to the Supreme Principle.[17]

To make our point of view clear: unity or the Father Monad as it was termed by the Alexandrian philosophers, is seen as a one, from which all else pours forth in exactly the same way that two can be seen as the inevitable product of one, and three the product of the previous. And it is indeed true that three is the perfect expression of unity.[18] This provided us with the useful Tree of Life schema, which owes, in its Hermetic form, more to Neoplatonism than it does to the Hebrew tradition or early Christian Gnosticism—though both these streams, which were not in any way entirely separate in Alexandrian Egypt, had a rich diversity of cosmological interpretation.

---

[14] There is a difference, it should be noted, between reason and intellect.
[15] *Timaeus*. See Sarah Iles Johnston, p. 14 [*ibid*].
[16] The path of *descent* into corporeal manifestation is frequently confused with 'reincarnation', a notion that has no basis in any traditional knowledge. Reincarnation was an invention of the Theosophical movement.
[17] *Man & His Becoming according to the Vedānta*, p. 53 [Sophia Perennis].
[18] If two lines extend from the point, through its self-polarisation, the base formed from their extremeties brings forth three, which is the unity of one—and note that 'one' cannot truly be a unity if it is regarded as singular.

A qualification is necessary: what we call the 'Hermetic Qabalah' is the development of the symbol of 10 sephiroth and 22 paths. The initiatic Hebrew tradition, on the other hand, is revealed through the sacred texts and commentaries and not in the various diagrams and correspondences developed from this.[19] The Tree of Life symbol is a Decad, based on the Pythagorean Tetractys. Numbers, however, can convey nothing of reality, even if they are 'facts in themselves'. To repeat what was said earlier, using the Qabalistic model, all numbers arise from or upon the face of the Abyss, which is the threshold of human reason. Numbers do not obtain beyond that threshold, which is the reflected source of all, as in a mirror, cosmologically speaking. Numbers, including one, reflect how human rational consciousness works—they therefore tell us how we think about things, which is conceptual or virtual 'truth', but cannot tell us of any truth in the real or spiritual sense—which is a domain entirely outside of and beyond the human sphere or individuality.

When Plato wrote of the Cosmic Soul he used terms that are very much alike those used by modern science; his followers then posited a causal process such as appears to be the case when matter alone is observed, as separate from any unifying or transcendent principle. The resultant disequilibrium requires that theoretical knowledge is perpetually modified and replaced so that it leads further and further away from any truth. Over time, all this causation was degraded by rational speculation until what was left amounted to the deified self-image of the human ego as alone and separate from all else. Plato, in his *Symposium*, applied the ONE to the aesthetic ideal, when he wished to mark a difference between beauty as an undying, eternal principle, and the objectification of beauty in worldly things.

Αυτο καθ αυτο μεθ αυτου μονοιδες αιεν ον.

Itself, by itself, solely ONE everlasting, and single.

Edgar Allan Poe wrote an amusing story, 'Bon-Bon', in which the Devil appears to a metaphysician and says that when Plato was stuck for words, he told him what to say; realising afterwards that it was a truth, which played on his conscience, he inverted the meaning by turning the letter *lambda* (λ) upside down (it becomes a *gamma*). The word *aulos* (αυλος), 'flute or wind instrument' was thus changed into *augos* (αυγοσ), 'light'. The implication is that reason, instead of being an instrument for the higher intuition of intellect, becomes the light itself—and this is exactly how philosophers later understood it.

---

[19] See *Thirty-two paths of Wisdom* by the present author.

Plato can thus easily be misconstrued, something that is made all the more easily possible through translation across languages, which removes the cultural and linguistic context. Ancient Greek, Latin and Hebrew words have more than one meaning and there is much play on words in scriptural and theological texts. We can easily see here affirmed, thricefold, the lie of the one as a singular or sole cause, thus isolating the principle—'my prophet is a fool with his one, one, one'.[20] Such notions have set the course for the emergence of an atomistic, technological civilisation that has by now usurped all that is beyond the human reason to conceive. Such a civilisation, in its hubris, must reject all ancient traditions absolutely, ultimately to abandon all ideals of truth and beauty, isolate itself from the natural world and destroy itself. When science replaces religion, causation is seen as chaotic or random. The solution to the problem is then sought in the mechanical generation of numbers that has no meaning whatsoever and can only lead to confusion and madness.

The numerical concept of soul and cosmos, entirely removed from the sacred context as conveyed through scriptures and initiated knowledge, leads to nothing but delusion. It is at best a reflection of human mind and can be no more than that. It even acts as a bar to ever truly knowing God or Reality, for there is no truth in any of it. Worse still, the profane world knows only of action, which is necessarily thought of as material, taking place in the measure of time. It knows nothing and cares nothing for intellectual or spiritual activity, especially that of contemplation. Psychologists have reduced the soul to the human mind, which is but a tiny fraction of even the human possibilities of being, let alone that which reaches beyond the human state. What then is the soul really? The celestial stars serve as an analogy for that which is neither of matter nor formed by matter. The alignments between the stars or 'space-marks' are as tenuous threads of light-borne consciousness, not fixed, not still and not mobile either in the sense that we know this. We are what we *know*, not what we think or see. The soul 'becomes' through knowledge. That is why a soul can be 'lost' through ignorance, or a human not even have a soul, for example, and so in truth be damned—neither alive nor dead and destined for oblivion.[21]

---

[20] Crowley was here mocked by Aiwass for assuming the title of 'prophet'.
[21] The positive aspect of Aukert, the Egyptian name of the land where the soul sleeps in a kind of suspended animation, neither truly alive nor dead, is shown in our *Egyptian Tarot* Atu IX. The soul must fully awaken from this sleeping condition in life before it can pass through it in death.

Every Number is Infinite

The number one is deemed to be the simplest number, although that is in itself an apparent truth. Most, if not all writers on philosophy, magick and ancient mysteries use the Monadic 'one' when referring to the goal of it all, or some universal truth. As we have previously mentioned, the use of what should really be numerical analogy and no more, rests on our understanding. That falls short of the mark when our understanding reaches no further than reason. Crowley declared that the number one is 'the goal, not the means.'[22] The reverse is true: the first number is the means, not the goal, in so far as it is necessary to concentrate thought in yoga. Yoga has the literal meaning of 'union', which is the better analogy, and expresses the means and the goal in one word. Once the being is changed permanently and forever through initiation then there can be no return to previous states. Any notion of goal as end result then places a limit upon the infinite. According to the (Egyptian) Book of the Law, I: 4,

Every number is infinite, there is no difference.

Numbers are discontinuous; we must understand 'infinite' here as an analogy at best. From the point of view of the supreme principle, there can be difference but not separation. We do not know what Pythagoras experienced or what he knew; he did not write anything down and was sworn to secrecy. We only know what others wrote who came after him. The Monad is usually attributed to Pythagoras as with the philosophy of numbers, but Pythagoras was of relatively modern times.[23] It is likewise with the Orphic mysteries, derived from what was originally an oral tradition. The writings on the Orphic tradition were all set down at a time when there was only fragmentary knowledge of the initiatic rites. As a consequence we see in those writings a father intervention in which the sky-father Ouranos is seed or germ and cause of all—as if a father could exist before a mother. If we understand the 'seed' as analogy, without removing it still further from its real meaning by positing biological reproduction or 'fertility gods'—as has so often been the case with profane writings—then we may also understand that seed and sky, or the metaphysical point in the circle, are not separate things, for the principal must contain all possibilities within it.

---

[22] *777 and other Qabalistic Writings of Aleister Crowley*, p. 43.
[23] Approximately 500 BCE.

From about the time of the Neoplatonists and onward it became acceptable to posit that 'the universe is made of numbers'. Again, this is not necessarily what Plato thought or knew but is what others that followed him made of his writings. This came about at the same time that philosophy was seen as an end in itself, when in reality it can only be a preparation for initiation. It was only a matter of time before man's reason was seen as the supreme if not the only means of knowing truth.

Discussion, argument and proof are in the speculative realm, the domain of profane philosophy. The human reason is completely satisfied with the philosophy of numbers: that all things somehow originate from a suppositious 'one', because numbers begin with one. Again it is necessary to qualify this by mentioning again that while the one perfectly serves as analogy, if it is taken completely literally as is now the case with conventional science, an error of a magnitude is possible. The 'universe made of numbers' is not apparent to any living creature except man, who has presumed for thousands of years that this makes him superior to all else. The corvid appears to use trigonometry to stash away food for the winter so it can easily find it again. The bird has no need for trigonometry however; no numbers are involved, not even a piece of string. We humans understand this as trigonometry so long as we remain in the individual sphere. Likewise, a migrating bird has no need for map or compass in navigating distances that man cannot traverse without the aid of machines. The numerical universe is merely conceptual, a system of convenient reckoning. When reason is taken far enough on its own ground, as the sole explanation for truth or reality without any resort to the principles that underpinned ancient civilisations, it eventually collapses in upon itself. And that is precisely the time in history we have arrived at now.

Those of the post-modernist school within the occult have posited non-existence as perhaps superior in some way to a unity, though none of these renounced their need for a Monad.[24] Non-existence is meaningless because it can be no more than negation of the positive value, 'existence'. If a thing does not exist then it simply does not exist, it is nothing at all, never was and never shall be.

---

[24] The post-modern orientialist Kenneth Grant, for example, was devoted to the Monad as 'Sole Self Alone'. He concealed this in his works, though not in his letters and personal notebooks. See 'Thelema Beyond Self-Love', p. 19.

From the same school of speculative philosophy has come about a misunderstanding of Non-Being or Not-Self, terms that owe to the Hindu doctrines. These are negations, where no positive value can be applied, but were never meant to convey 'nothing at all', which is an absurdity. Non-Being is descriptive of an aspect of the unmanifest and is in no way a contradiction of Being, for all possibilities are contained in the unmanifest state. Some have made much out of the abstract notion that opposite ideas cancel each other out, as though that were a form of Ynanayoga.[25] This notion rests on the profane misunderstanding that duality is 'evil', and at the same time confuses duality with dualism or dualistic philosophy. All symbols have a dual nature, as does the totality of manifestation. The confusion is either made deliberately or arises from ignorance. All manifestation rests on opposite and complementary things. The polarities such as East and West, Day and Night, North and South, do not cancel each other but complement. According to the Book of the Law, I: 26,

> *And the sign shall be my ecstasy, the consciousness of the continuity of existence, the unfragmentary non-atomic fact of my universality.*

This is a clear refutation of the atomistic Monad. The 'non-atomic fact' conveyed in the original transmission places Nuit as absolute principle outside and beyond the universe of matter, as we perceive it. Crowley hated these words, and later changed the wording of the verse, substituting 'omnipresence of my body'—thus reasserting Monism under the cover of 'all' (*omni*), and at the same time limiting universal being to the natural world. Nuit or I.S.I.S. is certainly not the material universe made of numbers as philosophers and profane scientists have declared.[26] How much less then is the non-material universe made of numbers, those elusive Figures of Emptiness that arise on the face of the abysmal threshold? The modern mind is thoroughly conditioned, to such an extent that one might even call it brainwashed, to a severely restricted quantitative evaluation of all things. This is extended to include even that which is supposedly spiritual—thus the total negation of anything properly spiritual has come about in our time.[27]

---

[25] 'Knowledge yoga', more especially descriptive of Advaita Vedanta.
[26] The Book of the Law, I: 22: 'Now, therefore, I am known to ye by my name Nuit ... I am Infinite Space, and the Infinite Stars thereof...'.
[27] See Guénon, *The Reign of Quantity and the Signs of the Times* [Sophia Perennis].

We are presently at a period where most people in the world today believe in a fear-phantasm that is no more real than witchcraft was by the end of the Middle Ages. As with today, 'scientific proofs' were brought in to support an idea that was in reality based on no more than pure fiction. The reasons for producing the fantasy were from fear of heresy spreading like a 'plague' and destabilising the feudal government system.[28]

It was the ideas of mind that were really feared by the authorities. In that sense Schopenhauer was not wrong in so far as ideas shape *our* world, which then becomes a construct upon reality, an artifice.[29] The witchcraft belief, as with the present madness, was much supported by the fact that everyone believed it—or appeared to do so, for any dissent from the official line was brutally suppressed or otherwise ridiculed.[30]

Similar prohibitions and 'treatments' are described in the biblical book of Leviticus, about two thousand years before Paracelsus was born. The scriptural prohibitions, in the name of the Lord, were also set down for political reasons, which include all notions of racial purity.[31] In that respect, our world has only changed since biblical times in so far as it has become increasingly degraded. All progress is an illusion, as is money, or capital, which is now, more than at any time in history, a matter of belief in digits, not actuality. In the twenty-first century, money is no longer a physical reality and has been translated into data streams. Yet entire social, industrial and technological systems depend on the illusion.

---

[28] This is an oblique reference to the global implementation of the 'lock-step strategy' in the year 2020, based on the greatest medical fraud of all time. A fraud that nonetheless won the full cooperation of individuals, corporations and institutions and that has brought our world several steps closer to the *mahapralaya* or 'great dissolution' at the end of time. The analogy with the witchcraft scare is apt, save that the direful repercussions from the so-called 'pandemic' are much greater for the whole of humanity.
[29] Schopenhauer, *The World as Will and Representation*. See 'Lapis Philosophorum', *Babalon Unveiled*.
[30] The 'present madness' is described in the author's preface.
[31] The notion of racial purity is a perversion of the spiritual means. For example, the name 'Cathars'—a group of Gnostics forced by circumstances to become dissidents—means 'pure', and there have been other religious or initiatic groups that described themselves or their *way* as 'pure'. This refers to a state of being, a degree of initiation or the pure intellectual intuition, and should properly have nothing to do whatsoever with race, nation states or any other outward identification.

Masque of the Beast

Thelema (Θελημα) is considered by its various cults to be a term for the 'True Will'. The word means 'will', and is used in scriptural context to denote divine will, the ordinance of Theos (Θεος).[32] It is best understood as spiritual and natural governance that is beyond reason or the self-identifying ego to comprehend. Having said that, such governance was well understood by ancient civilisations as is obvious from the symbolism they used to convey it. It is only owing to the degradation of human intelligence in modern times that it is even necessary to explain that Thelema is not the personal will that imagines it has deterministic power; the will current arises from the depth or innermost from the point of view of the individuality; from the point of view of the initiate it emanates from the primordial centre and is without location as such.

Eve (or Sophia) is the revealer of Adam to himself, the manifestor of the depths, the Intelligible. The 'depths', as pointed out in the introduction to this book, includes the reach of the 'sky' or heaven, and we do not mean to indicate any degree of sub-manifestation or otherwise inferior states by that; on the contrary, it is the superior that we are alluding to. The Intelligible, a metaphysical term, is a noun, not an adjective. It is that which cannot be comprehended by the corporeal or the psychic senses, only by intellect. Here, 'intellect' is meant in the higher sense, as something entirely beyond reason. On the threshold of man's consciousness lurks a 'beast'. The beast appears on the face of the Abyss of emptiness (Da'ath). The threshold is impassable without any real change in the state of being, for the spiritual realm is beyond ego identity, which includes all perceptions of matter, time and space. The 'beast' has a dual nature, as does the idea of 'depth'. Below the Abyss, it can only be experienced in its negative or inferior aspect—and this can be very compelling to the uninitiated.[33]

Symbolism and metaphorical language is necessary to produce paths in consciousness that mark out the terrain of interior worlds and spaces. The further inward we travel (so to speak), the more it is apparent that the so-called real world of objects, things and creatures is a projection from an inner source, consciousness objectified and at the same time made subject to restriction or limitation.

---

[32] The word *thelema* occurs 64 times in the Bible. Of these, there are only two cases that *do not* refer to the will of God (Θεος).
[33] See 'Thelema Beyond Self-Love', p. 19.

Furthermore, the only justification for this 'going inward' is to escape the labyrinth of the outer world, with all its contingencies that are subject to limitation, and to gain admission to the primordial centre. This is symbolised variously in all traditions, for example, the *omphalos* or the 'Heart girt with a Serpent'. At the further reaches of the spectrum of spiritual realisation—that are only possible through initiation—objective and subjective states are fused into an unbroken continuum of consciousness, all that remains at the ending of the worlds of matter. As it is put in the (Egyptian) Book of the Law, II: 9,

> *Remember all ye that existence is pure joy; that all the sorrows are but as shadows; they pass and are done; but there is that which remains.*

All pleasure and pain is an illusion when seen from this perspective, though it is real enough on its own plane, which happens to be the most inferior of all planes of existence. Even 'matter' is a relatively modern term and we only use it here for convenience, for it has nothing to do with 'substance', for example, called *prakriti* in Sanskrit, and only exists at all as a human-made artificial construct or superimposition upon reality. The sage Sri Ramakrishna described all manifestation as the Form of the Formless.

> God has form and He is formless too. Further, He is beyond both form and formlessness. No one can limit Him.

We must be careful then to differentiate form from matter, for form is the complement of 'essence' (Sanskrit *purusha*), and matter has almost nothing to do with either. And again, while the apparitions of the psychic realm can be said to have 'form', this has nothing to do with the Intelligible.

Modernists have increasingly abstracted intellectual reason from its natural or intuitive base. Matter is now commonly understood as the only reality, while all else is relegated to dreams and imagining and is termed 'unreal'. This is a complete reversal of truth, for the notion of 'matter' is about as unreal as anything can get. The rationalist mode of thought has reached an apotheosis in industrialised societies where it has by now become quite commonplace to see the existence of the soul itself as superstition, and to seek to understand the universe through the analogy of the man-made machine or computer. Such are the legions of the damned: these are the followers of Antichrist or the anti-spiritual force in man. These reject all traditional knowledge, accepting only anti-spiritual, usually therapeutic based fake versions. They are more dead than alive, and are doomed to death as finality by their own choosing.

Schiller and Self-Love

A comparison can be made with the work of nineteenth-century German philosophers and the postmodern Left-hand path doctrine of Self-Love. Austin Osman Spare typified and set forth the doctrine in his *Zos Kia Cultus*. It is unrelentingly isolationist, consigning the practitioner and all they love to hell, as has been previously explained.[34] Kenneth Grant took Spare's idea and welded it to his personal interpretation of the Law of Thelema, which can broadly be summed up as 'sex under will', where Grant's notion of 'sex' was limited to a kind of onanistic psychic voyeurism, sometimes outright vampirism. It is as far from anything spiritual as it could possibly be and rests on a negative inversion of symbolism.[35]

Similarly, the Self-Love doctrine, if we can call it that, rests on a negative inversion of Buddhism. As a counter-initiatic doctrine it can deny the existence of ego while at the same time seeking self-affirmation in all practices. The Besz-Mass auto-hypnotic practice, for example, invites the magician to plunge endlessly through the Abyss of the isolated human mind-ego seeking pleasure and wish-desire fulfilment in all illusions of self, perceiving all other selves as phantom projections of the One Isolated Self. It is also a negative inversion of all traditional knowledge and symbolism.[36]

The isolationist Left-hand path only differs from Monotheism in that it retains no positive or spiritual traces of that. It uses the humanistic rational device of translating the Monad or primordial 'point' to a self-isolating ego immersed in its own self projections—something very curiously similar to the perverse requirements of world governments and their 'medical scientists' in very recent times. The isolationist view of ancient mysteries is well evidenced by the work of the German philosopher Friedrich Schiller (1759–1805). The Biographer A.W. Thayer mentions Beethoven's interest in an ancient Egyptian temple inscription that he probably discovered in Schiller's Essay, *Die Sendung Moses*, which Beethoven copied and kept under glass at his writing desk.

---

[34] See *Babalon Unveiled*, Lapis Philosophorum, on the Zos Kia Cultus.
[35] For a complete explanation of how Grant inverted symbolism, see Part Three of *Thirty-two paths of Wisdom* [Ordo Astri].
[36] This statement is further explained in the chapter that follows, 'Thelema Beyond Self-Love'.

An English translation of the inscription from a statue of Neïth at Sàis (which Schiller incorrectly attributes to Isis) is given in Maynard Solomon's biography of Beethoven:

> I am that which is. I am everything that is, that was, and that will be. No mortal man has lifted my veil. [37]

To this inscription has then been added: 'He is of himself alone, and it is to this aloneness that all things owe their being'. This eliminates Isis or Neïth and the principle she symbolises from the enquiry. It confuses her with the Demiurge, a Theistic concept unknown to the ancient Egyptians, something that only arose with the advent of the dualistic world religions, most particularly Judaism. However, the translation is garbled; we conclude that this is not only an incorrect understanding of the temple inscription but is also a bad translation from Coptic to German at source and then an even worse translation from German to English. Here is a more credible English translation of the full Schiller text, including the passages from the temple inscriptions.

> The epic poets recognized a single supreme cause of all things, an elementary force of nature, the essence of all living creatures, which is in essence the self same demiurgos of the Greek sages. Nothing is more sublime than the simple greatness with which they spoke of the Creator. To distinguish him in a very decisive way, they give him no name. A name, they said, is merely a need of distinction; who is alone, does not need a name, because there is no one with whom he could be confused. Under an old statue of Isis, one reads the words, 'I am that which is', and on a pyramid at Sais one found the strange ancient inscription: 'I am all that is, that was, and that will be: no mortal man hath lifted my veil.' No one was allowed to enter the Temple of Serapis who did not bear the name of IAO or I-ha-ho—a name almost identical with the Hebrew Jehovah, probably the same type [as the rabbis] wear on their chest or forehead; and no name was pronounced in Egypt with more awe than the name of IAO. The hymn that the hierophant or chief of the sanctuary sang to the initiator was the first account of the nature of the deity. 'He is unique and of himself, and to this alone all things owe their existence'.

Firstly, Schiller confuses the 'supreme cause of all things' with a merely 'elementary force of nature', whereas any such principial cause is ouside of and beyond manifestation. Hiranyagarbha, for example, in the Hindu doctrines, is not the cosmos but the principle by which cosmos manifests.

---

[37] Solomon, pp. 156–157.

He then goes on to confuse the Graeco Egyptian IAO, and the immortal principal it symbolises, with the biblical Demiurge YHVH. The Trigrammaton IAO does not appear on the inscription of Neïth in any case. Nineteenth century philosophers habitually attempted to comprehend an *unknown*, such as the ancient Egyptian Mysteries, with that which was known and familiar to them, even though what very little they knew was based on sheer ignorance.

It is pure supposition, in fact, complete fantasy, regarding the entry to the temple and an initiatic rite. It would be as though a theology put together around 500 BCE could somehow precede knowledge at least 5000 years older. The translation is misconstrued for it would have *to this alone all things owe their existence* as 'one sole Creator, alone and inviolate'. The superimposition upon the sacred text not only confuses the supreme Atma with the Demiurge but also places that in an even more degraded form, as an isolated or monadic intelligence, 'phallic' in the sense that Freud would later expound. Crowley, Jung, Spare, Grant and all other modernists and post-modernists since have repeated the error—an error which we must conclude is in the way of a deliberate counterfeit.

Thelema Beyond Self-Love

The philosophical 'one' is best conceived of as the principle of union, not a singular 'existence'. This is alluded to throughout the text of the (Egyptian) Book of the Law. The doctrine is established at the outset, in the second verse of chapter one.

Every number is infinite, there is no difference.

To repeat what was said earlier, numbers are discontinuous; therefore we must understand 'infinite' as an analogy at best.[38] From the point of view of the supreme principle, there can be difference but not separation. The notion of a unitary intelligence within existence is a metaphysical absurdity, for such could not exist, having no higher principle. In modern philosophy, perpetuation of the singular myth can be traced to the works of early nineteenth century humanists such as Schiller, Schrödinger and Vaihinger.[39] These were much admired by the English occult writer, Kenneth Grant. In a letter, he argued that all other persons are phantasmal projections, so any consideration of them is merely a waste of energy that could otherwise be more properly used for self-pleasure:

> Your letters show an over concern for 'others'. As Schrödinger has pointed out, the Self is single, there is no plurality in consciousness. ... It is the false identification with the persona, the unreal, that prevents knowledge of the Real. Abide in Self-Love—that is all.[40]

This borrows from Advaita but with a fillip the meaning is inverted. Grant plundered diverse sources, always remoulding them to support his fallacious doctrine of Self-Love and wish-desire fulfilment. There is no real difference between Isolate Intelligence and the cliché, 'you create your own reality', and so accuracy is irrelevant. Grant, who only imagined what he knew about Egypt, declared,

> That the Egyptians practiced a form of sorcery involving a process similar to that of Spare's formula of atavistic resurgence is suggested by the fact that the hieroglyphics are usually in zoömorphic form.[41]

---

[38] At worst, the line merely reflects some of the popular notions of the time, that were doubtless circulating in the mind of Crowley.
[39] See the preceeding chapter, 'Schiller and Self-Love'.
[40] Kenneth Grant to Randall K. Holmes, 13th September 1991, reproduced in From 'Zos-Kia to the As-If', Michael Staley, p. 36 *Servants of the Star and the Snake* [Starfire Publishing, 2018].
[41] Kenneth Grant, introduction to *The Book of Pleasure*, Austin Osman Spare [Montreal: 93 Publishing, 1975].

The foregoing is a kind of wilful subversion, reducing all to the most inferior meaning possible. Furthermore, it rests on a hierarchic idea of nature, where man is supreme and all other creatures subservient to his interests. On the basis of this underlying prejudice, creature intelligences other than the human can only represent an atavism—a return to an ancient and more 'primitive' type, a notion that rests on evolutionist theory. On the contrary, when the Egyptian gods are depicted in animal forms it is to symbolise divine principles (*neteru*) observable in nature.[42] Pure consciousness embraces plurality so long as we can understood this as the Advaitans did: in the Supreme Principle there is difference but not separation. Beyond the abysmal threshold of human reason, infinity does not include separation but neither does it admit any unitary intelligence. All or most creatures on earth enjoy this continuity of consciousness and life. Only the human is excluded from it by ignorance of the principle.

German philosophers such as Schiller sought to interpret ancient Egyptian temple inscriptions in terms of monotheism, even though the Egyptians were neither monotheists nor polytheists. There is no unitary, 'alone consciousness', for such a singularity has nothing to be conscious of. Atomism began with the Greek Stoics, who knew of nothing beyond the infantile ego, and which they confused with the primordial. According to the Book of the Law, I: 28,

None, breathed the light, faint and faery, of the stars, and two.

Beyond the rational threshold, consciousness is 'none and two'—and in fact at this level, numbers as quantity no longer exist at all, so we must understand this as metaphysical analogy. There are indeed infinite possibilities at the supra-human level, which Grant simply ignored or denied the existence of, seeking instead to find such possibilities in infra or sub-human levels. Grant frequently referred to Da'ath as the 'height', which is only relatively true from the point of view of human rationality; he went even further to suggest that there can be 'nothing beyond Da'ath'. He would quite often create double and triple confusions to bring about an inversion of the spiritual—which is truly diabolical. That is a very good way to attract post-modernist followers, already allured by sex, power and glamour, to influence them all the more towards the destruction of any possibilities of real initiation, finally trapping them in the lowest and most infernal regions from which there is no escape.

---

[42] 'God', as that is by now conventionally understood, was as foreign to the ancient Egyptians as our idea of 'religion'.

A particular interpretation of the Qabalistic doctrine of the Qliphoth is central to Grant's thesis. His concept of the Qliphoth links the 'evil shells of the dead' to praeterhuman or extraterrestrial intelligences. He thus reverses the doctrine, confusing the supra-human and supra-mundane levels with the most inferior levels of manifestation, accessible to completely ordinary psychism.

In Grant's works, various names are 'creatively' given for such intelligences—if 'intelligence' is even an appropriate term to use in the present context. One of these is the Ancient Ones, which happens to be the name used by the Egyptians when referring to an elder race that preceded that of the human. According to Grant, the Edomites or Ancient Ones may be worked with, or approached, through the demon masks or 'dead shells' known as Qliphoth. Traditionally, the Edomites were the Lords of Chaos, Unbalanced Forces or Qliphoth that arose as the Beast or Red Dragon after the fall of Adam and Eve. The fall, as according to Qabalistic lore, cut off Malkuth the Kingdom from the Tree of Life. Such is the knowledge of the 'fall' of man, and while the symbolism is very apt, and indeed precise, a confusion was made through identifying the nomadic inhabitants of the land now known as Palestine with the Qliphoth—an identification that must have had some political intentions at the time the allegory found its way into the Hebrew Bible. In any case, in the Egyptian tradition the Ancient Ones have no negative implication at all and on the contrary they are seen as more or less equal to or cognate with the Elohim, or their descendants in the 'terrestrial Eden' or earthly paradise long ages before any Bible was written.

It is not possible to obtain contact with the Ancient Ones by adopting the mask of the same demons that are the agencies behind the profane governors of our world. It is to these adversaries of initiation that the Qliphoth or Unbalanced Forces truly belong, as projections of emptiness from the outer darkness—a darkness not to be confused with any state of unmanifestation in the primordial sense. Furthermore, the Ancient Ones will not be evoked, called forth or summoned by any individual person or by any means whatsoever. According to I: 15 of the Book of the Law,

> *Now ye shall know that the chosen priest and apostle of infinite space is the prince-priest the Beast; and in his woman called the Scarlet Woman is all power given.*

We must first understand that the 'beast' is a dual symbol. In the positive sense it refers to Christ (as lion) or an avatar that has acquired complete transcendence of the human state. In the wholly negative sense it refers to the Antichrist as the anti-spiritual force that arises in man at the end of time. In the above context it does not refer to the Antichrist or his ministers and certainly not to Crowley, who wrote down the oracle, or anyone that would come after him. Attention is the only true power that exists; all else is illusionary. The black magician or scientist has all power of attention fixed upon the victim. There is no power available to be placed elsewhere. Such a criminal cannot possibly give all power to the Scarlet Woman or soul of the world, for he is engaged in a brutal and senseless act, designed to steal this power—which of course is an impossibility in any case once we understand the nature of power. In attempting to do so, he destroys the body, the earth, and loses his soul or life-intelligence forever.

Much of Grant's vision rests on a way of return to source via an exploration of the demon worlds of the Qliphoth, which is in fact a proposal that is beyond the absurd. Both Grant and Crowley offered magical means to open the gates of the underworld but could provide no means to open the *other gate* that leads out of it, to eternity.

Cosmic Cycles

The Manvantara is not a matter that is subject to personal opinion. It is traditional knowledge, very accurately recorded in Sanskrit, and which also happens to exist in all other ancient traditions around the world. The differing ideas concerning the Cosmic Cycles owe to the fact that few persons can read Sanskrit, let alone understand its subtleties and metaphysics. One must also understand the use of analogy and symbol. Furthermore, the Cosmic Cycles are complex to explain in the analogous mode of time and numbers that we require with our limited understanding. In reality, the measurement of time in 'years', for example, is no more than a peripheral matter compared to the import of the whole.[43] We have to use approximation and analogy once we start translating very ancient times into years, because time is not a quantifiable thing in reality, it is qualitative. Only in the present Age of Kali Yuga, at the very end of the Manvantara, is time understood to be a measurable quantity, as is everything else.

With that caveat, we can nonetheless make an essential summary of the cycles in so far as they concern terrestrial humanity at the present time. A complete world is formed from two septenaries of Manvantara cycles, named after Manu in the Hindu tradition, whose name means 'the Legislator'—a title that refers to divine ordinance.[44] The basis of the system in all ancient traditions is very naturally the precession of the equinoxes. Half of a complete precessional cycle (a round of the Zodiac or 360 degrees) is equal to that which is called a 'Great Year' in many traditions. Each of the Manvantaras covers five complete Great Years, approximating 64,000 years in total in terrestrial time.[45] The Manvantara is further divided into four Yugas. The Yugas are not equal divisions in time, as each is necessarily further from the primordial centre from whence the manifestation was issued. So the present Kali Yuga is much shorter in time than the one before, and the one before that was much longer again. The first Yuga far exceeds those that follow. The present Kali Yuga, the last part of the Manvantara, is merely 6,000 years, a relatively very short time.

---

[43] René Guénon has explained the Manvantaras in such detail as is more than sufficient for the modern mind to comprehend. See *Traditional Forms and Cosmic Cycles* [Sophia Perennis].
[44] See Guénon, *The King of the World* [Sophia Perennis].
[45] We have rounded up or down the figures to a nearest whole number.

Yugas in *descending* order

Age of Gold	The entire duration of a Manvantara Cycle is approximately equal to 64,000 years or five Great Years. The last Yuga (Age of Iron) is much shorter than the first, for there is naturally a spatial relationship between cycles.
Age of Silver	
Age of Bronze	
Age of Iron	

The present Age of the Kali Yuga commenced approximately 6,000 years ago, which is when recorded or documented history begins as understood by profane science. The Kali Yuga is an age of great obscurity or darkness in which all previous knowledge is forgotten, including 'history'. Its beginning approximates the time of the first Egyptian pharaoh, thought to be named King Narmer (Heru-het-djet).[46] The Egyptian tradition, which carried the knowledge of the primordial tradition from previous Yugas, began long before that. The ancient Egyptians called the beginning of this Great Year the 'First Time'. The First Time was about 12,000 years ago, at the time of the last great Ice Age and the precessional Age of the Lion.

The Hebrew tradition happens to record its beginning from this time also, as after the great deluge that sank Atlantis—and that is narrated in the Bible in the tale of Noah's Ark. That great flood is not to be confused though with a much earlier deluge that took place at the end of the last Manvantara and beginning of the present one. The Hindu doctrine tells of how Vishnu took the form of a fish and told Manu that he would carry all the seeds of the last Manvantara over to form the new one. In the Bible, this is symbolised in the tale of Jonah and the Whale, and in the Egyptian texts—where the Cosmic Cycles are also supremely important—the fish is called Abtu. It should further be noted that the 'deluge' may be understood both literally and as analogy—in the ancient tradition there is no conflict between symbol and analogy, and literal fact.

---

[46] The first Egyptian pharaoh (though not by any means the first ruler), Known as King Narmer, is sometimes thought to be named Menes, which is remarkably similar to the names of both the God Mentu (Ra-Set) and Manu of the Hindu tradition. In fact, this is perfectly natural, for the variants of the name 'Menes' all mean, across quite different languages, 'regulator' or 'legislator', which is a very apt description of the 'King of the World' or his representative. See Guénon, *The King of the World* [ibid].

It is quite obvious from all these considerations that we are now at the extreme end of the Age of Kali Yuga, and at the end of the entire Manvantara cycle. It is necessary to dispel some illusions that are being perpetrated by those who would subvert all knowledge. Any notions of a general spiritual illumination or of a great awakening or a Golden Age on earth, at least without there being total dissolution and possibly cataclysm first, are completely absurd. Such notions are based either on wishful thinking or wilful subversion and confusion—and there is a great deal of that in the world now, as typified by the degradation at the end of a whole cycle. We are nearing the end of the darkest of the dark ages, before the great dissolution.

Our Great Work is not to 'save the world', for it is much too late for that. It is to prepare for the next Manvantara cycle. That will not take place in our world, for that world is at an end. The dissolution is not a figurative term; it is quite literal; our world will actually or quite literally cease to exist.[47] We know this is a difficult thing for people to grasp, and we don't expect many will, but it is the truth. It has nothing to do with opinion, speculation, imagination, psychic premonition or even something of an oracular order. It is not even particularly in the way of 'revelation'. All traditions from ancient time agree on it and the fact that knowledge has been forgotten or is no longer understood makes no difference whatsoever to the reality.

A Summary of the present Manvantara cycle

The beginning of the present Manvantara was about 64,000 years ago. Hyperboreans formed the primordial centre at the North Pole, of which it is said, 'the sun never sets'.[48] About half way through the whole Manvantara, a secondary centre was formed in Atlantis, the Western centre. This endured for about 12,000 years (or a Great Year equal to half of a precessional age) and vanished in the last great cataclysm about 12,000 years ago. The knowledge was nonetheless taken out from West to East. This corresponds with the change of ritual orientation from North, to West and then East, as it now generally is—although there has naturally been some overlap in different traditions. The 'Left-hand path' of the Tantras actually refers to the North, for if you are facing East as is customary with most orthodoxy, then the North is on your left side.

---

[47] We should note a difference between 'our world' and *the* world.
[48] The axis of the earth was not always tilted. This corresponds to the 'fall', as recounted in most traditional knowledge in one form or another.

From about 12,000 years ago, with the retreat of the glaciers and after the great deluge, a new centre combining the current from the North, Hyperborea, and the West, Atlantis, was formed in Egypt. This time, immediately after the flood, is what the ancient Egyptians called the 'First Time', and was the precessional Age of the Lion. From Egypt and this combined current it was possible for all the traditional forms we now know to go out into the world in their various cultural 'disguises'.

About 6,000 years ago came the onset of the Age of Kali Yuga. It was necessary for there to be pharaohs that are the type of the Universal Man, the ideal of Tiphereth—which is of course secondary to the primordial centre as Kether or the Trinity. Previously, the path of initiation was not even needed. Places for rites moved from the top of mountains or other high places to caves or other interior spaces as protection was needed from hostile psychic forces.

Throughout the Kali Yuga, the kings gradually move further and further away from the sacerdotal or priestly authority, until in the present time, near the end, even the power of the kings is usurped by merchants and middle classes. All temporal power owes to pure materialism, which reigns unchallenged. When materiality becomes very nearly total, the great dissolution will automatically occur and in an instant, the manifestation will be withdrawn and our world will end. A new world is simultaneously formed from the primordial centre at the dawn of the new Manvantara.

Egyptian Gods of the Great Year

The present Great year of 12,000 years began with the precessional Age of the Lion. Sekhet (or Sekhmet) is the Shakti of the whole Great Year, in which Egypt was, for the greater part, the primordial centre of initiation and knowledge. The previous Great Year commenced with the Age of Aquarius and thus Set (or Typhon) was the principal God of that Age, in which Atlantis was the primordial centre. The next Manvantara cycle, after the dissolution and end of this present one, will thus commence at the dawning of the precessional Age of Aquarius. Or at least, that is the case from the point of view relative to the end of the present Manvantara, which is now at the 'obscure' phase between the Ages of Pisces and Aquarius. Aquarius is already dominating, though in its most inferior and degraded form, which reflects in some ways the conditions existing immediately before the destruction of Atlantis at the beginning of the Great Year. The Uranian principle of Aquarius will bring about the final dissolution of the entire Manvantara, while the Saturnian principle will establish the new Manvantara from the primordial centre.

The Sphinx, Time and Alchemy

In *The Law of Thelema*, a work that was originally put together more than twenty years ago now, we produced an analogous time-line based on the Egyptian Twelve Hours of Night, in which the Sphinx as symbol of the four Yugas of the Manvantara took primary place. This still works well but we would like to make some clarifications.[49] The analogous 'history', based mainly on the Old and New Testament biblical narratives, stops at the 6th hour, which is precisely where we are in time now—the dawn of the Age of Aquarius, exactly opposite the beginning of the Great Year at the Age of the Lion. In the book, we wrote concerning the 6th hour,

> There is much danger at this point, for there is a strong pull towards going back the way one came. This atavistic tendency naturally arises from the fear of death and the unknown experienced by individual consciousness that is facing what seems to be a spiritual crisis.

Twenty years on, with a great acceleration taking place across the globe towards dissolution, and where materialism has passed its apotheosis, there is a great deal more we could add to that. However, it must suffice to say here that 'what seems to be a spiritual crisis' was and is a very real one, but it is too late now to stop the tide going backward in the wrong direction. It is never possible to return to previous states other than by undergoing atrophy and disintegration of the being. Although mankind by now almost unanimously believes in such delusionary notions as evolution, progress and scientism, all of which is in total contradiction to traditional and true or initiatic knowledge, the tendency is nonetheless downward and backwards. That tendency is taking our world and humanity towards the inferior and even the sub-human—and there is by now very little space left for time to fill, both literally and by way of analogy. Therefore it must be understood that our *Life-Cycle of Consciousness* map effectively stops in time during the 6th hour. Everything coming after that can only be understood in terms of the metaphysical descent and re-ascent of immortalised souls, and the complete destruction of all profane governance. And this is exactly as it is described across all initiated traditions.[50]

---

[49] This book has by now been re-written. See *The Law of Thelema—Hidden Alchemy*.
[50] The Gospel of St. John and Revelation are initiatic, not exoteric texts.

Metaphysical Basis of Love and Will

One of the key principles of traditional alchemy is that of complementaries, or of oppositions, depending on the point of view. All dual manifestation appears through apparent pairs of oppositions from the corporeal perspective, but from the initiated perspective all dualities are complementary as they arise from a third principle. The dualities appear, for example, as heat and coolness, day and night, Sun and Moon and so forth. The Quaternary of Air, Fire, Water and Earth consists of active elements, Air and Fire, and passive elements, Water and Earth. This continues through the Zodiac, where each sign is active or passive as well as forming part of a Quaternary and Ternary.[51] Wherever there is a duality there must always be a third principle from which the two have come forth, or otherwise (depending on the point of view), as a reconciler that unites the duality, in the way of a priest presiding over a wedding.

In the rituals of the Golden Dawn there was a dual mudra called 'Opening and Closing the Veil'. The veil refers to Paroketh, the veil or partition symbolising the liminal threshold dividing the outer world of profane men from the interior world of those that have realised the principle or spirit, that have seen behind that veil.[52] This veil also marks the departure from the astral world of images and phantoms, the grosser levels of the subtle planes, and entry to the higher reaches of the individual core or integrality, the realm of pure symbolism—which is in itself only a fractional part of the whole being, and only exists relatively in relation to the true Self. The first gesture consisted of stepping forward with one foot while simultaneously pushing out and away the hands, as though opening a pair of curtains. The second gesture reversed this, so the hands were brought back and closed together as in a gesture of prayer, while returning the step previously taken. This dual mudra reflects the alchemical principle of Solve et Coagula, to 'dissolve and put back together (in a different way)'.

---

[51] Aries, for example, is 'active' as a fire sign. It is also part of the triad of fire signs, Aries, Leo and Sagittarus and of the four cardinal signs, Aries, Cancer, Libra and Capricorn.

[52] The Veil of Paroketh should not be confused with the first Veil of Material Illusion, which exists on a far lower or more outer level. The second veil separates the psychic order from the intellectual order.

The mudra symbolises separation (or division) and union—which is the principle of 'drawing together', and the power of love as active and unitive force. The most outer level of understanding this is as analysis and synthesis, which, while very rudimentary is nonetheless essential to discrimination, which is the 'first virtue on the path'. The Egyptian Sphinx in many ways embodies all of this and very subtly.

There are other rituals where there is a trinity of Gods forming a triangle (within ritual circle) of Fire, Water and Air.[53] Horus and Isis symbolise Will and Love, while Tahuti is the Logos or Word and the third principle, or mediator. His 'voice' or silent vibration issues from behind the veil between the two pillars of dual manifestation placed in the North of the Temple. Tahuti's station also represents the path of the middle way, the Reconciler or intermediary. The extension of the polar North into a vertical axis typifies the ascent and descent of an avatar, or any form of Saviour.

Divine Will (Θεος) or ordinance, or even *dharma* as in the Hindu doctrines, has nothing to do with self-determinism or the will as understood in any psychological sense. The divine Will-pillar of the primordial extends from the height to the depth. The 'pillar' is thus the channel for all initiatic transmission.

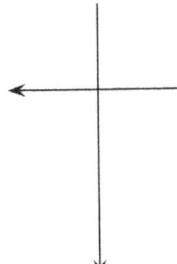

The pillar can be seen as the vertical arm of a cross. Love forms the horizontal bar of the cross, which is also the tradition in time. Love must be 'under will' because in manifestation the Will is that of divine ordinance. These two principles, Will and Love, may very usefully be compared with the outwardly active radiance of alchemical Sulphur working on the inwardly passive and reflective 'universal agent' of Mercury. This action manifests 'double Mercury'.

It must first be understood that Sulphur radiates or transmits from within, from the centre. This marks the important distinction between the divine Will and ordinance, the 'True Will', and human, personal or psychological will.

---

[53] The Golden Dawn corresponded the three 'primary' elements of Air, Fire and Water with alchemical Mercury, Sulphur and Salt. They extended this even further by equating both with Sattwas, Rajas and Tamas of Hinduism. While correspondence may be found between trinities, they are not exactly the same. If they are treated the same then confusion arises—or at least severe limitation—that prevents the person from gaining any real insight.

All matters of human will are contingent and can only effect modifications to the individuality of a being that are strictly limited and therefore self-limiting—in fact, the restriction or limitation is by definition. The action of alchemical Sulphur working upon Mercury may be symbolised by the Caduceus, the Hermetic Light, which has a dual operation as shown by the two serpents on either side of the winged sceptre. It is to form a magical 'environment', or otherwise, a specific seal made in the Astral Light. A further stage of the work is then for the combined Mercury to work on Salt so as to form a 'new body' from the corruptible body.[54]

Time and space are inseparable, and what we tend to think of as 'time' is an approximation, an attempt to measure the immeasurable. The Mercury, which gives rise to space and form when Sulphur acts upon it, is the principle of Love. Thus Nuit, in her appearance, is the circumference of the sum total of all possibilities. The horizontal bar of the cross in time is thus, in reality, circular. The ancient Egyptians did not think in linear or geometric terms as we do, and so all these ideas are perfectly symbolised in the *ankh* of life.

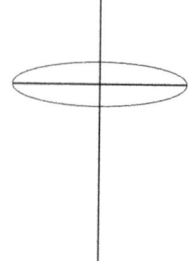

Across time, the circle is ever widening, moving further from the principal, which results in division and separation. Thus as we get to the end of a great age of time or Manvantara there is an increase of division, culminating at the last as isolationism, arising from belief in a separate and 'self-contained' self. The total rejection of the principle, which is inseparable from that of love, brings about the final dissolution—a world separated from Will and Love cannot exist in reality or in nature. Initiation, however, activates the principle latent in the theurgist so that return to the primordial state can be fully realised even while the theurgist exists in their corporeal state of being. It is only by initiation, which requires theoretical knowledge, concentration of the mind and meditation as a support, that the True Self in all of its infinite expressions or modalities may be known.

---

[54] The initial phase of the work is for Sulphur to act upon Salt, the body, to render it capable of supporting the universal agent or Mercury.

Ra Hoor Khuit: Cosmology of Thelema

Some have made the assumption, based on what is written in the (Egyptian) Book of the Law, that Ra Hoor Khuit presides over a 'New Aeon'. They have even gone so far as to suppose that such a 'new era' commenced with the spring equinox of 1904, when the book was received. While we may use a system of dating that begins with the winter solstice that occurred prior to that equinox—in conformity with the primordial tradition, which is solstitial—that does not mean that we accept the notion of any such New Aeon in time. The Greek word *aeon* is usually taken to mean 'eternity' in the Hermetic and other sacred texts. It does not denote a specific period of terrestrial time; thus any notion of a 'New Aeon' is a contradiction in itself as an aeon is indefinite and cyclical in nature. In the Gnostic cosmology of Valentinus, for example, the Aeons have nothing to do with time at all, but are metaphysical worlds that are in some ways comparable to the sephiroth and paths of the Tree of Life.

We have explained the universal cosmological basis in terms of the Cosmic Cycles, which do not in any way include some invented new era commencing as lately as a century or more ago, a period of human history that has only witnessed a further materialisation and degradation of something that has already been in progress for 6000 years.[55] As declared in the Book of the Law, I: 49,

> *Abrogate are all rituals, all ordeals, all words and signs. Ra-Hoor-Khuit hath taken his seat in the East at the Equinox of the Gods...*

The cosmic and terrestrial environment undergoes radical changes more frequently than the span of the Yugas; there is the precession of the equinoxes, for example, by which at the vernal equinox the Sun appears to enter a different zodiacal portion of the sky a little over every 2000 years.[56] As we are now on the cusp of the precessional Age of Pisces and that of Aquarius, it might seem as though it is reasonable to assume that Ra Hoor Khuit, as Lord of the Equinox, marks the onset of a new era. But this is pure speculation, based on a superficial reading of the Book of the Law and that owes to a certain portentous mood that has arisen at the turn of every century.

---

[55] See 'Cosmic Cycles'.
[56] That is to say, one sign or 30 degrees from 360, which is the whole round of the ecliptic. A complete precessional cycle is approximately 26,000 years.

We are in fact at the very end of a Great Year and of an entire Manvantara. Ra Hoor Khuit, as we shall see when we take a deeper look at what is in the Book of the Law, is the Lord or 'Legislator' not only of the current precessional epoch but also of a Great Year—that is to say, an era that translates into about 12,000 years of terrestrial time. So those who have wanted to proclaim a 'new era for humanity' or some such, were looking at this from such a narrow perspective that one might easily say it was a personal view, which means it was absolutely impossible for them to obtain any comprehension of what was really being declared in the Book of the Law.

It will first be necessary to take a closer look at the context of that verse numbered I: 49. Unfortunately, it is impossible to separate the Book of the Law entirely from the man that wrote it down, as many sections are dealing with questions from him, whether they were put directly or were simply 'on his mind'. For that reason alone it is a very bad mistake to treat the Book of the Law as though it were a 'holy book', and in any case, such a scripture is only a requirement of exoteric religious organisations. Crowley was well trained and deeply immersed in the syncretic magical rituals of the Golden Dawn.[57] In that organisation, the Hierophant assumed the mask of Osiris at the twice-yearly rite of the equinox. There is not the space here to go into all the confusions of the historical Golden Dawn, so let it suffice to say that the transmission, activated by a praeterhuman intelligence named Aiwass, had its basis in ancient Egyptian Thebes (Waset) at a time roughly corresponding to that of the prophet Ezekiel.[58] The traditional and initiatic knowledge that is contained in the book is of course much older than that. The initiated tradition in question was particular to a form of Set called Mentu at Thebes, and identified with Horakhty or Ra Hoor Khuit, as he is called in the Book of the Law. Nonetheless, the cult of divine Osiris, by that relatively late time in Egyptian history, was mandatory so far as any exoteric practice went; the older initiatic cults continued, often quite invisibly to the common person though the kings and priests knew of them.[59] There was then already a separation between the esoteric and the exoteric, though that separation would not become total for long ages to come.

---

[57] We are concerned here with the cosmological basis of Thelema and not the personal antics of Crowley, so will not waste time on the circumstances around the writing down of the book.
[58] Around 600 BC. This is very approximate.
[59] King Seti I, for example, was initiated into the cult of Set as his royal name suggests, but he always strictly maintained his Osirian exotericism.

The popular cult of Osiris was anathema to the priesthood of Set, which was not in any way concerned with the degraded rites of mummification and exoteric moral teaching as deemed necessary for the preservation of the social order. Thus, 'Ra Hoor Khuit hath taken his seat in the East at the Equinox of the Gods' is a correction, of which there are many made in the book delivered by Aiwass.

Now we must understand what is meant by 'Ra Hoor Khuit'. It is a complex matter, for he has many names, and all of these are to show different aspects of the same principle. The nome centre standard of Thebes is displayed on the frontside of the Stele of Revealing, behind the enthroned God Mentu or Ra Hoor Khuit.[60] It consists of Horus in the falcon form, perched on a mound, from which depend two ribbons with bands of different colour. The 'perch' actually consists of the hieroglyphs 'S' and 'T' as a composite, and spells the name of Set as 'Lord of the South'—it is his symbol.

The South, from the Egyptian perspective, is the whole region of Upper Egypt and is also the place of the burning hot desert winds blowing in from the Sahara desert. Such winds were also identified with Set, especially in his form as Ra-Mentu. Thus the solar creative and fiery destructive principles are embodied in one, rather in the way that in the Hindu doctrine creation and destruction is typified by Shiva, who is in many ways comparable to Set though the two are not of course exactly the same. It hardly needs mentioning then that Horus and Set are also depicted here in one God or *neter*, not two. The names of Horus are countless in their diversity, but fortunately we only have to deal here with three of them. Firstly, Ra Hoor Khuit typifies the 'Khu' or shining splendour of Ra-Hoor, as manifested light.

As Hrumachis, which is another spelling of the same name, and which is mentioned in the third chapter of the Book of the Law, Ra Hoor Khuit assumes the androgynous form of the Sphinx, 'Lord of the Two Horizons'. The Sphinx of Giza is the marker of the Cosmic Cycles, for she always points towards the place where the Sun rises in the East at the vernal equinox, while her tail points towards the West, where the Sun sets.

---

[60] The 'Stele of Revealing' is the name given to the funeral stele of the priest and scribe Ankh-af-na-khonsu, which was activated in Cairo, 1904.

The Bulaq 'Stele of Revealing'

As Mentu, a name particular to Thebes, Horus is the 'Legislator' of the great cycles of time; in particular, the Great Year that began 12,000 years ago in the precessional age of the Lion or Beast and that ends at the present time with the ingress into the sign of Aquarius, the Woman of Heaven. Thus the Woman and Beast, Aquarius and Leo, combine in the image of the Sphinx as the Alpha and Omega, the First and the Last. The latter happens to be a name of the cosmic Christ afforded him in St. John's book of Revelation, 22: 13. Mentu is a variant form of Menes, a name sometimes thought to be that of the first pharaoh but which is based on confusion with the principle that the king had to uphold. According to René Guénon,

> It is interesting to note that in other traditions the primordial Legislator is also called by names the root of which is the same as that of the Hindu *Manu*: we have for example *Menes* among the Egyptians and *Minos* among the Greeks; it is therefore a mistake to look upon these names as indicating historical personages.[61]

Guénon is referring to Manu, the Legislator of the Manvantaras or Cosmic Cycles. In the same doctrine, *purusha* and *prakriti*, 'essence' and 'substance', form the first duality from the corporeal point of view although neither exist in manifestation but form the unmanifest basis of it. Thus the Cosmic Cycles really reach outside of and beyond temporal time and space. The pair forms the two poles of the 'divine pillar', the height and depth. Manu is the *purusha*, which resides with the principial reality. It is that which legislates or orders the worlds of manifestation, the cosmos. The twin poles of the sum total of manifest existence are the Alpha and Omega; in their completion is their beginning. All other cycles reflect or mirror this in some way, even the annual course of the Sun and monthly course of the Moon. All true initiatic rites are based on the same universal principals. Some passages in the Book of the Law that are otherwise obscure can now easily be explained. In III: 34, it is said,

> But your holy place shall be untouched throughout the centuries: though with fire and sword it be burnt down and shattered, yet an invisible house there standeth, and shall stand until the fall of the Great Equinox; when Hrumachis shall arise and the double-wanded one assume my throne and place. Another prophet shall arise, and bring fresh fever from the skies; another woman shall awake the lust and worship of the Snake; another soul of God and beast shall mingle in the globèd priest; another sacrifice shall stain the tomb; another king shall reign; and blessing no longer be poured To the Hawk-headed mystical Lord!

---

[61] *Man and his Becoming According to the Vedānta* [Sophia Perennis].

The 'fall of the Great Equinox' is the present time, precisely the precessional ingress of the Sun into Aquarius. If we begin the wheel at Leo, approximately 12,000 years ago, Aquarius is at the cusp of the 7th house and end of the 6th, which is the 'fall'. When blessing is no longer afforded the 'Hawk-headed mystical Lord', then all worldly governance becomes entirely divorced or separated from exoteric religion, which has been the 'ark' that carried the esoteric doctrine throughout the precessional cycle of Pisces. The current Manvantara cycle then ends, or completes, and Horus becomes Hrumachis. To be more specific, Horus, the God that was once the principle of all warriors and kings, withdraws entirely from the terrestrial sphere and becomes the Sphinx. Ra Hoor Khuit is then as the Angel of Judgement who destroys everything that is not in accordance with the divine principle and withdraws the manifestation of the world at the end of time. In that same instant, the new Manvantara is formed from the *purusha* within the principle itself.

Between the twin poles of the North, *purusha*, and the South, *prakriti*, between Heaven and Earth, is the domain of the 'perfected man', where it is possible for the human to become conscious of the primordial as reflected into the mirror of the individuality. In the Qabalah this corresponds to Tiphereth. The initiatic realisation is called the 'Knowledge and Conversation of the Holy Guardian Angel'. The Angel is sometimes called the 'true King, Ruler and Helper'. In ancient times, though it is no longer the case, all kings upheld the divine principle. They occupied the middle ground as intermediaries between Heaven and Earth. We can see this on the frontside of the Stele of Revealing where the Egyptian three worlds are depicted. It is in the centre, between Heaven and Earth, where the priest adores the God Mentu or Ra Hoor Khuit. At the same time, he *is* the God, and can even speak for him. Thus he is able to convey the divine power of ordinance.

What then, is the import of the Book of the Law received in Cairo, 1904? The metaphysical and cosmic doctrine of the initiatic Egyptian tradition, that vanished completely two thousand years ago or more, was transmitted in such a way, and at such a time, that a century later, near the end of the Great Year, those few still capable of receiving it may effectively recover the 'lost word' before it is too late. We have entered a time where nearly all initiatic chains are broken or have been withdrawn entirely. When the last few that are capable of initiation are able to receive it, then the great dissolution will come. The Initiates will carry the seeds of all the knowledge of the present cycle through to the next.

The Nephilim and Sons of Anak

According to biblical and other sources, Nimrod, the legendary founder of Babylon, and the Sethians, represent kingly or noble governance that had no resort to spiritual authority, or that had rebelled against it. It is likewise with what are called the Kings of Edom.[62] All of these are associated with the Nephilim, who according to the book of Genesis were a 'race of giants' who were the progeny of congress between the Beni Elohim, an Order of Angels, and the women of earth. On the contrary, the Nephilim, as the children of the Elohim, were and still are the spiritual authority and governance of this earth—athough they withdrew from the terrestrial plane long ages ago. The Elohim, as is also known according to traditional sources, are concerned with initiatic tradition—a fact that has seemed to escape those who have taken the negative presentation of the Nephilim at face value. According to Genesis, 6: 4,

> There were giants in the earth in those days; and also after that, when the sons of God came in unto the daughters of men, and they bare children to them, the same became mighty men which were of old, men of renown.

The Qabalah, which is inextricably linked with the exoteric political contrivances of the old books of Moses, involves a rather gross misrepresentation of ancient peoples not deemed to be of the race of Israelites. This was made worse when the books were translated from the sacred languages into modern languages and all traces of the traditional symbolism erased. The Kings of Edom are thus associated with the Qliphoth as Lords of Unbalanced Force. The Edomites were in fact the original or indigenous peoples of Canaan. Owing to their great antiquity, their knowledge was vastly superior to that of their neighbours, who were always looking for a way to rob and plunder those ancient and fertile lands of 'milk and honey'. The Beni Elohim are traditionally an Order of Angels, the Sons of Gods attributed to Yetzirah of Hod. The Gods in question are called the Elohim of Hosts, corresponding to Atziluth of Hod. The Elohim are further attributed to Binah in the supernal triad, called the 'Mother of Faith' and 'Throne of the Primordial Wisdom'. All initiatic tradition has its source symbolically in this Throne or Seat, and all proper rites serve to establish a reflective 'world centre' or 'seat' (Tiphereth) on the terrestrial level, that is capable of receiving and reflecting that to individuals as a spiritual influence.

---

[62] See 'Thelema Beyond Self Love'.

To recapitulate: according to Genesis and the apocryphal book of Enoch, the Beni Elohim, 'Sons of Gods', beget upon the daughters of men a race of 'giants' called the Nephilim. The Nephilim, the result of the congress, then materialised or manifested upon the earth—for it was necessary that the terrestrial women should be involved before this could take place. According to other sources, the giants made their descent from the sacred mountain known as Hermon. As we have previously said, the descent from the holy mountain, which is to the Near and Middle East what Meru is to the Hindus, places the Nephilim in the order of avatars, indeed, in all probability the first avatars.[63] The idea that the Nephilim were a 'race of giants' owes to the translation from Hebrew or Aramaic into other languages. The root of the name has various meanings, including 'noble', 'renowned' and 'high'. While it is very easily possible that the Nephilim were much taller than the terrestrials, there being no contradiction in sacred texts between analogy and literal fact, it is obvious that the name refers to their superiority to those merely born of earth. The Universal Man or analogous perfected 'true man', of which Christ is one such example, is the 'Son of Heaven and Earth'.[64]

Although it appears that the accounts of the Nephilim owe to vast antiquity, in the book of Enoch it is said that they taught magick and sciences, including metallurgy. While this is sometimes taken to mean alchemy, the manufacture and use of metals really owes to the Bronze Age, which was immediately before the Kali Yuga or Age of Iron about 6,000 years ago. From this, and certain other evidence, it seems probable that either the Nephilim or at least their descendants called the Sons of Anak (which also means 'giant') were still on the earth at the time of the Egyptian 1st Dynasty. There may be an etymological association between 'Anak' and the Egyptian *menat*, which was a collar worn by Gods and royals. The *menat* was worn by some truly gigantic Egyptian statues dating to early dynastic times, and is a symbol of the primordial tradition and the sum total of all manifestation. It is similar in some ways to the solar hieroglyph (*swt*) often thought to be a sunshade or parasol, which is always shown accompanying pharaohs. The parasol is the symbol of royal authority *par excellence*, as it is also associated with Hathoor in her most primal aspect as 'Divine Pillar', which asserts the conveyance of the initiatic transmission from the primordial source.[65]

---

[63] The Sanskrit word *avatara* literally means 'a descent'.
[64] See 'Nu and the Number 11'.
[65] Guénon has written on the significance of the parasol. See *Symbols of Sacred Science*, pp. 253–4.

The *swt* parasol depicts the rays from the primordial centre, the 'sun' or king, passing outwards to the circumference of the sum total of manifestation, which is the 'appearance' of Nuit. It also includes the primordial pillar depending from spiritual power or authority, shown by the sceptre with the *sekhem* ('power') bull's horns. One of the earliest examples is inscribed on a macehead of the 'Scorpion King', the first pharaoh.[66]

A passage in Numbers, 13: 22, tells of an encounter between Israelite spies and the Sons of Anak. The spies were sent to find out if it was possible to plunder a valley rich in gigantic and succulent fruits.

> And there we saw the giants, the sons of Anak, which come of the giants: and we were in our own sight as grasshoppers, and so we were in their sight.

The spies returned to Israel, but not empty handed. They bore with them grapes of enormous size, as proof they had carried out their mission. On being asked if the land was ripe for plunder, they reported that the Anak were far too powerful. We can take this not only in terms of their physical stature but also in terms of their spiritual knowledge.

In Numbers, 13: 28, it is said the Sons of Anak lived in titanic walled cities in the Transjordan region. From this and other accounts it seems probable that they were the Sethians or 'builders' of gigantic earth structures, continuing on into the Age of Iron after the Bronze Age, before withdrawing from temporal manifestation. The problem with creating a genealogy or time-line is that the very nature of the Nephilim might be time-defeating in a sense. Both Shiva and Christ were anciently portrayed as holding the key of eternity and the threefold sceptre of time—they are masters of time because time originates with them, so they cannot be subject to time.

Time is not quantifiable, even though it is treated as such; time is qualitative; all unitary measurements of time are an approximation, a matter of human convenience. For this same reason, there is a contraction of time towards the end of a great age or Manvantara, and a simultaneous densification of terrestrial conditions. The world is not at all the same place it was a few centuries ago, let alone sometime between now and the last Ice Age.

---

[66] See 'King Scorpion and the Royal Way'.

The constellation of Orion, called the 'Giant' in various languages, was always regarded as a type of the cosmic Garden of Eden, as opposed to the terrestrial Garden—which either the Nephilim or their descendants tended. When the last of the descendants were gone, the earthly paradise also vanished, leaving behind only traces or a residue. One example of such 'traces' are what look like giant footprints in rock, found in many places around the world. In Tintagel in Cornwall, for example, a very large print in the area of the ruined castle, swathed in the legends of King Arthur, is called the 'Wizard's Foot'. While none of this needs to be taken literally, the names afforded such impressions by the ancients tell us at least of the psychic residue or impression left from prehistoric times. The remnants of the giants are also mentioned in Josiah, 12: 4:

> And the coast of Og, king of Bashan, which was of the remnant of the giants, that dwelt at Ashtaroth and at Edrei.

The cult centre of the Goddess Ashtaroth was, according to the Bible, destroyed by Josiah along with other 'pagan' centres, which were in reality centres of the primordial tradition. In some rituals, Ashtaroth, who was assimilated by the ancient Egyptians, is placed in the East of the place or temple, which is not only the quarter of elemental Earth but is also the place where Orion rises every evening. In the book of Deuteronomy, 3: 11, it is said,

> For only Og, king of Bashan remained of the remnant of giants; behold, his bedstead was a bedstead of iron; is it not in Rabbath of the children of Ammon? Nine cubits was the length thereof, and four cubits the breadth of it, after the cubit of a man.

The 'bedstead of iron' places this narrative clearly in the Age of Iron or Kali Yuga. There are further references to the remnants of the Sons of Anak in Deuteronomy, but the book of Josiah tells of their destruction. Whether or not the Sons of Anak were slain, as claimed in the book of Josiah, there can be little doubt that the primordial centres were destroyed. The remaining psychic residue would have been turned to evil ends by the destroyers or enemies of Ra, for the spiritual force was already withdrawn or removed elsewhere.[67]

---

[67] See Appendices iii, 'Biblical References to the Nephilim'.

 The ancient Egyptians made a close identification between the constellation of Orion and the Sahu, an attribute that was transferred to the pharaohs in dynastic times. The Sahu is generally supposed to symbolise the incorruptible soul but is at the same time a Star God. As such, Sahu is the personification of Orion, 'Father of all the Gods' as according to the Pyramid Texts. The name 'Sah' is identical to an attribute of Amoun, the 'Hidden One' as the god that is below the horizon at dawn, but which rises every evening. Sopdet, Sepet or Seshet, the feminine personification of Sirius, was considered to be the consort of Sah. Their son, Sopdu, was associated with Venus, and the seven-petalled star that is the crown of Sepet affirms this. It is at the same time the 'seven rishis' of Ursa Major. These represent the sevenfold nature of the Manvantara in the Hindu doctrine—the star (or flower) is thus a symbol of the primordial tradition of the North or Hyperborea. The first dynastic pharaoh, called variously Narmer or Menes, is the first known case of a king using the star of Sepet as his emblem. Menes has a relation with *menat*, the royal collar, but is also associated with Mentu, Manu and other legislative powers. The word 'legislation', in this context, has nothing to do with common judicial or temporal power; it is the authority of the primordial tradition itself, which is that of divine ordinance.

The Company of Heaven

There is an expression derived from the Orphic tradition, 'I am a child of the earth and stars, but my race is of the heavenly order'.[68] There is a profane or materialist notion of that—which we only mention here in passing—and a vaguely mystical or romantic one. There is no truth in either of these. There is a great difference between spiritual realisation and psychic experience. The latter takes place on the plane of imagination, whether it is voluntary or involuntary. Psychic experience carries nothing of the spiritual for it is, by definition, within the realm of the human mind. According to the (Egyptian) Book of the Law, I: 2–3,

> *The unveiling of the company of heaven.*
> *Every man and every woman is a star.*

There are three veils drawn across the Tree of Life. The first is the veil of Material Illusion. To be in any way prepared for initiation, the person must have passed through that veil and left, to a greater or lesser extent, the profane world of those that have not passed it and never will, which is the great majority of human beings in the present age. This is the first departure. If the seed of initiation has been well and truly sown, it will be a permanent one.

The second veil is called Paroketh and is likened to a cover or partition that encloses the sanctuary of a temple, by which it is implied that certain mysteries are contained there. The exoteric symbolisation of this veil may be found in churches of the various religious traditions, in which case the 'mysteries' that are concealed by it are no more than relics—although it is possible that a person duly prepared by acceptance into such a body may, by the cognitive values conveyed by artefacts, enter into their psychic equivalent. Under some circumstances, depending on innate capacity, this may act as a support to further insight—psychic 'experience' has nothing to do with initiation in itself.[69] The veil is encountered in the psychic realm but is not passed through in any real sense until the effects and experiences of the psychic realm are understood for what they are and have consequently been rejected. That is the second departure.

---

[68] Orphic inscription; Petalia Gold Tablet, 300–200 BCE [British Museum].
[69] See 'Psychism and Subversion'.

The name 'Holy Guardian Angel' is sometimes used to denote the primary initiatic realisation of the union between man and God. Any effective initiation corresponds to that second point of departure.[70] We must eschew those who confuse this with psychic phenomena of any kind, including all types of 'spirit guides' such as are encountered in what now passes for shamanism. Such persons are impervious to initiation in any real sense—though they may imagine the case to be otherwise. Such confusions range from psychological explanations of so-called ancient mysteries to the opinions of professional scholars that seek an explanation for all sacred rites in social or political conventions. The counter-initiatic movement also includes all self-appointed (or popularly elected) facilitators of 'mind, body and spirit' workshops, 'yoga for health' and the like.

When the above is understood it becomes clear how ridiculous it is of those in the postmodern school of occultism who imagine they can 'cross the Abyss', the third and last veil, through the trappings of magick. By this, we include the evocation of spirits, pathworkings, rituals, clairvoyance, sexual magick or sorcery, and the use of imaginative constructs. The spiritual realm is beyond the Abyss and wholly outside the reach of human reason or its psychic faculties—and these two are by no means as separate as most people imagine. A spiritual influence may extend into the psychic realm under some particular circumstances, but its presence will be entirely unknown to the person that is only capable of inhabiting the psychic realm. The psychic plane conforms to the laws governing it and which are peculiar to it, as does the material plane.

Pure knowledge is a means of recognition between those who are of the 'heavenly race', for these are exceedingly few. Yet it is easily possible that a person may be of the race but ignorant of any real knowledge concerning it. That is one of the reasons it is necessary to have initiatic Orders, though there are almost none in existence in the present time. We are drawing to the end of the Kali Yuga, an end characterised by darkness—by which is meant in this context the total ignorance and wilful rejection of all things spiritual.

At this juncture it is needful to mention how this doctrine of the starry race has suffered corruption. It is hardly necessary to enter into the matter of racial supremacists and the like, where these can be obviously identified with various groups, some powerful and some not at all, so we will not venture there.

---

[70] See 'The Holy Guardian Angel'.

There exists a subtler form of racial superiority, which is deeply embedded in the fabric of what is left of our civilisation. Histories, philosophy, science, even our dictionaries, are riddled through with it, and it passes by completely unsuspected for the most part. In order to explain the similarities in languages widely differing and very far apart geographically, such as English, Scandinavian, French, Greek, Hebrew, Sanskrit and Chinese, an Indo-Iranian or Aryan root race was posited by sheer imagining, though naturally 'proofs' were provided. This conveniently (for Europeans) attributed a source of knowledge, learning, science and culture to a people not indigenous to the Asian continent. As a consequence it is not uncommon to find Egyptologists trying to trace a Hebrew or Semitic source to ancient Egyptian words! The almost fantastic absurdity of this, by dint of the great age of even the known history of ancient Egypt, does not seem to occur to them.

We are not ancient Egyptians, and of course it should hardly be necessary to point this out. The source of knowledge and learning did not come from ancient Egyptian history or civilisation; it was passed on to the Egyptians long ago by another race altogether. Another caveat is required. We are not speaking here of Atlantis or some such lost island—which almost certainly did exist but there have been countless civilisations older than that of Atlantis. The problem with Atlantis is that so much written concerning it is suppositious and so imaginary. The records of the Atlanteans are fragmentary but in any case, we are speaking in terms of such vast antiquity—long before the last Ice Age—that all proof or evidence as is required by profane scholarship is irrelevant. Such 'evidence' is not only irrelevant in consideration of the scale of antiquity but is also quite meaningless because the real knowledge is purely metaphysical, as opposed to any supposition concerning ordinary facts.

It has been very popular for occultists to suppose that the ancient mysteries can be explained away either as symbolic of psychological 'process' or physical phenomena, or sometimes a confusion of both these things. That tendency is far older than the twentieth century and goes back at least to the Neo-Platonists.[71] In that case any real import is removed; the psychic and physical world are phenomenal.

---

[71] In 'Histories' (ii. 170), Herodotus tells of a vigil carried out in certain seasons in a chapel or shrine beneath the temple of Neïth. 'Herein everyone sees the likeness of his own affections and fantasies in the night, which the Egyptians call Mysteries.' Herodotus thus reveals, in spite of his constant assertions that he had initiated knowledge, that psychologisation of the ancient mysteries did not begin with C.G. Jung!

The knowledge behind the Orphic inscription, from which the expression 'my race is of the heavenly order' is derived, is that of remembrance. Legend has it there were two springs flowing forth in Hades: the water of Lethe (ληθη), 'forgetfulness', and the water of Mnemosyne (Μνημοσυνη), 'remembrance'.[72] Those souls who drink from the former are doomed to oblivion. Those who drink from the spring of remembrance are able to make their passage to that which is termed the 'company of heaven' in the Book of the Law, or if we put this in other terms, the realm of the immortal souls who are likened to the circumpolar stars—for these never disappear from the sky.[73]

The Orphic mysteries were originally transmitted orally, and were inevitably distorted by those who wrote about them later. The notion of reincarnation or the transmigration of souls, for example, was superimposed upon the Greek, Hindu and even Egyptian traditions by Theosophists and other moderns. It makes little difference, for it is only the spring of Mnemosyne that concerns us here. Mnemosyne is the name of an ancient Greek Titan, born of Uranus and Gaia and mother of the Muses—though it is worth mentioning that in the sanctuary of the Muses at Mount Helicon in Boeotia she was considered to be a Muse herself.[74] She has all knowledge, including that of the past, present and the future. As such, she is the basis of life itself—for to forget the true order and origin of things is to die the death of oblivion or Lethe. Such is the real meaning of a ritual or 'rite', which is to 'set things in order' in this very particular way, which is in the nature of divine ordinance.

Remembrance has persisted in the philosophy of both East and West, and in the Christian celebration of Holy Communion, for example, where another Greek term is used, Anamnesis (αναμνησις), 'recollection'.[75] The recollection of the passion and death of Christ is thus communicated, albeit exoterically, to the congregation. Spiritual communion in the true sense, or initiated sense, is far more than any ordinary recollection. It is beyond the ritual enactment of scripture or even far more ancient mystery allegories—though these may form a basis or support to the true recollection, which is their proper function and use.

---

[72] From whence the word 'mnemonic'.
[73] The Book of the Law, I: 2: 'The unveiling of the company of heaven.'
[74] Naturally, Mnemosyne was invoked to assist the memory.
[75] The idea may be found in the writings of Plato (Euthydemus) and in those of Shankara on the path of knowledge (*Crest Jewel of Discrimination*).

Schiller and other rationalists, as we have mentioned previously, have gone to work on Plutarch's account of the shrine of Neïth at Sàis, which carries the following inscription:

I am all that hath been, and is, and shall be; and my veil no mortal has hitherto raised.

Neïth—whom Plutarch likened to Athena, or is otherwise construed as Isis—here embraces both the lesser and the greater mysteries. She has firstly the three 'faces' or keys of the past, present and future time. This is the attribute of Tiphereth or the primordial centre as known by the individual, and which was later the domain of Shiva and then, thousands of years later, of Christ. Neïth also has the key of the 'third birth' beyond the abysmal threshold, which no mortal can attain. There is a further realm that belongs to her, of which the Egyptians would not speak, and that is the unmanifest or 'darkness' in the superior sense—a darkness that is nonetheless far from the 'nothing' or 'emptiness' that is sometimes supposed, as it contains all possibilities.

Remembrance in the true sense is life itself, and by that we mean the return to the immortal spring, which has its source outside of and beyond human reason. However exalted the reason may seem to the profane, it is bound to the limits of time and space and is thus of the order of 'that which dies', and not of that which lives forever.

Initiation

The term 'initiation' is frequently used without qualification. It is used to describe various things, some of which are mutually contradictory. There is thus no common agreement on what initiation even means, so it is not then surprising that confusion exists around the subject. The etymology of the word simply means 'to start something off', and yet there is no consensus on even that, the broadest definition possible. In fact it is so broad a definition that it necessarily narrows and limits the meaning to an ordinary material action. A trumpet can be blown to announce the commencement of some game, act or play, none of which concerns us here.

A common error to be made concerning initiatic organisations is that initiation, or a rite of initiation, is no more than a means of induction into a particular group or body. That may be the case with some organisations, but those are not in any way initiatic, which is to say, their purpose is in no way to transmit a spiritual influence and consists only of social, political or other profane concerns. From this mistaken idea of induction into a social or other group comes forth even worse confusion, for example that initiation is no more than 'psychological process'.

The Jungians and other rationalists that for various reasons made it their business to comment on things of which they were, by their disposition, not qualified to speak of, have denounced elite initiatic organisations. They did this on the grounds that all such groups can achieve is the immersion of an individual in a collective mind or egregore—we use the latter word here in its conventional sense. It would be as though some souls, too weak to help themselves, need the safety net of a collective body until such a time as they are ready for what Jungians term 'individuation'. We will return to this subject later.

The word 'egregore' has been used to reduce and nullify all public knowledge of initiatic organisations through misunderstanding and confusion. Before this could be done the word had first to suffer a degraded meaning. The meaning has by now become so far removed from its original sense that the word 'egregore' is even used to describe the motivations, attitudes and opinions of a corporate body, for example.

Originally, egregore, derived from the Greek *egregoros*, 'wakeful', was associated with 'Watchers', of the Enochian tradition.[76] Far from being any kind of collective mind (if such a thing can even exist), the Watchers hint at the central mystery of initiation, which is concerned with non-human, praeterhuman or 'beyond human' intelligence. The Polish author Count Jan Potocki (1761–1815) wrote *The Saragossa Manuscript* in the early 1800s. This features the term 'egregores' in relation to certain illustrious fallen angels—which is a reference to the book of Enoch and the brief mention in Genesis of descendants of the elder race called Nephilim. Eliphas Lévi, in *The Great Mystery*, 1868, identifies egregores with the Watchers, the fathers of the Nephilim, describing them as terrible beings that 'crush us without pity because they are unaware of our existence'. The description is complete fantasy on the part of Lévi, based on what he had read in the Bible and Apocrypha, which was overwritten from the surviving fragments by scribes completely unaware of the real meaning of the narrative. The accounts are therefore fascinating but corrupt. We shall turn to René Guénon for a precise explanation of what initiation means in our present context.[77]

> Initiation must have a non-human origin, for without this it can never attain its final end, which extends beyond the domain of individual possibilities. That is why truly initiatic rites cannot be attributed to human authors; in fact, we can no more know the authors than we can know the inventors of traditional symbols, and for the same reason, for these symbols are equally non-human in their origin and essence.

He goes on to mention that there are strong lines between rites and symbols. By 'rites' he does not mean something made up or created, obviously. The original meaning of 'rite' is more in the way of divine ordination, and of setting things in order. Thus any scholarly enquiry into the authenticity of rites through an examination of authorship or historical facts can tell us absolutely nothing of any real significance concerning this matter. The true origin of an effective rite is beyond the bounds of the corporeal world of time and space.

---

[76] The only authentic account of the Nephilim or 'Watchers' is preserved in the opening paragraphs of 'The Sethian Gnosis'. See 'The Nephilim and Sons of Anak' and also 'Sons of Gods', in the present work.
[77] Guénon, pp. 52–53, *Perspectives on Initiation* [1947—republished in 2001 by Sophia Perennis].

This leads us to the matter of an individual that confers initiation on another, or others. Such a person is a transmitter, for he does not act as an individual, which would render real initiation impossible. A transmitter is a 'link in the chain', as it were, and the support of an influence—but that influence has nothing to do with the individual domain. He does not act in his own name but in the name of the principle that the initiatic organisation represents. For this reason the effectiveness of any rite, even a religious one as opposed to an initiatic one, does not in any way depend on the individual merit of the initiator. The accomplishment of an initiatic rite is made possible not through individual or personal qualities, or even in ability or knowledge, but through power invested in the initiator. Thus the hierophant or officiant may sometimes close proceedings without the requirements of 'ceremony', which sometimes forms an additional part of a rite, but through simply declaring the closure, 'By the power invested in this sceptre', for example. The sceptre is the symbol of the principle and so of spiritual authority, though never the authority of the individual person.

The initiator, perhaps needless to say, cannot be 'anybody', but must be invested with the function of transmitter. The initiator must also 'know the rules' of the rite, and be able to perform it without error. Even if the members of such an organisation have only what Guénon terms as 'virtual initiation', the spiritual influence can be effectively transmitted so long as the traditional chain is unbroken and the organisation or body of initiates is truly a repository of a spiritual influence, which it carries. By 'virtual' initiates, Guénon, writing in 1946, does not of course refer to digital technology. He is referring to initiatic organisations where the members have, through deviation or necessity such as is brought about by the extremely unnatural conditions imposed by the modern world, forgotten the true meaning and purpose of the rites and teaching. These can nonetheless be transmitters of the initiatic current, *even when they do not know it themselves*.

Individualism, which reached its apotheosis in the modern world and has collapsed in upon itself in the technological age, is that which Guénon has termed as the force of *anti-initiation*.[78] Jung, for example, nurtured a profane idea of what he called secret societies, condemning them at first as 'anti-social'. This immediately proves his lack of qualification to speak on the subject—for a truly initiatic organisation does not have any social purpose whatsoever.

---

[78] Guénon, *Crisis of the Modern World* [Sophia Perennis, 2001].

Jung later conceded that such a secret society—and an initiatic organisation can hardly be any kind of 'society'—is at best a kind of collective route to what he termed as 'individuation', that might be necessary for those who were not paying for his exclusive services.[79] The notion of individuation, along with its supposed 'therapeutic' benefits, has subverted, through infiltration or other means, many organisations that might otherwise have continued as the repository of a spiritual influence. The psychoanalytic school is a considerable weapon in the persuasive armorium of the force of counter-initiation. Nonetheless, Jung ruthlessly maintained and promoted a quasi-elite group based solely on his personality and self-invented terms.[80] It is clear from Jung's writing on the subject that he was not initiated into anything in the sense that we mean it here. He regarded all matters of initiation as psychological process, demonstrating that he had no idea of real initiation at all and could never gain it, since his beliefs precluded the possibility of any real knowledge whatsoever. Initiatic transmission originates from outside and beyond the human sphere and is essentially non-human. An organisation that has personal, social or political aims cannot, by its very nature, be in any way initiatic. With hubris very typical of the modern word, Jung freely expounded on ancient rites that he had no knowledge of whatsoever, effectively denigrating them through his own ignorance:

> The Dionysiac religion contained orgiastic rites that implied the need for an initiate to abandon himself to his animal nature and thereby experience the full fertilising power of the Earth Mother.[81]

The 'orgiastic rites' of Dionysus were largely the invention of Roman propagandists in the 6th century that wished to denounce all pre-religious cults as 'pagan'. As with most profane commentators, Jung exhibited total incomprehension of ancient knowledge, imagining that gods in animal form could only symbolise 'animal nature'. Psychologists and others persistently refer to all ancient symbols of tumescent gods, whether male or female, as 'fertility gods'. Their conception is thus both materialistic and spiritually blind, for being of a wholly material nature it does not admit to even the possibility of any spiritual reality.

---

[79] Jung, *Memories, Dreams, Reflections*.
[80] Jung formed his own secret society in Switzerland during the First World War, with himself as the primary Aryan or Indo-Iranian Messiah. See Professor Richard Noll, *The Jung Cult*.
[81] Jung, *Man and his Symbols*.

While asserting the 'primitive' nature of all pre-scientific or pre-modern cultures, especially those of Africa, and the supremacy of modern civilisation with its supposed Indo-European heritage, Jung has cited Haile Selassie, the last emperor of Ethiopia, who adopted the title 'Lion of Judah':[82]

> The further back we go in time, or the more primitive and close to nature the society is, the more literally such titles must be taken. A primitive chief is not only disguised as the animal; when he appears at initiation rites in full animal disguise, he is the animal.

This reveals ignorance of a magnitude. In fact, the 'chief' becomes the *neter* or principle that the creature symbolises. Once psychological explanations of initiation gained dominance, the Western world was subjected to a plethora of 'self-help' literature and even professional guidance for those with disposable income and time on their hands. This counterfeit initiatic movement emerged from incomprehension of all spiritual traditions combined with the arrogant presumption typified by modernism.

Initiation by therapy or 'healing' swiftly gained popularity over the last half century, forming a covert anti-tradition. By placing all emphasis on the individual it destroys all possibilities of initiatic transmission in those who adopt its mind-set, for initiation must by definition have its origin outside and beyond the human sphere. This element of counter-initiation is also covert in so far as even the few remaining cosmic mediators in the last generation were persuaded by the claims of Jung and his followers that psychoanalysis might in some way be helpful, even essential, in matters of initiation—or even worse, that a therapeutic approach to the subject is in some way a healthier alternative. It was a serious deviation—destructive to whole generations in so far as it has rendered them impervious to any possibility of real initiation. We will turn once more to Guénon:[83]

> Thus it is altogether erroneous to identify initiatic organisations with secret societies, as is commonly done. First of all, it is very evident that the two expressions cannot in any way coincide in their application, for in fact there are many kinds of secret societies that have nothing initiatic about them since they can be formed by mere individual initiative and for any goal whatsoever...

---

[82] Jung [*ibid*].
[83] Guénon, *Perspectives on Initiation*, pp. 72–83.

Guénon here discerns a difference between groups that are societies, which are by definition purely exterior organisations, whether 'secret' or not, and initiatic organisations. He does this because even those who profess knowledge, or profane scholars who profess to 'facts' and 'evidence', commonly confuse the two things. He is prepared to concede, on the other hand, that genuinely initiatic organisations can sometimes take on the outward appearance of societies, in which case they automatically deviate from the original purpose of any initiatic organisation. He later qualifies the point further, by pointing out that in some circumstances, mainly those conditions that affect the modern Western world, this becomes inevitable. He therefore continues at some length describing in broad terms the different kinds of organisations that exist, for some of these are initiatic and some are not at all initiatic.

> In all of the quarrels relating to secret societies, or to what are so called, either initiatic organisations are not involved, or at least it is not their initiatic character as such that is involved, something, moreover, that would be impossible for other profound reasons that the rest of our account will better explain.

Guénon alludes here to the disputes, frequently carried out in public, among members of various organisations claiming to be initiatic. This often revolves around 'authenticity', 'lineage' and so forth. As he has already made clear, none of that can have anything to do with a truly initiatic Order. Sometimes an organisation might be initiatic, or was once, but the members have lost sight of the true meaning and purpose of initiation through social or other aims.

> Whether or not an organisation clothes itself in the particular and moreover wholly outward forms that permit it to be defined as a society, it can be qualified as secret in the widest sense of this word, and without attaching to it the least unfavourable intention...

Organisations are often accused of being secret societies once their presence, or at least their outer appearance, has become known. This rests purely on the fact of secrecy, as though that were objectionable in itself. There are two kinds of secret that an organisation may harbour. The first is that of initiation itself, which is incommunicable by profane means and completely ungraspable by the materialist—for even if such a person knew the rites from reading them in books (for example), they could not receive initiation, being impervious to any spiritual influence or transmission. The second kind is that of very ordinary secrets that are no more than outward signs, words or symbols conveyed to the members so they can recognise each other.

Once the difference between a 'secret society' and an initiatic Order is understood, it becomes clear why it is that the member of a truly initiatic organisation can never leave it. It is easily possible to leave, or be expelled, from any profane society, for it is only governed by the same rules that govern any other purely exoteric body, and so the being is not in any way changed by this. Any ties forged or broken are then entirely outward. In the case of an initiatic organisation, however, which transmits a spiritual influence, the person that has received an effective initiation is changed forever—no merely formal or administrative means can alter the fact. Furthermore, whereas a society can be the target of attacks from outside—because it is itself 'on the outside'—and can be removed by political or other means, an initiatic organisation, by its very nature, is not in any way affected. Guénon goes on to say that such an organisation exists so long as 'even one single member remains alive'. A truly initiatic organisation cannot be attacked or dissolved from without, for such a body is invisible to the profane world. Even if no representative is still living, we should understand that the ending of the spiritual transmission was willed from within and not as a consequence of attacks from without, or from any exterior cause.

It is necessary to qualify the different kinds of organisations, both initiatic and non-initiatic. While some have remained purely initiatic, others have deviated, for example by introducing political or social ideals or agendas, as previously mentioned. They nonetheless remain initiatic at the core, even when members or representatives do not understand this. There are also pseudo-initiatic organisations, which are in every way counterfeit, for example those that have a purely 'psychological' basis. In addition to these, there are organisations that are wholly opposed to all initiatic tradition whatsoever. This can include merely conventional, non-initiatic or pseudo-initiatic bodies. The pseudo-initiatic organisations, as profane as the declared anti-initiatic ones, are also opposed to all true initiatic tradition, including elements that have deviated yet retain an initiatic core.

There is a popular fantasy that confuses initiatic Orders with some political secret or covert project—the name of the Illuminati is often used, even though that was a real but profane organisation with a rationalist ideal. All this is conflated with 'conspiracy theories', which has nothing to do with either. It has lately been used as a political means of suppressing all dissent from the official line—it is only necessary to attack one that declares perfectly reasonable and quite ordinary facts to be a believer in 'conspiracy theories' and the public are ready to join in the condemnation, aiding and abetting the suppression of knowledge and reinforcing their subservience.

When a genuinely initiatic organisation holds a secret, that can only be a symbol or some outward token of the true initiatic secret, which of course can neither be disclosed or betrayed by any means available to the profane, for it is incommunicable. The outward 'secret' is then a purely secondary element, having no real value or significance in itself.

The seemingly endless quarrels and even litigation surrounding the Order of the Golden Dawn is widely documented; some of it is more or less based on fact, some of it is wild speculation. In the case of Crowley's autobiographical and fictional accounts of members of the Golden Dawn, much of it was lies or malicious fantasy, published with the intention of slandering persons that either disliked him or otherwise refused to submit to the absurd demands he made upon them. None of that has anything to do with initiation or genuinely initiatic organisations, and we will not waste further time on it. No truly initiatic secret can be betrayed and no exterior force can betray any truly initiatic body.

Finally, there are, and have been for centuries, organisations that parody initiatic organisations without concealing anything, though they sometimes pretend to hold a secret. There are some such groups that emerged in Britain and America from the 18th century onward, continuing in various forms even to the present day. One obvious example is the 'Hellfire Club', which served no other purpose than to entertain the whims and excesses of English lords.[84]

---

[84] The first Hellfire Club was founded in London in 1718, by Philip, Duke of Wharton, but gained notoriety through the English club established by Sir Francis Dashwood (1749 to around 1760). The Club was later associated with Brooks's (1764). Other Hellfire Clubs sprang up throughout the 18th century, most of them in Ireland after Wharton's had been dissolved.

Three Grades of Love and Will

According to the (Egyptian) Book of the Law, I: 28–29, there are three grades or degrees of initiation. These all derive from the word of the Law, Thelema—a word that conveys the sense of spiritual or divine will when it is taken in the context of its use, as previously noted.[85] Will is the ordinance of that Law which is truly right and proper to the being, or any group of beings in the cosmic or terrestrial scheme of things.[86]

> *The word of the Law is Θελημα.*
> *Who calls us Thelemites will do no wrong, if he look but close into the word. For there are therein Three Grades, the Hermit, and the Lover, and the man of Earth. Do what thou wilt shall be the whole of the Law.*

The three Grades, or Orders, correspond more or less exactly with the three veils on the Tree of Life described previously.[87] Before this subject can be entered into with any degree of accuracy, some further clarifications are needed. Firstly, no person is able to construe such matters wholly upon their own account. That is a worthy undertaking but any positive outcome is impossible. And this is because, by its very nature, the esoteric does not owe to any human influence, let alone the speculative realm of reason or of intuition as that is by now commonly understood, as something 'instinctive'. Here is yet another example of the profanation of our language. Intuition is derived from the Latin *intuito*, in turn derived from *intuiri*, literally 'consider'. The word originally denoted the insight only gained from direct spiritual communication, which is in the nature of initiatic transmission. To use the term in its original sense, we have to append it to read 'intellectual intuition'. For the same reason, almost anything that we might read on the subject, especially if it was written in the last century, will be counterfeit. There will be confusion, a substitution of that which is merely mundane for that which was originally esoteric. A great many modern writers on esotericism reduce the spiritual to completely ordinary material, physical or otherwise psychic matters.

---

[85] See p. 29, on the word 'Thelema'.
[86] This is cognate with Hindu *dharma*. See 'The Law of Manu', pp. 146–150, *Introduction to the Study of the Hindu Doctrines*, René Guénon [Sophia Perennis].
[87] See 'The Company of Heaven'.

The 'man of Earth' is a place of beginning. At the beginning there must always arise the question itself, as simultaneous occurrence. In that respect, the question is more important than any 'answer' that may be given, unless that answer or response is a non-verbal one. And that is the real meaning of seeking or aspiration, for this must begin from a question, even when such a question is as yet undefined and assumes the form of some vague impulse. The domain of the man of Earth is that which is wholly material. The terrestrial man or woman has not yet passed through the first veil, which is called the Veil of Material Illusion. They will never pass that first veil unless they make quite a considerable effort. Even then, whether the effort succeeds is more than merely down to how much time they spend studying, learning and even in contemplation, if they should know how to do this. Some have it in them while many more do not have it in them at all and so will never pass beyond that veil—not even in death. For if a person is not initiated in life, then how can they be initiated in death? It is not possible. Spiritual aspiration must always include study and learning but that alone is not enough. It is also necessary to reject the ambitions of worldly men and women as soon as these are understood as entirely illusionary and futile. Unless that understanding is reached, there is very little chance of initiation.

The domain of what is called the 'Lover' has nothing to do with any terrestrial duties or responsibilities. It has nothing to do even with the love of any man or woman in the ordinary sense. It has no counterpart in the mundane world as its field is entirely removed from that. There is sometimes a likeness drawn between this and the alchemical wedding of Rosicrucian literature, which is nonethelesss frequently confused with material or worldly matters. Needless to say perhaps, that confusion is made by those who are in themselves of a wholly material or worldly disposition. Alchemy has been confused with the profane science of actual physical metals, the transmutation of physical matter or base substance, laboratory equipment and so forth. Others then came along that scorned the attempt to physically reproduce the symbolism, in the hope that the 'miracle' might be produced, and declared it was all a matter of 'psychological process'. That is in some ways even worse, for it confines the operative aspect of the work to the human psyche, which is no better than any other kind of prison. All such miracles, while limited to material confines, can be no more than effects produced through the manipulation of natural laws.

Symbolism is a language in its own right, a language designed to convey that which is otherwise incommunicable. The profane—who rarely if ever admit their state of ignorance—misunderstand the very nature and function of symbolism as used in esoteric lore. They then even imagine that some kind of enlightened understanding can be gained through explaining the symbol. All that does is to produce a further set of symbols, always leading further and further away from that which was symbolised. Some have gone even further than this, to imagine that such speculative thought can be a kind of 'initiation' in itself.

Put in the broadest possible terms, the Lover is one that applies full attention to symbol and allegory. This can only bear fruit so long as no application to knowledge is sought. For example, it is useless to seek esoteric knowledge for betterment, for 'healing'—as we find constantly asserted by those who pretend knowledge—or for any purpose other than pure knowledge. And to make that even clearer, pure knowledge means spiritual knowledge for its own sake and for no other reason or motive. If there is some other reason or motive, some hope for gain or self-improvement, or for power, as in the case of the more degraded kind of individual, then that person has not truly entered the grade of the Lover. Their motives and disposition confine them to the material world of the man of Earth, and this may be a permanent state of affairs. In fact, it is worse than that, for there is no aspiration at all in motives of greed and acquisition.

The 'Hermit' is one that has passed the Veil of Material Illusion long ago; in fact they might never have been fooled by it in the first place. Frequently they will have spent some time as a Lover, learning the language of symbolism, and have renounced all applications of such knowledge as worthless. In obtaining spiritual realisation, they have seen through the glamour of the psychic plane and rejected all that it has to offer. The Hermit is as one that fully realises this instruction from the Book of the Law, II: 32,

> *Also reason is a lie; for there is a factor infinite and unknown; and all their words are skew-wise.*

The Hermit has thus passed beyond the third veil and to all intents and purposes has departed from the world of men altogether, and forever.

Three Ways of Initiation

The three degrees of initiation described in the previous chapter have a certain, though not exact, correspondence to the three ways or paths of the Eastern tradition. These are Ynana Yoga (knowledge), Bhakti Yoga (devotion) and Karma Yoga (right action). These are also called the sacerdotal way of the priesthood, the royal way of kings, and the way of the warrior.

In our time, the warrior path presents the greatest difficulties. The warrior path generally involves the Ideal expressed through exoteric religious (or other) dogma. Dogma literally means 'what seems to be good or true', 'what one should think'. The shortcoming is obvious. However, religious dogma has now been replaced by universal belief in scientism. Scientism is far worse than religious dogma, for that at least had a basis in true principles, even if the basis was often lost in practice—a condition made worse in the confusion of modern times. The dogma of conventional science, however, has no basis in any truth whatsoever since it rests entirely on theory and is therefore updated continually. Truth, however, does not change.

It could be said, and not without some justification, that all ways of initiation are closed in the present times—for we have reached the greatest darkness of the Kali Yuga that comes immediately before the final dissolution and regeneration of the world. However, even in times such as ours the way of initiation is open right until the last minute for the few that still have the innate possibilities.

The practices are not separate, as though having nothing to do with each other. They overlap and in some ways run concurrently. One path can also support another. The way of Bhakti, 'devotion', is akin to Raja Yoga, which is the way of the king or noble, yet it is also the way of the warrior or man of Earth. Karma Yoga is 'action', which implies immersion in time and place—the names, numbers and principalities. Yet that impinges on the way of the Lover, who, unless he is wholly devoted to union with God or divinity, must always be tested by the ordeals configured by the very nature of the darkness of the outer world.

The three paths, as with the practices, are comparable to the three Gunas in the same tradition: Sattwas, Rajas and Tamas. They are never truly separate in nature; each one flows seamlessly into the other. They must all therefore partake of each other's nature in some way. While each manifests according to its nature they all partake of the one essence or essential Esoteric Principle, as symbolised by the centre or hub of a wheel, for example.[88] No living creature or person consists wholly of one or the other of these three qualities, but one or the other will be the dominant force in them. That is not necessarily a fixed state of affairs, for initiation can change this, and as we have said, one path can act as a support for another. It can be readily seen then that the way of Ynana Yoga suits the Sattwic disposition, while the ways of Bhakti and Karma Yoga suit the Rajas disposition. The Tamas disposition, ignorant by its very nature, naturally precludes any possibility of initiation and only allows for exoteric affiliation. It is said, nonetheless, that Tamas has a closer relation with Rajas than it has with Sattwas.[89]

Those who follow the ways of Bhakti Yoga and Karma Yoga are those who must develop individual qualities. These two paths pertain to the Lesser Mysteries and the psychic sphere of the individuality. Ynana Yoga, which is the path of pure knowledge, exists for those who will leave the corporeal order permanently, and is the way of the Greater Mysteries. Yet Karma and Bhakti can provide a support to the further and full realisation that only Ynana Yoga affords. Indeed, there is no way to the pinnacle without first entering the centre of all, the *omphalos* at the heart of Tiphereth in our tradition. In the West, Bhakti Yoga once had its counterpart in the Grail tradition, the chivalry typified by Arthur and his knights, or in some of the ancient orders such as the Knights Templar—though we must exclude from that all modern claimants to that tradition.

---

[88] The Gunas are oft confused with the alchemical principles, as depicted on modern Tarot decks for the Wheel or Fortuna, the 10th Atu. This results from syncretism and obscures the meaning of the older Tarot cards. For example, the Marseille deck appears to depict the Hindu wheel of cyclical birth and death, and quite astonishingly, non-human states of being.
[89] René Guénon, Chapter 18, *Initiation and Spiritual Realisation*.

Sri Ramakrishna, one of the last of the great sages and an Avatar of Vishnu, frequently referred to the present age of the Kali Yuga when giving instruction to his disciples. To our great good fortune, his faithful disciple 'M' recorded much of what Ramakrishna said.[90] In 'Instruction to Vaishnavas and Brahmos', Ramakrishna tells of the Bhakti yoga path of devotion to the Shakti in relation to a cult of the Goddess Nanek in Benares.[91] He says that the path of devotion is particularly suited to the people of the Kali Yuga. 'M' then asked of the Master, rather surprised, "Are not sadhus of [Narada's] class followers of the [Advaita] Vedanta?"

"Yes they are", said Ramakrishna. "But they also accept the path of devotion. The fact is that in the Kaliyuga one cannot wholly follow the path laid down in the Vedas. Once a man said to me that he would perform the *puraschana* of the Gāytri. I said, 'Why don't you do that according to the Tantra? In the Kaliyuga the discipline of Tantra is very efficacious'. It is extremely difficult to perform the rites enjoined in the Vedas. Further, at the present time people lead the life of slaves." What is worse, he continues, they become degraded through wanting to be like their slave-masters, and they soon become just like them. Ramakrishna goes on to qualify that in the present time of the Age of Kali Yuga the most effective practices are Tantra and Devotion (Bhakti). That is to say, we do the rituals and adopt the mudra of the devotee of Shakti. He also says it is by now even impossible to work the path of Karma Yoga; to understand that better we must be aware of the Vedic context of the teaching. We are in times of such great darkness and materiality that outward or exoteric duties will no longer act as a path to realisation of God or Reality. While some of that might always be necessary for a householder, for example, only single-minded devotion to God in the form of Shakti will lead the way to truth. The profane world, in all of its aspects, only draws the soul to greater darkness and slavery.

Karma has its counterpart with crafts, and in that we would include poetry, music and all the arts, provided these express true principles and are not merely about personal expression. In the true and also the most technical sense, Karma Yoga is 'ritual action', which again, owing to the general conditions of our times, is nowhere to be found in our governmental, social or domestic conventions except in the most degraded and meaningless forms imaginable.

---

[90] Translated into English by Swami Nikhilananda and published in *The Gospel of Sri Ramakrishna* (Ramakrishna Vivekananda Centre, New York).
[91] P. 297 [*ibid*].

The principles hold true in all traditional actions. For example, there was a time not so long ago when at the Beltane cross-quarter of the year, on or around the 1st May, a pole was firmly erected in a field and coloured ribbons were tied to its mast. Young girls, dressed in white and decorated with flowers, would then each hold on to the end of a ribbon and all would go dancing merrily about the pole. One of these would be designated 'Queen of the May'. The Queen of the May is the 'one chosen' to play the part of the Daughter or Bride of the Kingdom, called Malkah or Persephone, and known by many other names in equivalent traditions around the world. The pole is the vertical axis of the universe and of the Great Yantra. This links heaven with earth and the spiritual order with the corporeal world. In the axis is the possibility of initiatic transmission, like lightning to the ground. The circle is the circumference of the sphere, of which the interpenetrating axis is the extended point or Esoteric Principle; it is the visible appearance of things, or Nature. The maidens are the whole range of possible expressions, as the multitudinous variety of flowers, yet each retaining the purity (white colour) of the Principle itself. The coloured ribbons that connect the maidens with the axis form the rainbow of Setian manifestation, the 'coat of many colours' of Joseph.[92] They are the seven rays, of which the seventh is white, or sometimes violet—an analogous term for that which is beyond the reach of the sky or otherwise at the head of the axial column.[93]

The Karma path in its fullest and original sense means that each must accomplish that which accords to its proper nature, called a 'True Will'. Unfortunately, the conditions now prevailing in the world have made that rare, almost impossible. This owes to the disorder that is now considered to be the normal state of affairs, so that every kind of deviancy is also considered to be normal. In that, it does well to bear in mind that this is so because the whole of our civilisation is deviant, not merely some parts of it or particular kinds of behaviour. The primary deviation is a step away from all spiritual knowledge; one step leads to another until eventually even the possibility of any knowledge or reality beyond the human corporeal domain is rejected absolutely.

---

[92] Genesis 37: 3: 'Now Israel loved Joseph more than all his children, because he was the son of his old age: and he made him a coat of many colours.'
[93] Traditionally, white is used as a symbolic colour in this respect, for it contains all other colours of the spectrum. More recently it has become quite common to think of violet as the seventh colour of the rainbow but the former is the more exact symbolism.

It remains to be said that as 'ritual action', various kinds of magical practice such as the making and consecration of talismans are related to Karma Yoga, though these may also, if properly done, act as a support for spiritual realisation. When talismans are made for wholly negative purposes, such as worldly ambition, material gain, persuasion of the will of others, and so forth, then the resultant disequilibrium means that wrath and retribution is automatically evoked. This is something many now find difficult to believe, since our world encourages such empty ambitions as a matter of course, and even heaps honours upon those with truly abhorrent or base motives. However, this action of retribution is inevitable. It does not arise from any moral consideration, since morals, by definition, are merely completely arbitrary human conventions. The retribution arises from natural action, which is another meaning of the Sanskrit *karma*. If the person has invoked either deity or devil, it matters not which, in complete ignorance of the principle or true knowledge underlying the symbol, then the principle will nonetheless be present at the ritual and in the operator, but only in wholly negative form.

The use of talismans as mere mechanical or hypnotic devices for some imagined self-improvement, gain or other personal goal, is a degradation of the art and necessarily divorces the highly specialised kind of intelligence involved from its principle. The talisman, when understood perfectly, is one of the foremost justifications for the magical arts. When we consecrate a talisman effectively, we make a link between our individuality and a non-human intelligence. The planetary spirits do not have an individuality; they are an aspect of being that is beyond the human scale and that has nothing to do with human consciousness. With a talismanic operation the intelligence takes on a temporary individuality through its relationship with us, and for this reason one must always be aware of the principle behind the intelligence. The classical form of talismanic working to some extent accommodates this, for there is a hierarchy of names and powers always depending from the highest source. If the operator is ignorant or careless, however, then the intelligence becomes easily separated from the principle, so that only the inverse or infernal reflection manifests in the human state. Much care, then, is taken over the preparation and consecration of talismans.

The Magi

At the head of the three ways of initiation are figured the Magi. A Magus will in some way show forth the 'three' symbolically, for example, in the trident, the *vajra* or some triangular form. In the Christian narrative there are three Magi from the Orient that follow the star to witness the birth of the light into the darkness of the world. 'Magick' is a term that we have used a little too frequently. Owing to various rationalist definitions of the word, as having to do with 'cause and effect', it is frequently misunderstood. The word is derived from the Magi (Greek *magoi* or *magos*), a term that once referred to Persian priests or 'enchanters' who were said to have interpreted dreams. Properly speaking, the Magi were wise men that taught others through symbol and analogy.

The first known Magi were of the Median tribe. The name is derived etymologically from Zend *maz*, 'great', a term that is allied to *magnus* (Latin) or *megas* (Greek). The Zend language is derived from the sacred Avestic texts belonging to those very incorrectly described as 'fire worshippers', and also known as Zoroastrians. The Scandinavian *maze*, meaning 'labyrinth', is a related term.[94] The same word also has the meaning of 'delirium' or 'out of one's wits', which is the condition that afflicts any profane who attempt to enter the well-guarded sacred place. Further related terms include 'zenith', the head of the vertical axis or pole of the worlds, and *zanana*, 'apartments for women', which is the equivalent of the Hindu *zenana* and East Indian *harem*. Fire worship is then suggestive of devotion to the unmanifested Goddess 'beyond the sky', the ancient Egyptian Neïth, who was also associated with Sekhet the lioness.

There were six tribes in ancient Medes, the place 'between the lands' (*media*, *medes*). The Magi had knowledge of the natural or traditional sciences, which included astronomy and astrology—these were not then separate disciplines. They were the Persian equivalent of the Brahmins, a class that corresponds to the path of Ynana Yoga. The Egyptian equivalent and most ancient source is *ma'atet*, 'a seer', related to *ma'a* 'truth' and also 'a lion', and Ma'at the Goddess in whom the word or utterance is made perfect.

---

[94] Maz is the root of Mazdaism, Avestic Mazda, named after Ahura-mazda or Ormazd, the 'good principal', or properly speaking, the 'highest principle' in ancient Persian theology. *The Concise Dictionary of English Etymology*, Walter W. Skeat.

The word issuing from the mouth of the primordial lion is the Ever-Becoming, which manifests in the human or corporeal world as the 'devouring' principle of time. It is the difference between the Idea and thought, the unmanifest and the manifest. The 'devouring' is at the same time the dissolution undergone by the initiate of the path of Ynana Yoga ('knowledge' or 'gnosis') when entering the supra-human state. As declared by Nuit in the Book of the Law, I: 30,

> *This is the creation of the world, that the pain of division is as nothing, and the joy of dissolution all.*

In the book of Daniel, 6: 12, concerning the lion's den, the Persian Law of Medes is referred to by the king:

> The thing is true, according to the law of the Medes and Persians, which altereth not.

The Law of Medes affirms that which is unalterable or imperishable, sometimes symbolised by the circumpolar stars that never sink below the horizon. It is the highest spiritual principle, the eternal truth. We have said that the Magus is a talisman—'the living incarnation of a particular type of intelligence, a word in flesh'.[95] All true symbols are manifestations of states of being that originate with the divine or supra-human order. When meditated on, such symbols act as a support for initiatic transmission. This is why the *bodhisattvas* or avatars of various traditions are sometimes the object of devotion. These can act as intermediaries between the spiritual world and the corporeal world—those who are able to express the Law of Medes. The *avatara* (Sanskrit) implies a 'descent', which is required of any intermediary, although it is more common in the West to hear of avatars described in terms such as 'ascended masters'.

Effective realisation of spiritual states is made possible by being a talisman of the primordial or Esoteric Principle. The individuality is gradually ordered through initiation. The being is then able to reflect the truth of its own nature or 'True Will'—which is the beginning of the path, not the end. The path of a Magus is ascetic in the true and original meaning of the word, from the Greek *asketikos* (ασκητικος), 'exercise, work or discipline'. Asceticism was originally descriptive of hermits and over time it took on rigorous connotations, although the term is positively descriptive of the way of Ynana Yoga and does not in itself imply negation or abstention. Indeed, negation is only seen by those who are completely outside such disciplines of knowledge, as they cannot conceive of anything existing beyond the sensorial.

---

[95] See *Babalon Unveiled*, 'The Magician', p. 8.

According to René Guénon, the root word *ascesis* 'properly designates a methodical method to attain a certain goal, and more particularly a goal of a spiritual order'.[96] He goes on to say that *ascesis* corresponds closely with the Sanskrit *tapas*, which means 'fire' or 'heat'. The 'heat' is that of an interior fire that is needed to consume the Qliphoth or 'shells', as termed in the Qabalah. To put this in other words, the fire is 'to destroy everything within us that is an obstacle to spiritual realisation'.[97] Ascesis is the positive action of initiatic rites and the subsequent interior work of an initiatic Order—it has nothing to do with austerity, though that is by now the common notion of the term 'ascetic'. Acsesis is the sacrifice of all the contingencies of the egoistic sphere, which is necessary for any spiritual realisation to be possible. Scholars will insist on calling such practices 'extreme', for they cannot understand that anything exists beyond the individual and egoistic domain. Such a 'sacrifice' is performed by the priest or hiereus—a Greek word corresponding in some respects to a Magus.[98] It is the spiritual realisation of the 'fire worshipper' or Zoroastrian priest. The *ascesis* or *tapas* is the alchemical Sulphur, the fire that over time melts or dissolves (MVG) the corruptible body (MVGShM) of the magus (MGVShM) so that he realises himself as the 'living incarnation of a particular type of intelligence' that we have alluded to previously. As such, the body of the magician is the *magena stone* (MGN) or telesmatic 'shield', called a 'buckler' in Psalms 18: 2:

> The Lord is my rock, and my fortress, and my deliverer; my God, my rock; in whom I will trust; my buckler, and the horn of my salvation, and my high tower.

And in the Eighth Key of the Enochian Calls of John Dee,

> Which I have prepared for my own truth, so saith the Lord; whose Eternal reign shall be as bucklers to the Stooping Dragon, and like unto the harvest of a widow.

Resistance to bring about the manifest (positive) or unmanifest (negative) is the discipline of the path, the *ascesis*. Such resistance is the form or method that, if adhered to, dissolves all obstructions to any spiritual realisation. The path originates with ancient Egypt, as does all language and traditional knowledge, as shown forth in the spells of transformation:

---

[96] René Guénon, *Initiation and Spiritual Realisation*, p. 101.
[97] P. 102 [*ibid*].
[98] From *hiera*, 'sacrifice made by a seer', which is the root of *hiereus* and by its number 124 is the equivalent by Gematria to *magoi*, magus.

> How shall I reveal to you the truth of my heart? I am as Horus; I direct his sacred bark. I appear on the throne of Ra, creator of all things. Set, son of Nuit, was bound up by the chains of his own making. I was tested in *sekhem*. I stretched out both my arms even as does Ptah, who createth his own image. I have passed the Gate of Judgement. I have passed the Gate of Sorrow, and Lo! I have passed by the Gate of the Shroud.[99]

Although this is an ancient Egyptian text, it is notable that the Gate of Judgment, Gate of Sorrow and Gate of the Shroud (or Death) are all titles traditionally afforded Malkuth in the Qabalah. According to our commentary on the *Swallow in the Moment of Becoming* (Ritual of Samhain),

> To be as Horus is to be a risen Khu, the fully formed magical 'child' or divine son, whose foundation has been prepared in the intelligence of the heart. As the enemy of Horus and his father Ra, Set is destroyed by the very act of opposition. In the equilibration of the dual serpent power—which is that of manifestation—the soul is brought to new life. Set is the double power, bound up in the talisman. As the son of Nuit, the word of Isis, he is thus restored, reserved for the Great Work.

The sacrifice of the priest is descriptive, in the broadest sense, of Karma Yoga when that is understood in the technical sense ('ritual action'). The *hieros gamos*, also related to the priest through the root *hiera*, *hiereus*, is the mystic marriage or yogic union with God and corresponds to Bhakti Yoga. The inner work of the Magus is to unite the soul with the divine.

The Magus of three paths corresponds Qabalistically to Metatron, the 'Angel of the Countenance' or Kether, the Primordial.[100] Metatron is 'the one that passes beyond', designating the ultimate goal of yoga, which is only accomplished on the path of Ynana Yoga. Metatron is the *avatara* of the initiation to the highest state. As such, he is the King of the World, which, as Guénon was at pains to point out, is not to be confused with the Prince of Darkness or Antichrist.[101] In this respect it is worth recollecting that Christ is a 'priest after the order of Melchizedek', and that the latter designates the cosmic order.[102]

---

[99] The translation is ours.
[100] Magos, 314, is the equivalent by Gematria to *gamos*, 'marriage' and to the Archangel Metatron. All entries for 314 in *The Flaming Sword* are cognate.
[101] See Guénon, *The King of the World* [Sophia Perennis].
[102] Psalms 110: 4. There are many references in Hebrews. In Hebrews 7: 17 it is written: 'Thou art a priest for ever after the order of Melchizedek.'

The stele of Hru-het-djet, known as the 'Scorpion King', or King Narmer

King Scorpion and the Royal Way

The first historically recorded king of all Egypt is known by Egyptologists as King Scorpion, or sometimes King Narmer or Menes. However, he established the first royal house name, which is called a *serekh*.[103] Every king that came after him used this 'Horus name'; it eventually developed into the cartouche. Scorpion was the first to unite the two lands under one kingship and so he was effectively the first pharaoh of Egypt. He was a Setian, as were many of the protodynastic and early dynastic kings, and did a great deal to develop agriculture, irrigation and sacred buildings.[104]

The Egyptian priesthood was almost certainly behind Scorpion's establishment of the royal way or way of kings as opposed to the sacerdotal (or priestly) way. By that time, which coincides with the beginning of the age of the Kali Yuga, there was a need of initiation to the second birth—previously there was no need of it, for all could clearly see the truth of things in visible nature. The secondary centre, called Tiphereth in the Qabalah, is the exact midpoint between the Heaven and the Earth, and is the domain of the Universal or Cosmic Man. This is really an inner realisation, but in ancient history a king was identified with the divine principle, and was the upholder of that principle. Likewise, the king was one with the land itself, and with the people, as carried through the legends of the Holy Grail.

Among the Scorpion King's artefacts is a mace with a scorpion on the head. That is why he is called 'Scorpion' or Selk. The Scorpion, however, is also *hetjet*, 'breath of life'. It is a form of Isis, while the mace is the light-giver. However that may be so, the royal name of the first king at least is quite easy to work out. The king's 5,000-year old stele, on which is engraved his Horus name, was discovered at Saqqara and stolen away to the Paris Louvre.[105] The shape of the stele is most interesting. It is not an arch but is clearly a representation of the shape made by the body of Nuit arched over the sky, which is asymmetrical to allow very precisely for her bodily contours.

---

[103] Egyptian SRH, with a hard 'h' like *cheth*. In some texts the king's name is confused with that of his *serekh*, so he is sometimes called Zru or Zorah.
[104] This happens to accord with ancient tales regarding the Sons of Anak, who were of divine or angelic descent. See 'The Nephalim and Sons of Anak', and 'The Sons of Gods'.
[105] The stele appears to have been broken in two pieces by the Egyptologists and damaged in transit, as was the stele stolen from the top of the sacred mount Hermon in Phoenicia.

The stele depicts Horus in the falcon form (*hru*) perched upon his own house (*het*).[106] The house has the serpent (*djet*) at the top and below it are three elaborate pillars, which symbolise both the power of manifestation and the primordial tradition. Behind these are the two gates, the royal way (second birth) and the sacerdotal way (third birth). From this may be derived the real name of the first king of Egypt: Hru-het-djet, 'Horus, Lord of Light and giver of Life'.

Another of the king's symbols was the seven-petalled Sepet or Septet, which was later identified with the goddess Seshet. It is said that the task of the Masters is to 'spread the light and to gather what is scattered'.[107] King Hru-hed-djet accomplished this Great Work by establishing the royal way of initiation and uniting the two lands of Upper and Lower Egypt.

Lucy Lamie's book *Egyptian Mysteries* includes a photograph of Hru-hed-djet's stele. Also shown there is a three-dimensional line drawing of his rectangular Mastaba tomb.[108] This includes dozens of compartments, including a great number of bulls horns set in clay heads—as many as 346. According to Lamie, King Scorpion's tomb was probably configured astronomically—for example, the number 346 is used to calculate lunar eclipses far into the future. This was, we should remember, at the time of the precessional Age of Taurus the Bull. Scorpio, as the opposite zodiacal sign, is the 'power behind Taurus', and its occult counterpart. While Egyptologists will deny the existence of all knowledge not comprehensible by them, it is quite obvious that ancient Egyptian architectural symbolism was adapted to the changing constellational background for the sun's rising at the vernal equinox. This changes six times (approximately every 2000 years) in a Great Year of about 12,000 years.[109]

The workmanship of that time in Egypt's history was finer and of greater accuracy than anything that came after. The stele of Hru-het-djet is of great beauty, characteristic of the very early period. That is to say, 'early' in the sense of what is known historically, which is very little; according to ancient texts, the hieroglyphs were all written 40,000 years earlier. Taken as a whole, the stele is a symbol of the Great Work *par excellence*.

---

[106] In 1938 his basalt Sarcophagus, of breathtaking beauty and fine detail, was being taken on a ship to England when the ship sank off the Spanish coast. Only drawings remain.
[107] Guénon, *Symbols of Sacred Science*, p. 288 [Sophia Perennis].
[108] Pp. 38–39 [Thames and Hudson].
[109] See 'Cosmic Cycles'.

Recollection and Spiritual Realisation

Recollection, insight, realisation and revelation pertain to quite different degrees or levels of initiation; yet the terms are frequently confused. Some clarification is therefore needful. *Recollection* is essentially of the exoteric order. The Christian Mass is a good example of recollection in the religious context. It is said that a priest performing the Mass must not strive too hard after the recollection, which is the primary aim of the Mass, and is better advised to concentrate on simply performing the operation correctly. The same advice can be applied to any ritual, where too much seeking after what is supposed to be the desirable outcome restricts or limits that outcome by the very fact of the personal wish getting in the way. Spiritual experience in itself is wholly unconditioned by any human will or intention, and spiritual experience must always be the aim, even where the activity really belongs in the exoteric domain.

The Latin *recollectio* is from the verb *recolligere*, 'to gather again', that is, from memory. There is a close association with the idea of Holy Communion itself, the shared participation in spiritual experience as according to the level that each participant is capable of reaching. Recollection also takes place in the individual sphere, where the 'gathering' is in the bringing to mind of any true symbol, or image or idea—though we use the word here in the technical sense and not the ordinary one of simply remembering a fact, for example, unless the fact is a spiritual one. This forms part of a very specialised use of recollection (Sanskrit *smrti*) as part of meditation practice. Using discrimination requires cutting off of all harmful thoughts at the root. One may then recollect helpful mental impressions, such as previous knowledge of yoga states. When devotion is practiced on an image or form of God, then it is not direct cognition but recollection that is the means. 'Ritual', as according to the dictionaries, is nothing more than 'repeated action', which limits ritual to a completely profane or outward notion. Ritual in the true sense, as with a 'rite', is of the sacred and initiatic domain, and its purpose must always be aimed at that. While ritual cannot convey any real initiation as such, when ritual is 'contacted' by way of an initiatic organisation it can act as a support to the possibility of initiation. Ritual then takes on the meaning of 'ordination', literally, 'to put in order', but the ordinance here is in the sense of a holy rite. This putting in order is a form of recollection at the most outward level. Yet recollection is essential, for without it no real insight is gained.

Insight is akin to inspiration, and implies that a more profound level of understanding has been reached, or touched upon. This is also the meaning of the word 'attain', which is derived from the Latin *tangere*, 'touch', as is the word 'tangible'. When something becomes tangible it has been touched upon. We must note here that the language used is within the realm of the sensorial, although insight is taken as pertaining to the plane of intellect. Insight may touch upon wisdom, in which case it becomes truer in the literal sense of 'inner-sight' or of 'seeing within', which is then from the interior and not the exterior point of view.

Realisation, on the other hand, is (literally) 'to make real' the knowledge. In the spiritual sense, realisation exists purely in the realm of initiation. Realisation is spoken of in the Vedanta, for example, as being synonymous with the goal of yoga itself, which is 'union with God', ultimately the complete realisation of Atma and Brahma as one. Realisation is thus synonymous with initiation and knowledge (Sanskrit *ynana*) in the true sense.

Realisation must not then be confused with any ritual as such any more than it should be confused with persons that are 'authorised' to conduct rites—unfortunately, this confusion is very commonplace. Likewise, such realisation must not be confused with 'degrees' or any other outwardly marked stages in development as used by initiatic organisations, even if these are genuinely initiatic, which happens to be a very rare thing in the present times.[110] The grades or degrees are in a sense part of the *ritual* in the literal and outward sense of 'putting things in order'—for that is absolutely necessary if initiation is to take place. There are lesser degrees of initiation, however, by which we can include all that is within the individual's mental or psychic domain, in which case this is called 'virtual' initiation.[111] Realisation, in the sense we mean it here however, is far more than merely symbolic, or as pertaining to the human psychological order. Realisation effects a complete change in the being that is in every way irreversible. Likewise, initiation in the true sense is once and for all of time; it can never be lost, stolen or taken away from the person that has truly experienced it.

---

[110] See 'Initiation'.
[111] We use this term 'virtual' in the etymological meaning of the word, which has nothing to do with modern computing slang. Cf. 'Initiation'.

Revelation is sometimes confused with all three of the other terms we have explained here. It is even confused with completely ordinary things, such as is implied by the usual dictionary definition of the word as the 'discovery of a previously unknown fact'. Worse than that, it is used to refer to the discovery of a well-known fact not previously known by the person having the revelation! Now while words can have many levels of meaning, as is necessary, in modern times all emphasis has been placed on the most profane level of understanding, to the extent that the original meaning becomes forgotten entirely. Eventually that meaning drifts altogether out of the reach of most people. Revelation as the 'discovery of a previously unknown fact' came about as recently as the late nineteenth century, yet it is by now the primary dictionary definition. St. John's book of Revelation, however, conveys something of truly spiritual import.[112]

The word 'revelation' has a double meaning, for *reveil* means 'to uncover', 'to lift the veil' on something but also has the opposite meaning, 'to cover'—for spiritual experience cannot be conveyed in words or symbols directly; to attempt to do so automatically veils it. This is shown in the etymology of the word, which is derived from the Latin *revelare*, literally to 're-veil', from *velum*, a veil or covering. Nonetheless, the study and often the memorisation (recollection) of sacred scriptures is considered essential in all traditions as the best means of preparation so that initiation may even be possible. Indeed, this is not merely 'reading' but involves the study of etymology, the sacred languages and the understanding of symbolism of other kinds, such as astrology, *yantras*, geometric or other traditional forms.

In the very ordinary sense we might speak of something being revealed to us, but 'revelation' is best reserved for direct knowledge of God or of Reality. Even more particularly, the nature of this kind of revelation is usually taken to refer to a matter that is even of some profound significance to others. It is therefore not any kind of merely 'personal' revelation—for that would automatically relegate it to the realm of perfectly ordinary or commonplace things.

---

[112] The title of the book of St. John is derived from the Greek αποκαλυψις, from whence the alternative English title, 'Apocalypse'. This has the same meaning in Greek as in the Latin, literally, 'to lift the veil'.

Psychism and Subversion

Our past curriculum, as published in various textbooks, contains a great deal of what can be termed as magical or even 'psychic' applications of Hermetic Science.[113] Skrying, for example, if properly done, involves the yogic concentration on a symbol so that a 'flow of knowledge' (*dhyana*) comes about. 'Skrying' means 'seeing', and is comparable to the Sanskrit *darshana*, which means literally 'a window' or 'point of view'. Rising on the planes, if correctly understood, is a Hermetic form of tantra-yoga, making use of symbolism as a support to gaining *samadhi*, the goal of yoga, with the equivalent of *mantras* (words) and *yantras* (images).[114]

So long as we keep the goal in sight, which is identical to that of yoga in the real sense, we should not go too far astray. Unfortunately, it is very rare now to find anyone that can make use of such magical practices without incurring harm to their self or to others, and this owes to the widespread lack of any true knowledge of the principles involved. There is also a risk of over-developing the psychic faculty and becoming excessively reliant on it, even to the exclusion of all else. It is not intended that results of the psychic order should be given objective validity. It goes without saying that neither are such results to be counted in any way as being important or significant in the scheme of things. The psychic realm has nothing to do with the spiritual realm, as by definition that which pertains to the psyche is strictly limited to the body and mentality of the individuality and reaches no further—a matter we shall come back to.

Psychism, on the other hand, is a very different thing, and we have always spoken out against this. Psychism is a branch of the occult that originated as recently as the latter part of the nineteenth century. It should be noted in passing that public knowledge of this is non-existent—for opinions are guided by 'news' and 'information' that reduces everything to the most simplistic and grossly material level. While it is obvious that mediums and charlatans have used the tricks and illusions of stagecraft to produce manifestations, what is not so obvious to an easily deceived public is that the exposure or debunking of this usually rests on a confusion of the psychic realm with the material realm.

---

[113] *Ritual Magick—Initiation of the Star and Snake*, for example.
[114] Yoga means 'union', in the traditional and real sense, and means, more particularly, union with God; to put it in the terms of Advaita Vedanta, it is the realisation of Atma and Brahma.

A psychic occurrence cannot, by definition, even though it exists on the most inferior of the subtle planes, exist on the material plane where it can be subjected to all the 'tests' and 'proving' of profane science. Those who write or speak about this with total confidence in what they imagine to be a superior understanding know absolutely nothing about the subject whatsoever, for to them the psychic realm has no existence, let alone the spiritual. The irony that these same commentators are wholly deceived by the tricks and illusions of so-called 'science' escapes them completely. We are not then denying the existence, relative though it is, of psychic phenomena.

Psychism, which has no doubt captivated the interest of many persons that are perfectly sincere—though that is no justification in itself—admits no real knowledge. It reduces everything to the psychic level and even the *infra* or sub-human levels of manifestation, though it knows not the real source of its 'visions' and 'spirit-guides'. Psychism is the habitual and passive resort to the lowest of the subtle levels. Its advocates frequently embrace or claim to practice many elements of the Occult Science though not understanding them at all, reducing them to their most inferior level of manifestation. The use of the law of correspondences, for example, which has traditionally served to train the mind, is translated into a vague search for 'signs' and 'omens', not only in what passes for a form of magick but that is also extended into every area of life so that it becomes a matter of habit. While the person cannot coherently explain the meaning of such 'coincidences' they nonetheless insist on treating them as if they had some profound, even spiritual import. The products of psychism are illusory and meaningless.

There are, however, even worse and more degraded forms of psychism than those described above, such as 'channelling'. The agents of confusion and subversion that adopt this mode will even claim that the reams of quasi-mystical gibberish they produce derive from a source of higher wisdom. It is evident that such advice comes from a source nearer to the limited imagining of the channellers than any extraterrestrial or trans-mundane source. The banal content is invariably heavy with illiterate New Age jargon, popular clichés and faux-psychology.

Quietism is really a further form of psychism of a very low order. Although the term 'Quietism' fell out of use long ago, the attitude it describes has persisted and increased within the field of what now passes for spirituality.[115] Quietists admit no knowledge but pretend, by implication, belief and behaviour, to all knowledge. They take refuge in a complete distortion of the non-action doctrine of the East and refuse to do anything at all so that all is supposed to come to them miraculously, as it were, dropping into their lap as manna from heaven. They cannot see that this 'manna' consists of nothing but flattery and vain pretensions. These persons will often form loose alliances with professional psychics, mediums and channellers for mutual flattery and sometimes to increase the spread of their poison to the gullible and poorly educated. In fact, the so-called education of everyone by now is no more than a matter of enforced acceptance of a profane outlook on all things, for that is even a requirement to achieve 'qualifications', whether at school or university level.

The growth of psychism in all its forms was aided and abetted by the Theosophist movement and those influenced by it. It eventually opened the floodgates for the full onset of the anti-spiritual and anti-initiatic second level of the occult revival that took place from the 1950s and onward, replete with well publicised 'witchcraft' poseurs and sham Golden Dawn revivalists. The degradation was made complete by the New Age movement that emerged from the 1970s and onward. This hungrily devoured all the remnants of traditional knowledge, including various forms of Shamanism, and quickly subverted them towards wholly profane ends.

It has become increasingly difficult for our students—many of whom were born at a time when the subversion of all previous knowledge was more or less complete—to know anything about the spiritual realm at all. It has been sealed off by the 'plan' that Guénon wrote of 70 years ago now.[116] By subverting spiritual knowledge, or to put this more accurately, its symbols and doctrines, and relegating everything to the realm of the human psyche, the individual and the 'material', a hard shell was formed across the ceiling of human intellect—this even makes an impact upon the cosmic and terrestrial environment.

---

[115] 'Spiritualism' is another term rarely used now but which is descriptive of an anti-spiritual movement that has sought to substitute inferior forms of psychism for 'spiritual contact', as if there was no difference.

[116] 'Fissures in the Great Wall' and associated chapters in *The Reign of Quantity and the Signs of the Times* [Sophia Perennis].

Once the sealing shut of the upper worlds is accomplished, only the psychic realm remains for refuge. Although the spiritual domain is completely out of reach of the profane—for to them it does not exist—the psychic realm can be reached and manipulated by profane governance, which is in turn controlled by the anti-spiritual force in man. The psychic plane can also be reached and manipulated by individuals and organisations with pretended spiritual aims. The ways are closed off by now to most people in the world but it is still possible for an initiatic organisation to open them. So long as real initiation takes place, such an organisation is able to support further initiation. The reception of a spiritual influence makes it completely immune to the attacks made on it from the outer darkness. However, the prospective candidates must totally eradicate from their minds all allegiance to social or political strategies, resisting every lure to engage in the artificial constructs of hypnotic media technologies or to believe in, let alone partake of, the products of fake sciences.

A doctrine exists in all traditions regarding an incursion of the Qliphoth at the end of time.[117] The incursion is made possible by fissures opened in the human artificial construct from *below*. As mankind has effectively sealed off that which is 'above', no spiritual influences can neutralise the mindlessly destructive power of infernal forces. The use of the word 'infernal' here is meant to specifically describe the realm of the infra-corporeal or of sub-manifestation, which is to say that such agencies exist at the most inferior level possible, for any further degree would render them completely non-existent. Their existence is only relative but their effect is real enough in the corporeal and psychic realms, which is the limit of their reach.

That which was implemented in our world from the spring of 2020 and onward is undoubtedly the greatest deception of all time. Though the 'plan' was prepared long ago, this latest phase is a vast acceleration towards the final dissolution at the end of the present Great Age. The sweeping 'measures', including population control and genetic modifications, could only be accepted because human intelligence is degenerating at an exponential rate. This has been aided and abetted by the confusion and subversion of all traditional knowledge.

---

[117] The orientalist Kenneth Grant incorporated this in his writings but as with so much else he inverted the symbolism. He thus confused the spiritual with the demonic to such an extent that his followers unwittingly work on the side of self-destruction and anti-initiation. See pp. 16 and 19–22.

The Star of the Order

The (Egyptian) Book of the Law contains some metaphysical allusions but the Law is 'Written and Concealed' (III: 75). Metaphysical reality can only be conveyed indirectly in words and symbols. To write it is to veil or conceal it. The first and only time that Aiwass makes a direct statement in his own name is in verses I: 7–8, where he declares, 'The Khabs is in the Khu, not the Khu in the Khabs'. He has named himself as the 'minister of Hoor-paar-kraat', the royal priest or God of Silence or of meditation. This is to be understood as symbolic of 'pure consciousness'—of which more will be explained later. The God, often shown emerging from a lotus flower, is easily comparable with early depictions of the Buddha and also of Shiva. As a prince and priest (literally), Aiwass was entitled to wear the forelock of Harpocrates; however, in this case we are dealing with one that far exceeded the fulfilment of a mere office or official function.[118] To approach further understanding of all this we need to know something about the Egyptian Khabs and Khu.

The Khabs has a threefold symbol, as written everywhere upon stone and papyrus. It consists of a five-fingered or five-rayed star, which is sometimes called the 'Hand of Orion' (Sahu). It is described in the Book of the Law, I: 60, as blue and gold, five-pointed with a red circle in the middle. Stars exactly as described there adorn the walls and ceiling of Egyptian temples such as the Temple of Hathoor at Iunet (Denderah).[119] Within the radials is a small circle, and within that is the point or primordial centre. From the centre, the radiations form the circumference of the circle of all possibilities, and so these possibilities exist as latent in the centre.

---

[118] Aiwass is known to Egyptologists as Kha-em-uast (various spellings).
[119] Iunet, which includes a large temple complex north of Waset (Thebes), means approximately, 'She of the Divine Pillar' (or 'pillar of light'). The name relates both to Hathoor as Sky Goddess and the axis of the universe, of which the 'hub' of the wheel governs all manifestation, cosmologically speaking. Spiritually speaking, it marks the primordial centre that is the source of all initiatic transmission.

The circle and point is used to symbolise the Sun but is also used to symbolise the 'Sun behind the Sun', or Kether in the Qabalistic schema. The latter is the Supreme Centre, the primordial fount of all wisdom, while the former is the secondary solar centre, or Tiphereth. The Khu is the principle of radiance as applied to the transcendent individuality. As a 'resurrection body', the means of return to the source, it is symbolised by a phoenix, ibis, heron or other kind of bird.[120] The Khabs or 'star' also shows the principle of radiance, and radiance is naturally contained within the circle about the point, whose rays form the circumference.

The Khabs does not symbolise a star as such, which is called *seba*, but is a type of opening or doorway to the timeless 'hollow' at the centre of all, sometimes depicted in various traditions as a heart, vessel or Grail.[121] The Khabs is nonetheless the principle of a 'body', 'house' or 'abode', and is called in the Book of the Law, II: 2, the 'House of Hadit'—that is, the abode of the principial point. We are dealing here with Egyptian metaphysics and so it is not possible to simplify the meaning without distortion. However, if we understand that the five-rayed Khabs has a correspondence with the *jivatma* or centre of the individuality in the Vedanta, the instruction of Aiwass becomes clear: While the *jivatma* appears to be the centre of the self, it is in fact only a reflection of the Atma or true Self. Atma cannot be contained, enclosed or limited by anything. From the terrestrial or corporeal point of view, the 'Khu is in the Khabs', which is to say, 'the spirit is in the body'. This is a common error; from the point of view of Atma, the true Self, it is an illusion. The instruction from Aiwass is therefore the higher or initiated teaching. However, most persons take the meaning to be the very reverse of what was intended!

The 'extension' or manifestation of Hadit takes place through the two-way mirror of the Khabs. Outside or below that, he manifests as the Serpent of Knowledge whose abode is the Tree of Death, which is also the abode of man in the fallen state. Thus the Khabs itself has a dual aspect, above and below, or within and without—and with initiation, the point of view reverses. The Khabs is in the Khu from the supra-human or post-Abysmal point of view.

---

[120] See *Babalon Unveiled*, 'New Light on Stele 666', pp. 41–43 (pp. 107–113 in the Second Edition).

[121] The word 'Khabs' is actually the reverse of *seba*, 'star', with the addition of the 'kh', similar in pronunciation to the Hebrew *cheth* (ח). Note that the termination, *abs*, is cognate with both 'abyss' or 'opening' and the Egyptian *ab*, 'heart' or vessel. Furthermore, *seba*, as in the case of Khabs, is frequently depicted in hieroglyphs as a bird ('celestial body').

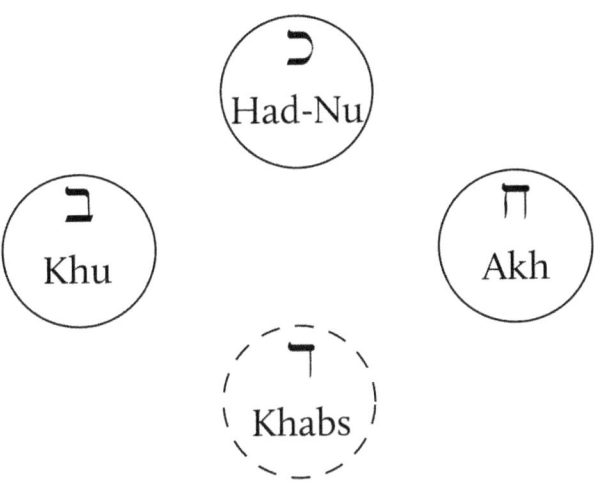

This can best be understood if we use the Qabalistic model as shown above. The Khabs star is here identified with Da'ath, for it acts as the means of Nuit's manifestation or appearance, as measured, and eventually *quantified*, in the Abyss of man's consciousness. It is at the same time the means of return to the primordial state; thus Nuit instructs us in the Book of the Law, I: 9,

Worship then the Khabs, and behold my light shed over you!

The Khabs as self-centre is now understood as its immediate higher principle, which is the Sanskrit *boddhi*, the ray or light of the higher intellect, and by which all things are known truly. According to traditional Qabalistic texts, Da'ath is hidden in the secret places of Binah, the primordial Mother and feminine aspect of Set-Typhon. Seen this way, the Khu cannot be in the Khabs, for the lesser cannot contain the greater or superior. The Khabs is here the emanation of the Khu, Nuit's body or 'company of heaven' as projected in time and space.[122] The verse is an Egyptian play on words. The Khabs has several meanings, including 'star', 'to adore' and to 'give light'. Thus the instruction includes all meanings of the word in one sentence.[123] Knowing and being are one; knowledge changes the state of the being through metaphysical realisation.

---

[122] Book of the Law, I: 2: 'The unveiling of the company of heaven.'
[123] All sacred languages do this such as Arabic, Hebrew and Sanskrit. Once specific meanings are applied to scriptural texts, as with vowel pointing, all traditional subtlety is lost, for interpretation is then dependent on both the interpreter's ability and, most often, social or political expediency.

The word Kha, which is sometimes transliterated as 'Ka', is identical to Khabs but without the *abs*, which means 'heart' but also 'emptiness'. Thus the real meaning of the Ka is rarely understood, because it is usually explained as 'vital force', which is not incorrect but is very limiting. As the Khabs includes the idea of the 'space' or cavity within the heart, then by upward transposition it includes what is called in the Hindu doctrine the *purusha* ('essence') residing in the heart of Brahma, the supreme reality. Thus Nuit also hides the *purusha* in her star on the cosmic level, and this essence is how all beings are produced, through polarisation. Thus Nuit declares of the manifest world, in the Book of the Law, I: 53,

This shall regenerate the world, the little world my sister, my heart and my tongue, unto whom I send this kiss.

The principle of all life resides within the sacred heart of Nuit. She repeats the words 'heart' and 'tongue' three times in the first chapter, to emphasise that hers is the power of creation and life.[124]

To complete the metaphysical basis it is necessary to place the Egyptian Akh principle in Chokmah. Akh, like Khu, is 'radiance', but whereas the Khu tends towards form, the Akh tends towards essence, the primordial or immortal state. This is shown by the word 'Akh' itself, which is the reverse of Khu and is formless, as is the principle of 'will' or 'ordinance'—which is a further meaning of Akh.

We can now see why the threefold Khabs is sometimes called the 'hand of Orion', the giant constellation or 'sky-strider', which has great importance in the ancient Egyptian doctrine. Every king was identified with Sahu or Orion. This was frequently depicted by an anthropomorphic figure of a God or a man with his left foot forward and one arm flung back over the shoulder, bearing what is frequently misconstrued as a 'flail'. This, combined with what is nearly always mistaken for a 'crook' became one of the most important symbols of Gods and kings. The *nekhakha* ('emanation') and *hekat* ('hook') are another type of the Khu and Khabs. Nekhakha, the triune Sophia or Khabs, is the means of the creation of a new state of being; *hekat* is the power of ordinance or 'activity' in the inner or spiritual sense.

---

[124] 'Creation' is the conventional term, though it has gained unfortunate anthropomorphic implications. The power of 'production' is more accurate. And let us note that this power, ultimately, does not reside with the Serpent—although as 'Beast' or Satan ruling the inferior worlds, he falsely claims the power for his own.

Thus, the 'servants of the star and snake', as it is put in the Book of the Law, II: 21, are those who serve only the primordial reality of Nuit and her Star, to whom the 'snake' must arise. Their sole purpose is that of initiation. This is accomplished, in the highest degree, through an ascending and descending realisation.[125] For the 'descent' to be perfect, the realisation must be to the fourth state, beyond even the 'third birth', and in which, to use the Sanskrit term, the dual soul of Brahma is known. This fourth state must have been known by Shankaracharya as it is in the texts he was commenting on, but he would say nothing about it.[126]

In this respect it may be worth noting that the Advaitan *turiya*, the 'fourth state' of consciousness, is equal by Qabalah to the number 226, which is that of Tzaphon, 'hidden', 'profound' or 'the north'. The ancient Egyptian word *tura* is clearly the origin of the Sanskrit term, and means 'pure'.[127] Terms such as *bodhisattva* and *avatara*, as according to various traditions, describe one that has effectively risen beyond even the 'saints'—for while the saints attain a high degree of initiation it is on their own behalf, whereas the avatars have a special mission that is concerned with assisting others with the Great Work to the very end of time.[128]

---

[125] See Guénon, chapter 38, *Initiation and Spiritual Realisation*.
[126] Perhaps for the obvious reason that Advaita is 'non-dualism'—see Guénon, p. 178 [*ibid*]. However, the dual soul of Brahma, neither manifest nor unmanifest yet partaking of both, has nothing to do with 'duality' or 'dualism' and is not in any way 'dualistic'.
[127] If the Egyptian *tura* is not the origin of the Sanskrit word *turiya* then it is certainly derived from the same source, a source that is so exceedingy ancient that almost nothing can be known of it.
[128] The notion of 'compassion' that is often used in association with the work of avatars reduces and degrades both their purpose and their function, so that some have supposed an 'avatar' to represent a lesser degree of the deliverance or Supreme Realisation, whereas it is in fact of the highest and most complete order. It is not a matter of sentimentality or emotionalism, which again is so often confused when the symbol of the 'heart' or vessel (Egyptian *ab*) is present, but is a matter of divine ordinance.

The Kiss of Nuit

The use of some comparative Sanskrit terms has proved helpful in gaining an understanding of the significance of the Khabs in the Khu. The primary, though not by any means the ultimate purpose of yoga, is to know Atma, the True Self, as the personal realisation of God. In the second verse of the second chapter of the (Egyptian) Book of the Law, Hadit, the equivalent of Atma, discloses his 'secret', which is concerned with his unmanifest aspect:

> *Come! all ye, and learn the secret that hath not yet been revealed. I, Hadit, am the complement of Nu, my bride. I am not extended, and Khabs is the name of my House.*

Hadit or Atma, when reflected into the *jivatma* or centre of the individuality, is symbolised by the metaphysical point at the centre of the Khabs, when that is depicted as a five-fingered star (or hand) with a circle in the middle. The reflected light of Atma shining upon the universe is the Khu or Phoenix, when that is understood from the cosmological perspective. In that case the 'Khu is in the Khabs', for the Khabs appears to be the higher principle. When Atma shines but does not give off light, then the perspective has changed, and the Khabs (as Da'ath) is in the Khu (as Binah).

The Khabs is called the 'House of Hadit' where the crosscurrents or emanations of the unmanifest sun-star form the appearance of Nuit. We are not here speaking of visible light or even astral light, but the source of all that. According to Advaita Vedanta, Atma and Brahma must be realised as one. Brahma is cognate with Absolute Nuit and not the appearance of Nuit, which is exoteric and pertains to the cosmological domain. However clearly explained, much of this must remain abstruse to the practitioner in the early stages. There is, however, a form of simple and effective devotional Tantra, for to worship the Khabs is to adore Nuit. This is conveyed in the voice of Nuit in the Book of the Law, I: 9,

> *Worship then the Khabs, and behold my light shed over you!*

The Egyptian God, crowned by the solar-stellar disc girt with a serpent, is a type of the fully formed Khu, phoenix or resurrection bird. The soul must become a Khu to escape the binding limitations encountered in the underworld or *duat*, the kingdom of shadows cast off by the terrestrial or mortal life. She may then pass on to the infinite reach of the sky, to realise her identity with Nuit.

The cobra serpent projecting from the brow of Egyptian Gods and pharaohs is the Serpent Power. This is also posited in the Tantras as a coiled serpent, latent or dreaming at the base of the spine in the subtle anatomy. The latter constitutes the being in an unawakened or ignorant state. When fully awakened, the Serpent Power rises from the base of the spine, travelling up to the nape of the neck. It passes from there over the top of the skull to the forehead, as a current of force or light, where it coils upward and stands erect. It should be understood, however, that the raising of *kundalini* does not, in itself, constitute either initiation or spiritual realisation, but is one part of the traditional sciences that can act as a support to these. As such, it is a type of individual alchemy that can lead, when taken to its limit, to the full realisation or *moksha* ('deliverance'). However, it is also possible, especially if the yoga is taken entirely out of its traditional context, or there is not even any yoga as such, as in the rare case of 'spontaneous' *kundalini* awakening, that magnification of delusion is all that takes place.[129]

The first realisation of the Khabs is more or less equivalent to that which is sometimes termed the 'Knowledge and Conversation of the Holy Guardian Angel' or the 'Vision of Adonai'.[130] The Initiate does not yet know Nuit, for Hadit has veiled her in the appearance of the universe. Samadhi, 'union with God', is the general Sanskrit term for the first direct spiritual realisation. There are gradations to this; the knowledge of God is not static but dynamic, and corresponds to the stage of development of the practitioner. Atmadarshana is the term used for the further realisation, and means literally, 'Atma point of view'. There is Shivadarshana beyond even that, which implies the supreme attainment. In either case, a real transformation in the state of the being is effected. The fullest realisation of the True Self does not come until the path is completed, which means final deliverance. However, in the Book of the Law, II: 76, it is said,

> *But remember, o chosen one, to be me; to follow the love of Nu in the star-lit heaven; to look forth upon men, to tell them this glad word.*

---

[129] This is particularly the case with forms of Laya Yoga taught in the West, or possibly by now, anywhere in the world, where it has been 'systematised' and grossly over simplified, often with pseudo-scientific and psychological assignments that have denatured the practice and placed it in the pseudo-initiatic domain. There are other means that are really in the domain of 'black magic' and of which it would not be seemly to discuss here.

[130] The term 'Knowledge and Conversation' is unfortunately misleading as it has been used to mean nothing more than psychic phenomena.

What does it mean, to 'look forth upon men, to tell them this glad word'? We are not all to become total renunciationists though some, knowing the Real, have chosen this. What is important to understand is that the only real use of all our dealings with the world and the worldly, once a real transformation has been effected in the being, is to convey, however subtly, the knowledge of the true state of affairs, or Reality. Only very rare persons have the innate 'qualifications' or possibilities in them to become involved with such a mission, which requires a particular *dharma* or True Will.

Ultimately, the *yogin* must strive to get beyond the Khabs 'star', to the source of all light and its reflected radiance. In the early stages the practitioner learns *dharana*, control of thought; eventually all thoughts are drawn together into a single idea. The prolongation of *dharana* is *dhyana*, where the object is fixed as a steady, unwavering flame. This is described as 'flow of knowledge', but one must not think this implies any ordinary kind of knowledge. Ultimately, one must follow the symbol back to its infinite source. Thought must be made single-pointed. Thoughts and images are suppressed altogether for increasing periods of time, all the while maintaining the mudra, the pure Idea called here the 'star'.

The *mudra* does not merely refer to a physical gesture or seated position. Its literal meaning is 'seal'; by adopting an attitude that involves the self as completely as possible, the seal or impression is formed. Thus a person may be a devotee, disciple or aspirant, but this must not only be descriptive of something they do, it must be descriptive of something they truly are—otherwise it is no more than mere wishful thinking or pretence. Furthermore, one must not think of this 'making a mark', as upon a surface, as the activity of the practitioner, as an exertion of will. On the contrary, it is an impression made upon the practitioner through receptivity to the spiritual activity transferred from higher states or modalities of being. Further realisations come about through the higher intellectual intuition (*boddhi*). This must not be confused with the conventional understanding of 'intuition'; it has nothing to do with instinct or emotion and is beyond the level of the reason. To paraphrase the words of Shankara, 'It is no use to describe to you what the Moon looks like. You have to see the Moon with your own eyes to know the Moon.' Thus Shankara emphasised the importance of yoga as a means of gaining direct knowledge of reality.[131]

---

[131] *Crest Jewel of Discrimination* (Ynanayoga), Shankara.

The mind of the *yogin* is trained to remain absolutely awake yet free of thoughts and images. In this way, veil after successive veil is stripped away. When the self becomes as a hollow vessel or Empty Throne, it becomes possible at last to know what the 'kiss' of Nuit really is. It is even possible to know Nuit herself, the Soul of the Eternal, through direct knowledge, which is unlimited.

The Enochian schema known as the Thirty Aethyrs was the work of the Elizabethan astrologer and alchemist John Dee. It would be beyond our scope to go into a detailed discussion of that here, but it is worth mentioning it in so far as its practical application has a bearing on the goal of yoga. It has a resemblance, outwardly at least, to the Gnostic Thirty Aeons of Valentinus, an Alexandrian Egyptian reckoned to be the first Christian theologian. Although the Thirty Aethyrs is often reduced to a merely psychic skrying experiment—which would in fact render it quite worthless in terms of initiation—it has Tantrik, yogic and devotional aspects, as does the Thirty Aeons of Valentinus. With the Thirty Aethyrs, the Gnostic Sophia and Christ are transmuted to the Woman and Serpent, or Babalon and IADA.[132]

The outermost or highest Aethyr is named LIL, which means 'Night', and is a name of Nuit. LIL symbolises the unmanifest state, which is the positive or superior sense of night as opposed to the wholly negative darkness of ignorance. While the First Aethyr, the highest or closest to the supreme principle, is called 'outermost', that is as seen from the terrestrial perspective. Thus symbolically, the Terrestrial Watchtowers are placed in the centre and the Aethyrs then surround them in ever widening concentric circles. From the perspective of the Initiate, LIL is the 'innermost', for the greater or higher contains the lesser or lower, and not vice versa. Thus the First is the principle that contains all of the Thirty Aethyrs—and there is also that which is beyond even the First.

Comparison may then readily be made between the practical work of the Thirty Aethyrs and that of the Laya Yoga tantras, or raising of the Serpent Power, as previously mentioned. Each chakra and its associated powers is assimilated and reabsorbed into the next on the ascent, until all is subsumed into the Supreme State.

---

[132] In early forms of Christianity, Christ was identified with the serpent, which was sometimes depicted with the cross, Egyptian Tau or *ankh*.

The Way and the Way Forward

There are, broadly speaking, four sub-degrees to the knowledge of God. The degrees are somewhat cryptically referred to in the (Egyptian) Book of the Law, III: 64–67.

1. *Let him come through the first ordeal, and it will be to him as silver.*

This covers the degrees from that of Neophyte to Zelator. It should be noted that all 'ordeals of initiation' do not concern initiation directly. They can only apply to the corporeal state and the individuality. All ordeals are thus illusionary from the higher or initiated perspective, for they only involve contingent matters. The verse number III: 64, taken as the whole number 364, corresponds to H-ShTN, which is Satan as the Opposer or Dweller on the Threshold and the Initiator through Trial. The possibility of delusion is great at this level.

The work here may involve further development of the individual possibilities, as a support to initiation. The use of traditional sciences such as magick can be the means for such development, though in the present times it is unwise to make too much use of this. This degree has a correspondence with the light of the Khu, which when realised as having its source from beyond the personal sphere, is the radiance of Atma. If the practice of yoga is persisted in, which involves concentation of the mind, then the verse number as 364 corresponds to Lux Occulta, 'secret path of illumination'.[133]

2. *Through the second, gold.*

This corresponds to the degree of Adeptus Minor. Gold is the solar and purest metal; it is a symbol of the imperishable or primordial state. It naturally implies that the being has passed through certain purifications, which must involve the liberation of the self from all contingencies or irrelevant factors. The work involves the continued development of the Khu and gradual realisation of the Khabs as Atma, the 'House of Hadit'. The practice of yoga is the development of *dhyana* leading to *samadhi*. The verse number III: 65, taken as a whole number, then equates to 365, Adonai. In case of failure, which can only be a fall from the path, then NShIH, 'oblivion'.

---

[133] Lux Occulta (אור מופלא), the Veiled or Occult Light, is a name associated with Kether the Crown, the first sephira of the Qabalah. In the present context it is a downward transposition, as the 'secret' is the ignorance of the practitioner, which is only revealed to him through initiation.

3. *Through the third, stones of precious water.*

This corresponds to the admission or entry point to the grade of a Magister Templi, corresponding to Da'ath. Da'ath is the Abyss when viewed from below and the Supernal Garden of Eden as viewed from above. There is a dissolution of ego (*ahankara*) implied in the water-stones, which are a traditional symbol for that which is enduring (stone) and that which is fluid or changeful (water). These principles are at first seen as opposing but are in fact complementary and so must eventually be realised as one. Worshipping the Khabs may here be construed as continuous observance from the point of view of Atma in the state of *samadhi*.

The verse number III: 66, taken as the whole number 366, then corresponds to the Nakedness of Nuit (ORVMIM)—which is the condition of the pure or virgin soul—as well as the Daughters of Nereus (Νηρης) or sea nymphs. Although this last might seem to symbolise seduction, the mythological context is that of prophecy or truth-speaking. Conversely, 'Reckoning' (ChShBVN) is the ultimate retreat from the path into rationalism, hubris and irrevocable fall. It might seem strange as to how such a thing could happen at such a relatively advanced level. There are two possibilities: firstly, it was only 'virtual' or symbolic initiation, and so delusion had already entered the work. Secondly, a *karmasaya* or affliction arising from a past action that was dormant becomes active and the practitioner succumbs to it absolutely.

4. *Through the fourth, ultimate sparks of the intimate fire.*

This fourth state covers the grades of Magister Templi and beyond, and involves knowledge of the non-volitional nature of the True Self. The yoga involves spontaneous Nirvikalpa Samadhi, leading to a more or less full or complete spiritual realisation, which is the very rare condition described in the *Yoga-Sutras* as Dharmamegha.[134] If we take the verse number III: 67 as equal to the whole number 367, then it corresponds to the 'Eye of God' (AIShVN) and the Undivided Will or True Self.

---

[134] Nirvikalpa Samadhi involves transcendence of even the I-sense. The state of the Dharmamegha *yogin* means literally 'cloud of virtue', and has some correspondence with the divine presence or Shekinah. See *Way of Knowledge* and, for greater detail, *Thunder Perfect Gnosis*.

The Return to the Holy City

René Guénon has written about the 'Triple Precinct of the Druids'.[135] This is an exposition on an ancient symbol that has been found on Druid stone at Suèvres, on a Roman seal at Villefranche-sur-Cher and cut into a foundation stone at the church of Saint-Gemme.[136] The same symbol has been found in Rome at the cloister of San Paulo (thirteenth century). It has also been found at the Acropolis of Athens, and on flagstone of both the Parthenon and the Erechtheion. The figure depicts a triple precinct in the form of 'three concentric squares, linked together by four lines set at right angles'.

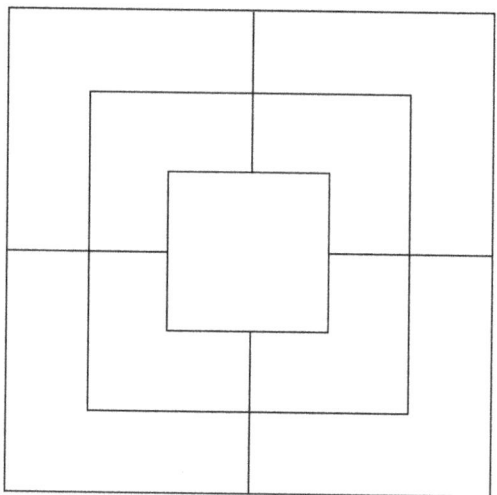

The triple precinct corresponds to the three major degrees of initiation—for all other degrees are subsidiary to the second birth, third birth and fourth state in which the dual nature of Brahma is realised. Some Masonic systems describe their higher grades as successive precincts traced around a central point—that point is marked on the greater number of figures at the Acropolis of Athens. The degrees in any truly initiatic organisation are, properly speaking, states of being and are not in any way 'accomplishments'.

---

[135] *Symbols of Sacred Science*, chapter 10 [Sophia Perennis].
[136] These locations are all in the district of Loir-et-Cher, central France.

This naturally has its correspondence with cosmologys such as the 'three worlds' in all traditions. The lines are the channels by which the doctrine is transmitted outward from within, or downward from above—the fount of all wisdom. The quaternary is further symbolised by the four rivers or streams that flow forth from Eden as according to the Qabalah, and their equivalent in other traditions. The Supernal Garden of Eden is cognate with Da'ath in the higher sense, 'hidden in the secret places of Binah'. The walled enclosure is an ancient symbol of the Holy City. This was vastly predated by symbolism of forests, trees, plants and gardens—as for example those gardens that once surrounded the Temple of Neïth in the Delta region of northern Egypt. The terrestrial Eden or paradise is always the correspondence of the heavenly Jerusalem or Holy City, though on a lower or more outward plane.

The Sphinx is a personification of the same ideas in one form or image, where the four feet are the quaternary and the woman's face and lion's body are the 'head and the tail', the Alpha-Omega. The Sphinx of Giza also declares the Cosmic Cycle of Manvantaras, for she is aligned with the point on the horizon where the sun rises at the vernal equinox—and this also marks the precessional ages. This point was called by the Egyptians Akh, of which we have spoken. Hormaku or Hrumachis is another name of the Sphinx, as is Ra Horakhyty, or sometimes Ra-Hoor-Khuit.

At the end of a Great Age or Manvantara, the 'circle is squared', or to put it another way, the circle becomes a square—which is the symbol used in degrees of initiation. The celestial Jerusalem figured in St. John's Revelation, with its twelve gates, is but one well-known example. Upon completion, and so dissolution, all is withdrawn to the unmanifest state. In an instant, the new cycle or Manvantara is produced from the primordial state. Such is reproduced in any true Mass, for a Mass must be a symbol of the completion of the Great Work, the creation of a New Heaven and a New Earth.

There is another form of the triple precinct that is identical in meaning and function to that found on the Druid stones and in other ancient locations. This clearly shows the twelve gates of the Holy City along with some other possibilities, for the middle or intermediary square has its corners placed at the middle of the outer square of time and space. This shows the relation of the Perfect Name to the Holy Mountain or Supreme Centre.

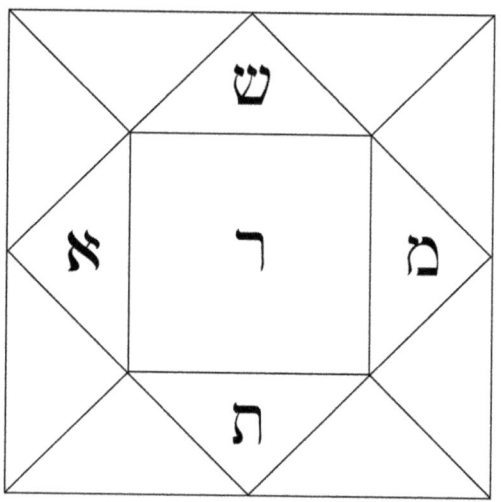

This can be viewed in various ways, including the truncated pyramid for four elements and Spirit.[137] We have here placed the 'Perfect Name' ShMRATh upon the figure. This triple precinct is identical to the figure used by ancient astrologers to draw a horoscope, in which case the Ascendant would be here marked by the letter *aleph*, the Descendant by *mem*, the Midheaven by *shin* and the Imum Coeli (IC) by *tav*. The Perfect Name is one of many names given to the Logos. ShMRATh is composed of letters that correspond to the four worlds of Qabalah: Atziluth (fire), Briah (water), Yetzirah (air) and Assiah (earth).[138] The letter *resh*, 'the head', symbolises the Spirit or 'King' as intermediary between heaven and earth, and is naturally placed here in the position of the central point marking the vertical axis.[139]

---

[137] The Truncated Pyramid is a symbol of the twenty-eighth path of Tzaddi, which symbolises the 'Way of the King'. The Practicus must negotiate this path to gain admission to the next grade of Philosophus. The truncated pyramid symbol is used with the Enochian Watchtowers and Spirit Tablet.

[138] Properly speaking, the three Mother letters of the Qabalah are formative *principles*. They are not the same as the four classical elements of air, water fire and earth. Likewise, the fact that they are 'three' does not mean they are the same as the alchemical principles of Mercury, Salt and Sulphur. The correspondence owes to Golden Dawn syncretism.

[139] References to the name ShMRATh are given in *The Flaming Sword Sepher Sephiroth* (number 941), and *Ritual Magick—Initiation of the Star and Snake*, pp. 13 and 149.

By permutation of the letters as well as by the number 941, ShMRATh is equal to AMShRATh, 'Master of Truth' and MShRATh, the Angel of the Arrow. The arrow is said to be fired from the 'bow of promise', which refers to the base of the sephirotic schema of the Tree of Life and also to the rainbow that was seen by Noah when the new cyclical phase was to commence after the deluge. The Ark is the vessel that carries over the seeds of the previous cycle to in-form the next commencement. The Ark is Thuba, which is cognate with Thebes, the Greek name of Waset, and Thuban, which was the name of the Pole Star at the time when the pyramids were built.[140] The ancient Egyptian Waset or Thebes, variously known as the Place of Ordinance and Abode of the Gods, was clearly a terrestrial centre, as was Aunnu (Heliopolis) in even more ancient times.

As a fivefold symbol of four lines converging at a central point, the figure corresponds to the Khabs, which as Aiwass has instructed, is 'in the Khu' and not vice versa.[141] When a square (or a building or shrine) is joined by two lines drawn from the corners, the central point is the axis—the *vertical* axis, or Axon Sophias, of which the holy mount Hermon is one symbol.[142] The Cube of Space marks the six directions of space from the primal three and places the ritualist in the Tiphereth or secondary centre—as that is 'below' the Supreme Centre at the Pole.[143]

The lines are the channels for teaching or transmission from the Supreme Centre (head of the vertical axis). An initiatic Order must be a 'subsidiary centre' for that, conveying knowledge through the 12 Gates (or Zodiac)—which are ritualised, for example, in monthly and seasonal rites. Individual members then form further centres, always depending from the Order that is in turn linked to the 'fount of wisdom' and initiatic transmission.

---

[140] See the entry for the number 407, *The Flaming Sword Sepher Sephiroth Volume Two*.
[141] See 'The Star of the Order'.
[142] The 'Pillar of Light', or of Wisdom.
[143] Note that Resh when spelled in full (RISh) is equal to 510, the number of Draco and 'the door', and Nux, the Greek Goddess of Night, who symbolises the withdrawal into the unmanifest.

Finally, the three precincts may be seen as relating to the three ancient Egyptian *nome* centres of Aunnu (Heliopolis), Hut Ka Ptah (Memphis) and Waset (Thebes). These are figured in the initiatory symbol of the triangle within a circle used by the O∴A∴ and certain rituals of the same Order. There is a further symbol by which all these ideas are resumed and summarised:

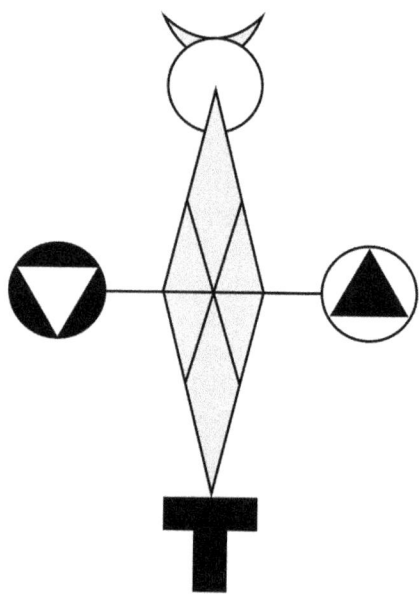

Gates of the Sun

The solstices are the dual gateways that lead into and out of the 'cave' or 'heart of the world'. The analogy of the heart is used across all traditions and of course has nothing to do with the anatomical organ itself as it is not properly speaking of the corporeal order. In spite of this, the chakras of yoga, for example, have been confused with the physical structures and chemistry of the human body in an attempt to create facts that would agree with the methods of conventional science. Such facts are by definition limited to an illusionary notion of 'matter', as though it were real substance. When temples, shrines or other buildings are properly constructed they can act as centres for the transmission of primordial wisdom. As symbolism is the means of such transmission then ritual also plays a very important part in this. It is for this reason that while we have made clear that the 'heart' does not owe to any physical location, this should not be taken in any way as to imply a rejection of the body or to deny its importance in the development of spiritual possibilities. On the contrary, the purpose of ritual is to include the physical body in the sacred act or ordinance. Although the *prima materia* (of alchemy) is not the physical domain as such, in the first instance our identification with the body as though it contained or housed the spirit is more or less complete—even though it is quite the reverse in reality, when viewed from the spiritual point of view.[144]

A non-physical centre for transmission can be provided through an initiatic Order that maintains the correct symbolism and rites. Mount Hermon, for example, is the Near Eastern equivalent of the Hindu Mount Meru, and is an actual mountain towering above what is called in biblical and other accounts the 'valley of the giants'. Hermon is steeped in legends of how the Sons of the Elohim alighted on the peak and from there descended to earth to instruct humanity in wisdom.[145] In that way, these Sons of Gods were the original and true type of the *avatar*. It would do little good, however, if engineers were to tunnel their way into the centre of the mountain in the hope of finding the Holy Grail! Similarly, it is recorded in historical accounts that a Persian king had the colossal monument of Isis-Hathoor in Heliopolis (Aunnu) torn down and destroyed in the vain hope of finding gold buried beneath.[146]

---

[144] See 'The Star of the Order'.
[145] See p. 108.
[146] See *Babalon Unveiled!*

It is very efficacious to perform the zodiacal rites on an evening nearest the time of the Sun's ingress. These include the rituals of the two solstitial doors of Cancer (Ra) and Capricorn (Set). The gate of Ra is the symbolic entry to the universal or cosmic centre while that of Set involves the exit from the cosmological sphere to the supra-mundane or primordial centre at the North Pole of the vertical axis. Both these points of entry therefore constitute an ascent in terms of initiation—the 'second birth' and the 'third birth' of deliverance.

In terms of the seasonal rites, the north gate of Capricorn is actually a *descent*: The Capricorn solstice indicates the path of the increase of visible light away from the spirit, while the Cancer solstice and southern gate marks the decrease of visible light and path towards the spirit. This is further emphasised by the zodiacal signs and their ruling planets through the course of the year, which we begin at the Capricorn solstice. Saturn rules Capricorn and Aquarius at the beginning of the descending Lightning Flash of the Tree of Life. Cancer ruled by the Moon, in which the Sun achieves maximum elevation, marks the re-ascent.[147]

The harmony of symbolism of the 'two doors' is expressed in effective seasonal rites and other rituals, and these must include a properly designed temple floorplan as the basis for all else. It may be worth mentioning, though it is a digression from our main subject, that ritually tracing out the pentagrams point-downwards reflects the *descent* of spirit to earth, the way of the avatars. This is further figured in the mode of tracing out the elements assigned to the five points of the star: we start (invoking) at spirit, proceed to the angle of fire, then air, then water and earth. We complete the star by returning to the angle of spirit. Furthermore, the angles of each pentagram correspond to the order of elements on the Enochian Watchtower Tablets, which each form a Kerubic Angel: the wings and upper half are composed of fire and air while the lower half and feet are naturally in water and earth. As we reverse the pentagram with point downward, the Angels are descending or 'falling' towards the corporeal realm. However, any pentagram, whichever way up it is drawn, automatically includes its opposite by way of the pentagon formed by joining the outer angles. The way of ascent and descent is therefore strictly relative to one's point of view and in reality—or from the purely metaphysical perspective—ascent and descent are simultaneous. Likewise birth and death are strictly relative and only mark a change of state.

---

[147] The Order of planets (by descent) along the Lightning Flash is Saturn, Jupiter, Mars, Sun, Venus, Mercury and Moon—marking the return.

There is a further aspect of the two doors to consider, which is when they are related to Da'ath, the Tree of Knowledge and Death. Da'ath has at least two aspects, one when viewed from 'above' and another when viewed from 'below'. The higher or Supernal Da'ath is said to be hidden within Binah, the Mother of Understanding or of the Gods, Aima Elohim. Here, Da'ath is really none other than the Supernal Garden of Eden, the Gate of which is the entrance to the supra-human realms, guarded by the flaming sword of the Kerubim. The lower and inferior aspect of Da'ath embraces the world of shells or Qliphoth. This is everything between Malkuth and the Supernal sephiroth. In another sense it is a sub-plane of manifestation below Malkuth and impinging upon the outer darkness.

There are those that have dedicated their lives to exploring the infernal regions and the denizens that haunt them, seeking human victims. That should really give us something of a clue to the nature of what the real purpose of such 'specialists' really is, whether that is known to them or not. The nature of the subversion of spirituality, which utilises the inversion and confusion of all symbolism, is that it is seldom guessed at by its agents, who frequently hold a sincere belief that they are 'liberating humanity' or something like that. What they have actually brought about is a premature acceleration of the negative dissolution. As with Da'ath, a dual symbol, the 'dissolution' we are speaking of here needs to be carefully considered. There is the positive dissolution of the individuality in the deliverance or 'third birth', and there is the completely negative dissolution involving dispersal and destruction of the being; these are not in any way the same thing or even complementary opposites. Perhaps needless to say, those same agents for the subversion of the spiritual also confuse any difference between the two aspects of dissolution.

There is yet another aspect of Da'ath, the 'non-sephira', where it symbolises the mode of transformation from one world to another. This is the mode that should really apply when eleven knocks or knells are sounded at the opening of the temple.[148] The double cone or hourglass symbol of the Orbicular Tree of Life depicts this dual mode, as we shall here explain.[149]

---

[148] This is certainly not to invoke the lowest of the subtle planes of sub-manifestation. However, there are some organisations and individuals that are so degraded that the inferior planes are the limit of their operation—it would make no difference to them how many knocks or knells.

[149] See *The Enterer of the Threshold*, pp. 77 and 79.

The Kether of Assiah is shown connected to Malkuth of Yetzirah by spirals passing through the Ain Soph within a double cone. As a reflection of the Ain Soph, or 'limitless light', Da'ath is the means of translation from one world to the next. To use the geometric analogy of the circle or sphere, it is in the continuous radiation from centre to circumference that this is accomplished.

This thread of the Ain Soph Aur is also a form of double door, for as it is possible to ascend to the world above by this means so it is also possible to *descend* to the world below, which is in the nature of a 'fall'. Such a descent is not always to be understood in the negative sense; for example, an avatar first ascends to spiritual realisation and then descends to assist others. In the descending phase, the avatars do not return wholly to the previous state for they have been permanently changed in their initiation. On the other hand, there is the very different case of a real descent to a lower plane of existence, which is brought about by the restriction of sin or limitation, ultimately shutting out the truth of things and reinforcing the delusion of separate existence.

The word 'sin' is an old word with the root form found in many languages, but in all cases it means 'to go astray', in other words, to make an error or deviation. On the collective level, man has deviated from sacred ordinance to such an extent that he has reached the nadir of descent in the twenty-first century of our era. That is to say, there is no further step downward. This is described in the book of Revelation as the 'pit' from which the Antichrist arises to temporarily (and seemingly) rule the temporal world with absolute power. It is a short-lived and illusionary triumph, though we nonetheless suffer the consequences on the lowest plane of manifestation. As there is nowhere else to go, then the final dissolution at the end of the Manvantara comes about in an 'instant'. This is one level of the meaning of the legend of Isis and Horus as recounted by Herodotus, though it has never previously been noted. Isis hides Horus—the immortal principle—in the Delta swamp; when he is stung to death by a scorpion, her sister Nephthys then cries out to heaven and stops the sun boat of Ra in its tracks. The momentary cessation of time enables Tahuti to whisper in the ear of Isis the spell ('moment of time') that will resurrect Horus to immortal life.

Nephthys is the 'dark', invisible or unmanifested aspect of Isis. Her cry marks the cessation of time and withdrawal of manifestation. It is no different from the trumpet blast described in St. John's book of Revelation, which is depicted on the older Tarot trumps for Atu XX, Judgement. In that same moment, the whole world is returned to the unmanifest state and the new cycle or Manvantara commences from the primordial centre.

The Whole World

At the close of the Mass of Hormaku it is said, 'May the whole world come to this joy'.[150] The world is thereby restored to her true place among the starry heavens. To use the Qabalistic symbolism, Malkuth is raised up to the throne of Binah as the host is raised to heaven in the transformation at the Mass. This corresponds to the complete and final resurrection of the soul. According to early Gnostic theology there is a true or real world and a false or artificial world. When 'our world' reaches a point where there is almost total belief in this construct, which is a superimposition upon reality, then comes about the (apparent) triumph of Antichrist at the end of man's time. The Great Work is to extract all that is true from the world, rescuing it from the artificial prison to which it has been condemned through mankind's ignorance. According to the oracle of Nuit, in the (Egyptian) Book of the Law, I: 30,

This is the creation of the world, that the pain of division is as nothing, and the joy of dissolution all.

These words are said at the Mass after the transformation in the cup, but before the wine is consumed—an act which in itself replicates the absorption of the elements in the higher order or quintessence. In terms of the individuality, the dissolution of the ego (*ahankara*) does not imply the annihilation of the being. The qualities are subsumed, 'taken up', to a higher modality than that of corporeal existence or of psychic existence.

'The law is for all' (the Book of the Law, I: 34) does not mean that spiritual realisation is for everyman. Indeed, 'everyman' does not even exist in reality. Nothing is the same in reality; the sameness of things is a delusion arising from belief that only numbers or quantity can tell us anything about reality. Traditionally, the 'law is for all' means that no man or woman is barred from the Gnosis through quantitative or purely external evaluations.[151] Compare, for example, Luke, 21: 17,

And ye shall be hated of *all men* for my name's sake.

---

[150] See *Ritual Magick—Initiation of the Star and Snake*. The word 'Mass' is generally supposed to be etymologically derived from the ecclesiastical Latin, *ite missa est*, 'the congregation is dismissed', i.e., at the end of a liturgy. The response is *Deo gratias*, 'thanks be to God'.
[151] 'Traditionally', that is to say, in context of all other sacred texts.

And again, in John, 1: 7,

> The same came for a witness, to bear witness of the Light, that *all men* through him might believe.

And in I Corinthians, 9: 22,

> To the weak became I as weak, that I might gain the weak: I am made all things to *all men*, that I might by all means save some.

If individuals have allied themselves to a creed such as scientism then initiation in any real sense is impossible so long as that condition remains. It is impossible, as the person has created a 'false centre' about which all possibilities are determined, and are thereby limited or restricted. Such a false centre eclipses the heart and drives out the soul. Such ignorance, in the Sanskrit language, is *avidya*, which includes man's reason—for reason does not reach to direct knowledge of any sacred or divine thing. Verses 2–4 of the first chapter of the Book of the Law concisely summarise all of the above:

> *The unveiling of the company of heaven.*
> *Every man and every woman is a star.*
> *Every number is infinite; there is no difference.*

The 'star' is the essential principle of a being as latent, for it must be realised, awakened and brought to life, so to speak.[152] Entering the company of heaven is the equivalent of salvation or immortality. It means that all that we love in truth partake with us. Numbers are not infinite but are countless, indefinite, to be far more precise, and this indefinitude applies even to the modalities of an individual.[153]

In the Book of the Law, II: 21, a superficial reading implies a severe judgment and condemnation, quite in opposition to the words spoken by Nuit:

> *We have nothing with the outcast and the unfit: let them die in their misery. For they feel not.*

One must beware of reading this from a profane or external point of view, however. To be fit or unfit in this work has nothing to do with physical conditions or even psychological ones. It has nothing to do with the observances or judgments made every day by humans upon others, whether 'officially' or 'unofficially', whether declared openly or kept as a secret thought.

---

[152] See 'The Star of the Order'.
[153] See the geometric analogy of René Guénon, *The Symbolism of the Cross*. See also p. 10, 'Every Number is Infinite', for this has to be a figure of speech not a real fact.

Those who 'die in their misery' have chosen death in so far as they have rejected all true and living principles. The 'chosen' are the elect, not through a selection process or some favour, which is a political or judicial concept strictly limited to man's reason, but through the fact that they have chosen truth over and above all falsehood. That involves discrimination, the function of Horus, who also appears as Lord of Judgement or Avenging Angel. This principle is as essential to every man and every woman as the 'star' itself, indeed, it is not separate from that and never can be. Discrimination is called the 'first virtue on the path', and is also a practice essential to Ynana Yoga, the path of pure knowledge that alone affords the final deliverance or *moksha*.[154]

Our intention to restore the whole world arises from love of the world—not love of the artificial construct of man but love of all that is beautiful and true, the soul of the world. It acts as a bar against selfishness and isolationism.[155] It is the very nature of the soul to love. The soul cannot live without love—love and life are the province of Isis and love is the nature of her intelligence. Whenever there is love, Isis is present, for she is life itself, and the soul of the world. Isis is Iset, the Seat, Throne or Foundation, existing both beyond and outside the cosmos and within the cosmos.

Isis is the *neter* ('principle') that unites all the stages along the axial pole extending from earth to heaven, and makes all initiatic transmission possible.[156] When the chalice is raised up from the altar at the Mass, three stages are marked along the vertical axis from earth to heaven by the sounding of three special words: As the chalice is lifted from the foundation (Malkuth), *Isa* is sounded, for there can be no resurrection unless the Holy Spirit be present. At the midpoint (Tiphereth, heart), *Hkoma* is sounded, which indicates the wine as indwelling spirit. As the chalice is raised fully it is pushed, so to speak, through the 'doors of heaven' or the roof of the sky (Supernal Eden), and the word *Blior* is sounded, which is a name of the sacrifice made out of love, or of the Saviour or Messenger. The meaning of the three words may be construed thus:

---

[154] Deliverance or *moksha* is final liberation, whereas 'salvation' is not. The former is the 'third birth' and the latter is the 'second birth'.
[155] See *Babalon Unveiled*, 'Lapis Philosophorum'.
[156] Thus the alchemical text of the Rosicrucian mystery begins with the vision of Isis, for she is the Foundation that existed 'before the beginning of things'. See *The Chymical Wedding of Christian Rosenkreutz*.

> *In the name of Isis, may this wine be transformed by the power of love and sacrifice.*[157]

As the chalice is brought back down (*avatara*, the 'descent'), the symbol of the Cross and Triangle is formulated. The chalice is then thrust into the centre of the cross and the words previously referred to, 'This is the creation of the world...' are said.

It only remains to be added that we never do anything in our own name, always in the name of the powers that are in themselves the infallible link. The closing of the celebration of the Mass symbolises, and is in fact, the culmination and fulfilment of the Great Work. The universe (or real world beyond that of the human construct) has been brought to presence in the name of all the requisite powers. So long as this is done in the names of the powers then the rite is infallible. The restored world is gathered. The whole world is taken up into the company of heaven at the end of time through being woven into the light radiation of the Khu, which is the source of all phenomena. As the 'Star of Man', it is the means of salvation, which is to say, through our Lady Babalon Soteira, Saviour, it becomes a portal of going out from the universe of matter and entering the company of heaven. The Khabs is the 'house of Hadit' just as Hathoor (Het-Hor) is the 'house of Horus'. In this the whole world, which is to say, the true world, is taken up and restored to her place among the stars: Igne Natura Renovatur Integra.[158]

---

[157] This is an amplified meaning of the three words. More may be gleaned by examining the numerical value of the words. By the Golden Dawn Enochian Geomantic values, Isa is equal to 73, Hkoma is 342 and Blior is 288. These, added together, add to 703, the 'child' of Silence born in the womb of Isis. The number is also the result of $\sum (1-37)$ and is therefore the summation of the middle pillar of the Tree of Life, which is the vertical axis along which the chalice ascends and descends in the ritual here discussed.

[158] 'The whole world is returned through fire to perfection.' Fire is not meant here in the ordinary sense of that word. Comparison can be made with the Sanskrit deity Agni ('Fire'), the 'mouth of the Gods', considered to be a divine intermediary. To be an intermediary involves ascent and descent of the worlds.

The Whore of Babylon from Revelation, Durer

Enochian Keys to the Apocalypse

Some have speculated that John Dee's book of Enochian Keys (or Calls) is a theurgic operation comparable to opening the seven seals of the Apocalypse. Commentators and critics regard the subject from a strictly scholarly and so exoteric point of view, and so this notion of 'opening the seven seals' probably derives from the narrow perspective of psychology or the neo-spiritualism of Steiner. The book of Revelation, from whence the seven seals, is a prophetic vision that is in exact accordance with the Hindu doctrine of the Cosmic Cycles. The end of time occurs at the end of a sevenfold Manvantara, and we are nearing that—literally, not figuratively.[159]

St. John's book of Revelation is also known as the Apocalypse. The word 'apocalypse', from the Greek root *apokalypto*, means 'to reveal'. The book's title is frequently confused with 'Armageddon', a word from Revelation 16: 16 that refers to a kind of 'last battle on earth', a war between spiritual forces and evil (anti-spiritual) forces before the Day of Judgement. The meaning of the word is sometimes reduced so that it refers to any catastrophic war between contending human forces. Such a battle, when properly understood as taking place between the spiritual and the material, is not the same as a 'revelation', though it might form a part of that revelation under some circumstances. The battle must, by definition, always be 'won' finally by the spiritual, since the material has no existence without its higher principle.

Materialism only admits to the existence of matter and quantity. That is effectively what the war between spiritual forces and material forces is about, and in many ways that is no different than a battle for possession of the human soul. However, while the spiritual must always prevail in the end, there are those who are of 'the damned', which is to say they cannot survive mortality as they have absolutely rejected all spiritual possibilities while alive on earth. These form the great majority at the present time, as we near the end of Kali Yuga.

The Enochian Keys seem to include elements both of revelation and of the 'last battle'. This is no doubt tempered by the fact that Dee's translation (and so understanding) of the Enochian Keys was placed in language very similar to that of the King James English Bible—though that was not published until after his death, thought to be around 1609.

---

[159] See 'Cosmic Cycles' p. 23.

The general agreement between the Enochian Keys and the book of Revelation, albeit placed within a perspective other than Christian theology, concords with the knowledge of all other traditions. From the individual, initiatic point of view, it expresses a need for psychic regeneration so that spiritual realisation is even possible. One should then bear in mind that such an end is the beginning of renewal, wherein by fire all of nature is renewed and restored to original perfection: Igne Natura Renovata Integra. This does not mean that our world will literally be consumed by fire. Catastrophe, including fire or flood, frequently marks the ending of the great cycles of time but it would be pointless to enter into speculation. The dissolution will take place, whatever the physical circumstances should happen to be.

It is not the intention here to create a commentary on all of the Enochian Keys, which would take at least a small book to accomplish. We will focus here on one of them, the 8th Key. This Key invokes the subquadrant angle of Earth of Air in the Terrestrial Watchtower of Air.[160] This region corresponds elementally to the Tarot court card Princess of Swords, the 'Throne' of the Ace of Swords. Her full title is Princess of the Rushing Winds, the Lotus of the Palace of Air. The suit of Air in the Tarot corresponds to the whole realm of the intellect in the microcosm, or on the human scale.

In the cosmology of the 'Orbicular Tree', the four Aces circulate, as it were, about the North Pole of the universe or Kether, while the four Princesses are positioned at the South Pole, and Malkuth.[161] Malkuth is Kether but after another fashion—for we are looking at two extremities of the world axis here. For this reason the four Princesses of Tarot are said to be the Thrones of the Aces. The 8th Enochian Key begins,

> Beautiful is the first, which is as the third heaven made of pillars of Hycacinth, in whom the Elders have become strong, which I have prepared for my own truth, so saith the Lord; whose Eternal reign shall be as bucklers to the Stooping Dragon, and like unto the harvest of a widow.

---

[160] There are four tablets of Enochian letters and spirit names corresponding to each of the classical elements, and each of these is divided into four subquadrants of lesser elements: Air of Air, Water of Air, Earth of Air and Fire of Air, for example. There is also a Black Cross or Spirit Tablet (in the Golden Dawn scheme) that binds them all together. There are 91 Genii or Governors that determine which of the Thirty Aethyrs or Aires is invoked when the one Key that calls them is sounded.

[161] See 'Orbicular Tree', *The Enterer of the Threshold*.

The first and the third heaven is a technical reference to the order of the Watchtower Tablets and their subquadrants—in this case, the third angle (Earth) of the first Tablet (Air). Hyacinth is traditionally associated with peace but also desire, in the spiritual sense of longing for eternal truth, in which alone is peace of mind in any real and lasting sense. The violet flowers in some varieties of hyacinth do indeed form pillars of six-petalled stars. The 'six' symbolises the meeting of time and eternity in the world centre or heart of all, and is figured by the hexagram of two interlaced triangles.

The Elders or Old Ones are frequently mentioned in the spells of the so-called Egyptian Book of the Dead.[162] According to tradition these are the children of the Sons of the Gods (Beni Elohim) that spawned or manifested the original life-wave on the earth. In the Bible, their children are called the Nephilim, and their descendants the Anak—a word that has an identical meaning to that of Nephilim, 'giants, tall, noble or renowned'.[163] The 'Lord' is named IAD, 'Holy'. This has the numerical value of 70, equal to the Greek *omicron* and Hebrew *a'ain*, 'an eye'—in this context, the Seer or Knower.

Curiously, the name 'Watchers' has been applied to the Elders or Nephilim referred to in the book of Genesis. The term is thought to have originated with *The Manuscript Found in Saragossa* by Count Jan Potocki (from the early 1800s). He used the word 'egregores' (Greek *egregoros*) for what he called 'fallen angels'. The Nephilim were a race said to be born of congress between the Sons of Gods (Beni Elohim) and the daughters of earth (Genesis 6: 4). The sense of the Nephilim as 'fallen angels' is true in so far as they *descended*—compare to the Sanskrit *avatara*, by which a spiritual force is reified. The meaning of the word 'egregore' was later corrupted so that it came only to mean a kind of collective psychic entity.

The apocryphal Book of Enoch, which has a detailed and probably older account of this very ancient mystery, was not discovered until centuries after the time of John Dee. Dee named the language of the Angels 'Enochian' as his intention had been to psychically recover what was at that time the 'lost' book of Enoch.

---

[162] The Egyptian title of the book is *hru-em-prt*—'coming forth into light'. The meaning is the complete opposite of the title that was first afforded it by tomb robbers and then later taken up by Egyptologists.

[163] Anak is spelled in Hebrew ONQ, and has the value of 220. In the Bible this is given in the plural, ONQIM (270), which is translated in the King James Version as 'Anakims'.

The last line of this first stanza, where it says that the eternal reign of the Lord shall be as 'bucklers to the Stooping Dragon, and like unto the harvest of a widow', may be understood metaphysically. The word 'buckler' is used in the book of Psalms, 18: 2:

> The Lord is my rock, and my fortress, and my deliverer; my God, my rock; in whom I will trust; my *buckler*, and the horn of my salvation, and my high tower.

The Hebrew word is *mageni*, from the root MGN.[164] A buckler was the name given to a heraldic device born upon shields; it sometimes refers to a goatskin shield (Greek *aegis*) worn by Athene. Athene was thought by the Greeks to be identical to the Egyptian Neïth. Neïth is one of the goddesses who protect the Four Children of Horus, who in turn guard over the elemental body of the pharaoh after death.[165] The Greek buckler conferred the protection of a god, and sometimes depicted the Gorgon Medusa, who had the power to turn men into stone by a single glance. The *aegis* also has the meaning of a 'violent windstorm', which is the power of Set-Typhon. The 'buckler against the stooping dragon' (or dragon of death) corresponds by analogy to the three-dimensional cross, as shall be seen in a moment—for the buckler of a shield is also the 'hub' or centre, which in cosmological terms denotes the axis of the universe. The Hebrew word for 'horn' in this verse carries the meanings of 'head, grandeur, might, peak and capital, and so affirms the allusion to the axis and primordial fount. The same word (QRN) is also used in relation to a ceremonial horn, which is indicated in the Marseilles Tarot XX as calling the souls to the new life and resurrection at the end of time.[166]

The Tarot trump called the Priestess II corresponds to alchemical Mercury and is placed on the thirteenth path of the Tree of Life, called the 'Uniting Intelligence'. This denotes the axis or central pillar. The lunar-magnetic power of the Priestess as the Saviour or intermediary between the worlds of Heaven and Earth is reflective, as is alchemical Mercury. Yet while Mercury forms all that is 'outside' or extending away from the axis, its force is centripetal. Thus Love is the force that draws all together. This double Mercurial activity is able to dissolve (*solve*) and 'put together in a new form' (*coagula*).

---

[164] MGN has the value of 93.
[165] These in turn correspond to the four directions, north, south, east and west, and these are also the stations of four goddesses.
[166] Book of Psalms, 148: 14: 'He also exalteth the horn of his people, the praise of all his saints; even of the children of Israel, a people near unto him.' This properly refers to the 'elect', initiates, not to any race or tribe.

'The Lord is my rock' may also be associated with the holy mountain, for example Hermon in the ancient land of Canaan or Phoenicia, where Ashtaroth is both the name of a place and that of a hornéd goddess.¹⁶⁷ It was on mount Hermon that Christ Jesus was transfigured before his disciples, according to some sources.¹⁶⁸

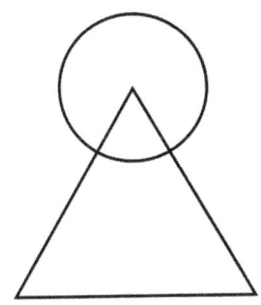

Mount Hermon: comparison may be made with the 'double cone', p. 96, and also with the double action of Sulphur as radiating or centrifugal, and Mercury as body-forming and centripetal. The intersection of the circle with the pyramid or mountain is the 'place of the oath' or will of the avatar.

It was from near the white summit of mount Hermon, where still exists the highest shrine in the world, built from stone blocks, that the angels descended as according to the apocryphal book of Enoch. This is also recorded on a stele that was stolen from the shrine and is now preserved at the British Museum.¹⁶⁹

---

¹⁶⁷ Hermon is from the Hebrew (HR HRMVN), derived from the Aramaic *har* and Arabic *al-haram*, 'sacred enclosure'. The holy mountain is also known as 'white' or 'shining', owing to its snowy peaks.

¹⁶⁸ Transfiguration of Christ Jesus: R.T. France, Matthew: An Introduction and Commentary [IVP Academic, 2008].

¹⁶⁹ Known as Qasr Antar, it sits at 2,814 metres above sea level. According to Sir Charles Warren (1869), the temple is a rectangular building, sitting on an oval, stone plateau, and without a roof. Warren ignobly vandalised it, removing a limestone stele from the northwest of the oval and breaking it into two pieces (for portability). He then took it back to the British Museum, where it now resides. The inscription on the stele reads, 'According to the command of the greatest and Holy God, those who take an oath proceed from here.' This tallies with the legend of an oath taken by the angels under Semjaza who then took wives among the daughters of men as recounted in the Book of Enoch (1 6: 6) and Genesis 6: 4. Hermon then became known as 'the mountain of the oath'. The name of God is supposed to be a Hellenic version of Ba'al or Hadad, which identifies it with the place name of Baal-Hermon (Lord of Hermon) and the deity given by Enoch as 'The Great Holy One'.

References: Nickelsburg, 1 Enoch 1. A Commentary on the Book of 1 Enoch, 1–36; 81–108 [Minneapolis: Fortress, 2001].

E. A. Myers (11 February 2010). The Ituraeans and the Roman Near East: Reassessing the Sources, p. 65 [Cambridge University Press].

It was from this shrine that the angels were said to have taken the oath to descend and mingle with the daughters of men. From this it may be seen that the Nephilim were born of the first avatars.[170] This is, of course, entirely contrary to what is said of the angels in the book of Enoch, where they are described as 'iniquitous', spawning a race of evil giants that ate men. It would be better to understand that the race of men are eaten up by their own pride. The book of Enoch is a corruption, of which only a fragment remains from what was probably an oral tradition originally.

Mount Hermon is used today for military surveillance across some considerable distance. This is sadly indicative of the inevitable degradation that takes place at the ending of the Kali Yuga or Age of Darkness. However, the view from the mountain is also analogous with the *darshana* ('window, view') of the Supreme Principle. The transfiguration of Christ Jesus on Hermon is then, at the very least, a recollection of the Elder race, to which he properly belongs according to tradition. For example, some of the Orphic texts support the same Gnostic theme: 'I am a child of earth and stars, but my race is of the heavenly order'.[171]

The 'harvest of a widow' is an allusion to Binah, the Mother of Faith and Foundation of the Primordial Wisdom (Sepher Yetzirah). Here is indicated the hidden or left side of Hekate, revealed to no mortal man. It is the night or the unmanifest side, which may be described as pure observance or watchfulness, yet without manifest projection, light or extrusion. It is the 'hidden light' (AVR MPLA) of the Qabalah, an attribute afforded Kether as the 'height', beyond the visible stars or cosmological sphere.

There is mention of Machpalah, a 'double cave', in Genesis (19: 30–50: 13), where one chamber is the light or manifest, and the other is the dark or unmanifest. In terms of initiation this equates to the two paths: the 'second birth' corresponding to Tiphereth, and the 'third birth' corresponding to Kether. The second birth and third birth is also described as a 'first and second crossing', in relation to the symbol of the double cave.[172] In the present context, a withdrawal of manifestation is implied. The Key continues:

---

[170] See the 'The Sons of Gods' for a detailed account.
[171] Orphic inscription from the Petalia Gold Tablet, 300–200 BCE [British Museum]. See Appendices.
[172] This is comparable to the Egyptian *hekat* and *nekhakha*, commonly mistaken for a 'crook and flail'. See pp. 228–231, *Babalon Unveiled* [First Edition only].

> How many are there which remain in the glory of the earth, which are, and shall not see death until the Fall of the Great House, and the dragon shall sink!

There are those, 'saints' or men that have become *devis* as according to other traditions than the Christian, that gain 'immortality' but not the final liberation (*moksha*). At the end of time all is withdrawn to the supreme principle; salvation or immortality is thus temporary.

> Come away, for the thunders have spoken; come away, for the crown of the temple, and the robe of Him that is, was, and shall be crowned, are divided.

'Him that is, was, and shall be crowned' is a reference to the Lord and Master of Time, for example Christ and Shiva—for both these bear the symbols of the key of eternity and the sceptre of time, three-fold (past, present and future).[173] There are references to the son (or *sun*) of God as holder of the key of the threefold aspect of time and eternity in ancient Egyptian papyri and the book of Revelation. In the 8th Enochian Key, 'Him that is, was, and shall be' is written I ZIROP KHISO. Curiously, the eleven-lettered name has the value of 666, a number that corresponds to Tiphereth and the Kamea of the Sun. The number 666, as with the lion, is a dual symbolism and may refer either to Christ or the Antichrist. The words obviously refer to Christ Jesus as the holder of the keys of eternity, or of heaven and hell. The Antichrist, on the other hand, will not rest content with temporal power alone but seeks to produce a counterfeit of the 'spiritual', so that control is gained not only over human minds and bodies but also over their very souls. The division takes place in the heart, the world centre, and by implication all centres of spiritual power on earth. Through the power of division, spiritual centres are divorced from the source that sustains them. Once abandoned, such centres may be exploited by the Adversary.[174]

The division of the 'crown of the temple' is the division of the earth from all spiritual influence during the reign of Antichrist. The division of the robe seems to be a direct allusion to the Romans, who divided up the robe of Jesus to sell, before his crucifixion.[175] In John, 19: 23, there is a curious reference to the coat being 'without seam, woven from the top throughout'.

---

[173] See Guénon, *Symbols of Sacred Science*, p. 120 [Sophia Perennis].
[174] See René Guénon, *Reign of Quantity and the Signs of the Times*.
[175] Matthew 27: 35; Mark 15: 24 and John 19: 23.

The seamless robe is mentioned in the Gnostic *Pistis Sophia*, Chapter 10. It is there told how the Master was given a new robe after returning to the 24th Mystery. He then saw five words in the robe: ZMH ZMH OZH RChM OZIAH. The Master explains the meaning thus:

> O Mystery, which is without in the world, for whose sake the universe hath arisen, this is the total outgoing and the total ascent, which hath emanated all emanations and all that is.[176]

Thus our world is sold into slavery and condemned to hell through rejection of the Truth and denial of all spiritual possibilities. The 'robe of Christ' is his resurrection garment or body, which is to say, the possibility by which a soul may enter the 'kingdom of heaven'. To return to the 8th Enochian Key:

> Come forth, appear to the terror of the earthbound, and to our joy, and to those who in thy knowledge are prepared!

We may recollect that those who remained 'in the glory of the earth' attain the salvation (second birth) but not what is called the final deliverance (third birth). They enjoy a kind of perpetuation of the earthly life, similar to that which the popular cult of Osiris envisaged. Perpetuity is not the same as eternity or the infinite, though, and in time they undergo a change of state. The 'earthbound', however, are really nothing other than the dissociated psychic elements of those who have rejected Christ, or any true principle. At the end of time there is nothing of such psychic remnants that can be 'saved' or that can be subject to a change of state in the being. In Christianity, such souls are the 'damned', although this is played down in the diluted and denatured forms of Christianity of today; damnation is not very popular with secular or profane persons, who in fact do not believe in any continuance or further journey of the soul, and only wish to 'remember' their loved ones when they have departed. That amounts in every way to a total rejection of God and spiritual reality; stopping short at a celebration of memories, it encourages the prolongation of dissociated psychic elements, and these can have a negative effect on the souls of those remaining, making them 'earthbound' literally, which means there can be no change of state for them. These are not only damned but also *damning*, for their ignorant actions prolong suffering and negate all spiritual possibilities.

---

[176] The five words have the value of 527, which is the value of the name of the book, *Pistis Sophia* itself (1,581), divided by its factor of 3. The Sanskrit term *apurva* has an associated meaning. See Guénon, *Introduction to the Study of the Hindu Doctrines*, pp. 195–197.

The 'earthbound' do not rise again—for these, death is finality. The Angels of Truth and Justice, appearing at the end of time, will seem terrible to the profane and wicked, but are a wonder and joy to those that have retained spiritual realisation. That, indeed, is the positive kind of recollection—an essential part of spiritual practice.

The Prophecy of Hermes

Our focus here is on four chapters of the Perfect Sermon, XXIII to XXVI, sometimes called the Prophecy of Hermes, thought to date from the mid 2nd century.[177] The discourse takes the form of a dialogue between the Master Trismegistus and Asclepius, his disciple. These texts were written down at a critical turning point in history. It was the cusp or event horizon of the precessional Age of Pisces, just as we are now on the cusp of the precessional Age of Aquarius. While the popular cult of Isis still survived and proliferated far beyond the boundaries of Egypt, it would be but a short time before the Egyptian language was completely forgotten.

When these texts were written there was still what Hermes-Thoth refers to as a 'pure philosophy', based on Gnosis or direct revelation, and an emergent impure or pseudo philosophy based on ordinary reason. Before long the rational or profane philosophy would become the only acceptable 'truth' for most persons, as it is today.

In XXII, Thrice Greatest Hermes has expounded to Asclepius on all matters concerning the immortal nature, and of those that will perceive it, and of those who cannot. The dialogue continues in XXIII on the nature of the images of Gods that man fashions in his own likeness. We begin by summarising what was said at the end of the previous chapter, as the narrative continues without a break.

XXIII

The knowledge of the immortal nature is conveyed only to a few. These are chosen through the devotion of their heart.

1. Tris. Still, of the rest, the vicious folk, we ought to say no word, for fear that our sacred sermon should be spoiled by even thinking of them. Our sermon treats of the relationship and intercourse of men and Gods. Learn then, Asclepius, of wherein is the true power and strength of man.

As the Most High God created the Gods in Heaven, so man is the maker of the gods who, in the temples, allow all to approach, and who not only have light of blessing poured on them, but who also send forth their light on all; thus the devotee does not only go forward towards the Gods but also confirms the Gods on earth.

---

[177] A translation from the Latin of this Graeco Egyptian sacred text can be studied in *Thrice-Greatest Hermes*, Vol. 2, G.R.S. Mead (1906).

Are you surprised, o Asclepius? I see that you—even you!—do not believe.

2. Asc. I am amazed, Thrice Greatest; but willingly I give assent to all your words. A man is very blessed that has attained to such great felicity.

Tris. This is rightly so—for such deserves our wonder, in that he is the greatest of them all!

As for the race of the Gods in Heaven, it is clear from the commingling of them all that it has been made pregnant from the fairest part of nature. The only signs by which they are discerned are, as it were, from their source, before all else.

3. On the other hand, the species of the gods that humankind constructs is fashioned out of that most ancient and divine nature, and also from out of that nature in men. That is to say, it is fashioned out of the stuff of which they have been made and are configured, not only in their minds but also in each of their members and in their whole body.

It is thus that humankind, in imaging Divinity, stays mindful of the nature and the source of its own self.

Furthermore, in the same way that our Lord [supreme principle] did make the Gods immortal, that they might be in his likeness, then so has mankind produced its own gods according to the likeness of the look of its own self.

XXIV

1. Asc. Surely you do not mean their statues, O Master?

Tris. I mean their statues, o Asclepius. Can you not see how much you—even you!—doubt my word? Statues ensouled with sense and filled with spirit! These work mighty and strange results. Statues that foresee what is to come, and perchance can prophecy. They will foretell things by dreams and in many other ways. There are statues that take the strength away from men, or that may cure their sorrow, if they should deserve it.

Do you not know then, Asclepius, that Egypt is the image of the Heaven? Or that which is even truer, the transference or descent of all that are in governance or exercise in Heaven? And yet more truly still it must be said:

This land of ours is the Shrine of all the World.

2. It is proper that the wise should give utmost care in considering and understanding all that I have said concerning these matters. As for you, Asclepius, it is not right that you should be ignorant of the same.

The time will come when it will seem as if Egypt served the Divinity with single-minded devotion and care for nothing—for all her holy cult will fall to nothingness and be in vain.

That Divinity is now about to depart speedily from Earth and return to Heaven, and Egypt shall be left alone. The Earth, which was once the seat of devoted and honourable cults shall be widowed, bereft—no longer knowing the presence of the Gods.

And barbarians shall fill this region and this land. Not only shall there be the neglect of the pious cults but—and what is still more painful—by profane laws, penalties shall be decreed against such devoted practices and worship of the Gods. These will even be totally prohibited.

3. This most holy land, the seat of our shrines and temples, shall then be choked with tombs and corpses.

O Egypt, Egypt! Only tales will remain of your cults, and these will be as unbelievable to your own sons as for the rest of humankind. Words alone will be left carved on your stones, to recount your beautiful deeds.

And Egypt will be made the home of those who are alien to her.

Yes! The Godly Company shall climb back to Heaven, and their forsaken worshippers will all die out. And Egypt, bereft of God and man, shall be abandoned.

4. And now I speak to you, O River, holiest Stream! I tell you what will be. Your banks will overflow with bloody torrents. Not only shall your sacred streams be stained with blood but also they shall all flow over with the same.

The cult of the dead shall far exceed the cult of the living. The surviving remnant shall be Egyptians in their appearance but in their deeds they shall be as the profane.

XXV

1. Why do you weep, Asclepius? There is more than this, by far more wretched. Egypt herself shall be impelled and stained with even greater evil.

For she, the Holy Land, once deservedly the most beloved of the Gods by reason of her untiring service to the Gods on Earth, she the sole abode of holiness and teacher of wisdom upon the earth, shall be the type of all that is most barbarous. And then, out of our loathing for mankind, the world will seem no more deserving of our wonder and our praise.

This entire good thing, of which none fairer was ever seen, nor is there anything, nor will there ever be, will be in peril.

2. And that will prove a burden unto men. On account of this they will despise and cease to love this Cosmos as a whole. They will cease to love the eternal work of the Divine; the glorious and entire creation, comprised of manifold variety of forms; the steadfast deliverer of the Divine Will. They will cease to love the multitudinous whole reflecting changeless unity in its variety of forms, that should be reverenced, praised and loved—by them at least that have the eyes to see.

For Darkness will be set before the Light, and Death will be thought preferable to Life. They will not even raise their eyes to Heaven. And then they will think that the holy, wise and strong are mad. They will think that fools and profane are wise sages. The unruly mob will be held as strong, and ignorance will prevail over all.

3. Of the soul, and all concerning her, whereby she presumes that either she has been born deathless or that she will attain to deathlessness, as according to all that I have said to you:

All this will be considered not only a matter of jest and mockery, but even as vanity.

Believe me, if you will, that the penalty of death shall even be decreed to him who shall devote himself to the Pure Knowledge.

New legislation will be enforced, a novel law; nothing that is sacred, nothing holy, nothing that is worthy of the Heaven, or Gods in Heaven, shall ever be heard, or even believed in the mind.

4. The sorrowful departure of the Gods from humankind takes place. Only noxious spirits remain, who mingled with humanity will lay their hands on them, and drive the wretched folk to every reckless evil—to wars, and robberies, deceits, and all those things that are opposed to the soul's very nature.

Then the Earth shall no longer hold together. The sea shall no longer be sailed upon. The Heaven shall not continue with the courses of the stars, nor the star-courses in Heaven.

The voice of every God shall cease in the Great Silence that no one can break. The fruits of Earth shall rot. Earth shall no longer bring forth. The air itself shall faint away in despair of that sad listlessness.

XXVI

1. This, when it comes, shall be the world's old age and impiety, denoting irregularity and irrationality in all things.

Asclepius, when these things all come to pass, then our Lord [the supreme principle], maker of the First God, to thwart the criminals, and to cancel the error of the corruption of all things, to restore all things so as to be in accordance with Divine Will, shall put an end to the evil. It will be washed away with water-flood, or burnt away with fire or forcibly expelled with war and famine. God will restore the Cosmos to its ancient form, so that the world shall once again be loved and worshipped. And once again, ceaseless praises and hymns of blessing will be sent forth.

2. In this rebirth of Cosmos is the renewal of all good things, and the holiest return of Nature's self, by means of divine ordinance—of Nature, which was without beginning, and which is without an end. For the Divine Will has no beginning; it is ever the same and as it is, without end.

This then, is the Divine Will, and the whole world her Image.

Commentary

XXIII. 'Many are called but few are chosen' (Matthew 22: 14). A person can be called or invited but they can still choose not to attend. Those who attend the wedding, or the Great Work, are chosen 'through the devotion of their heart'. Those who will not attend are those who devote all their attention to physical activity, to industry. Trismegistus will not even speak of the profane ones. In the modern world, the 'busyness' of everyone has increased to the point of real madness; a state of irritable distraction is 'normal'. Trismegistus has been discussing the immortal nature, of those who can know it and those who will never know it. That is a matter of the 'heart' as termed by the ancients, which has nothing to do with emotions, but is more to do with qualities inherent in the individual nature that support the possibility of initiatic realisation.

The words of Trismegistus on the relations between the Gods and humankind are very clear, and need little in the way of clarification. The devotee of the 'gods in the temples' has a vital rôle to play, for such a man becomes a link in the chain between Heaven and Earth, between the world of spirit and the world of the mortals.

In spite of the straightforward nature of what the Master has said, Asclepius is astounded. It is revealed here that Asclepius, in common with others of his class at this time, holds to the rationalist view that the statues of Gods in the temples are no more than stone images or 'vain idols' that cannot possibly convey anything of substance. Seeing this, the Master rebukes him:

"Are you surprised, o Asclepius? I see that you—even you!—do not believe."

Asclepius then weakly pretends to give his assent to the Master's words:

"I am amazed, Thrice Greatest; but willingly I give assent to all your words. A man is very blessed that has attained to such great felicity."

The cryptic response of the Master indicates he is not fooled by this bluster:

"This is rightly so—for such deserves our wonder, in that he is the greatest of them all!"

The Master sees that his disciple does not comprehend and thus he is referring here, with some irony, to his own title, 'Thrice Greatest'—for he is alone here in his understanding of the matter.

XXIV. The Master has explained why it is so that the gods in the temple, created by men, nonetheless provide a living link to the reality they veil. Asclepius, however, remains baffled.

"Surely you do not mean their statues, O Master?"

Trismegistus, by now thoroughly exasperated with his student, delivers a further rebuke:

"I mean their statues, O Asclepius. Can you not see how much you—even you!—doubt my word?

He then explains that Egypt is the image of the Heaven and that,

"This land of ours is the Shrine of all the World."

The obstinacy of Asclepius, his complete inability to understand, then provokes the Master into speaking forth a terrible prophecy of future times. Firstly, he foresees the ancient fall of Egypt, the decline of her language and civilisation and the Persian conquest.

"This most holy land, the seat of our shrines and temples, shall then be choked with tombs and corpses."

Both Christians and others that were to occupy Egypt and other holy places around the world literally used the catacombs and ancient temples as places to put their dead. To the present day, Egyptologists still hold to the view that the Great Pyramid was built as a tomb for a king. They called the Egyptian papyrus spells the 'Book of the Dead', yet the Egyptians named it 'Book of Coming forth into Light'. The Greeks named the region of Saqqara as Necropolis, 'City of the Dead', yet the Egyptian root of the name (*sek-r*) means variously, 'mystery', 'silence' and 'truth'. Trismegistus then falls to lamentation, crying,

"O Egypt, Egypt!"

He tells how the Gods will depart from the Earth, and from the world of men, who will have forsaken them.

XXV. The prophecy continues even to our present time, when all of civilisation is faced with final collapse into ruin. It is an age in which darkness or ignorance seems to triumph over all, even if that triumph last only for a relatively short duration until the final dissolution.

"They will cease to love the multitudinous whole that is the principle of love itself, that should be reverenced, praised and loved—by them at least that have the eyes to see. For Darkness will be set before the Light, and Death will be thought preferable to Life. They will not even raise their eyes to Heaven. And then they will think that the holy, wise and strong are mad.

"They will think that fools and profane are wise sages. The unruly mob will be held as strong, and ignorance will prevail over all."

All knowledge of the soul, of the immortal life, is lost, forgotten or rejected. The vision becomes reminiscent of the Apocalypse of St. John, to the extent one wonders if the Hermetic scripture was not an influence on that work. However, both scriptures are in agreement with the ancient Hindu doctrine of the Cosmic Cycles and Kali Yuga.

"Then the Earth shall no longer hold together. The sea shall no longer be sailed upon. The Heaven shall not continue with the courses of the stars, nor the star-courses in Heaven.

"The voice of every God shall cease in the Great Silence that no one can break. The fruits of Earth shall rot. Earth shall no longer bring forth. The air itself shall faint away in despair of that sad listlessness."

XXVI. Finally, the world of men, set to evil ways, is destroyed, that it may be renewed and restored to the governance of the supreme principle, and that all this comes about through divine ordinance.

"In this rebirth of Cosmos is the renewal of all good things, and the holiest return of Nature's self, by means of divine ordinance—of Nature, which was without beginning, and which is without an end. For the Divine Will has no beginning; it is ever the same and as it is, without end.

"This then, is the Divine Will, and the whole world her Image."

The Oracle of Isis

HERE IS THE WISDOM OF ISIS.
Hidden in the soul there is me, who is the eternal life without end, deathless.

A soul may pass through life not knowing me. And if by reason and desire of the heart, they have not sought me, who is the Mind or Wisdom Sophia, the Intelligence or Daemon within them, then when the body has died, their image of reason—being self-image—and their passions, is reduced to its elements.

For if they will not hear me, if they have shut me out, then I am not in them, and they will not live. For I am Life. And the life that was in them goes out from them.

It is possible too that even while in the corporeal flesh they reject me and deny me so vigorously that I fly far from them—so that to all intents and purposes they are as dead, even while living in the world.

I do not judge them, for I am Life Everlasting. The judgement on the soul is self-declared. It is the snare, the net cast by the body and sense that lacks true reason, that does not love me.

And so we asked, Then what of your son, Hoor? Is he not the Angel set over the Judgement of the soul?

My son is Light, as are all the Sons of Light. His is the radiance. It is by him that the soul learns to hate evil and to know what is true and what is false! The soul desires him greatly; he is the light-sustenance.

Now if you know me, and have heard my voice, and love me, rejecting the evil ones, the destroyers and the tormentors that lurk in the spaces of matter, then by him, Hoor, you shall arise. Then knowing me that is within you, you shall live forever and ever.

By my sacred heart and tongue I declare it: these are true words, and a million times true.

The Oracle of Shenut

Behold, I am in Shenut, and Shenut is in me!

Hear me, my friends and companions: I am the Oracle that ye seek.

I am in every word that ye speak.

Behold my glory in the rising and the setting of Ra, my sun-star.

Reach out to me in the horizon, and in my arms I shall gather thee.

Thine every breath is the life that I give.

I am the dawn and the dusk.

I am the sweet fragrance of the morning, and in the evening I am musk.

I am the moon in her mysterious light.

I am the myriad stars shining in the night.

I am the radiance of the sun in his full strength, at his hour of triumph.

And when the light fadeth, I am there in darkness and in the deep.

I am all that is above thee, and all that is below thee.

I am the skirts of the infinite reach.

I am the Song of Songs and the Trees of Eternity.

The muses are mine, and the heavens dance before me!

Every flower, every bird and creature is my song and my joy.

For I am the one that speaketh, and the one who listens.

I am vision and I am voice.

Know this: thou art blessed in thy blessing. Thou art loved in thy loving. Thou art eternal in thine eternity, which is mine also, which I hath given, and is all that I give to thee.

The Holy Guardian Angel

The idea of the Saviour or intermediary is more ancient than any religion. Hekate is the original type of the 'angel'—a word that is itself derived from the Greek, *angelos* (αγγελος). As a proper noun, Angelos was a name of Artemis, the goddess of the Arrow. In all likelihood the name belonged originally to Hekate. According to Hesychius of Alexandria, Angelos was a surname of Artemis in Syracuse where she was identified with Hekate as goddess of the Moon:

> She whom we called Hekate above, is now referred to by us as Artemis, because there exists a certain similarity between the goddesses.[178]

Hekate was able to fulfil this rôle by occupying both the upper world of the living (heaven) and the lower world of the dead (underworld or Hades).[179]

The primary type of the angel is found in the Egyptian tradition, where countless Gods appear in the form of birds, or are otherwise winged. These are the *neteru*, 'divine principles manifest in nature', frequently mistaken by the profane for symbols of 'animal worship' or some atavistic reversion.

Instances of angels as both guardians and punishers of men abound in the Christian and Judaic tradition—far too many to recount. The Hebrew or Aramaic word for an angel, *melekh* (מלך), literally means 'messenger', and the word for a 'king' shares the same root.[180] Originally the royal way or way of kings was precisely to fulfil the rôle of messenger between the Gods and man. An angel acts as an intermediary between heaven and earth, occupying the middle ground.

Melchizedek, the 'priest-king', notably makes his first appearance in the biblical book of Genesis serving the Eucharist.[181] The Order of Melchizedek is the inner or cosmic Order, of which any teaching, religion or organisation is the outer veil or exoteric level.

---

[178] Scholia on Theocritus, Idyll 2: 33.
[179] See the next chapter, 'Hekate Soteira: Fire of Mind'.
[180] Malachim, the name of the Order of Angels in Tiphereth, is variously translated as 'Kings' or 'Messengers', for example.
[181] Book of Genesis, 14: 18.

The name Melchizedek refers to one who is concerned with holy rites of an order or ordinance.[182] Traditionally, Christ is th'priest after the order of Melchizedek'.[183] The medieval French Rabbi Rashi said, in a comment on the book of Daniel, 10: 7,

> Our Sages of blessed memory said that although a person does not see something of which he is terrified, his guardian angel, who is in heaven, does see it; therefore, he becomes terrified.[184]

Also according to rabbinical lore, Lailah (לילה) is an angel of the night who guards over such things as conception, pregnancy and childbirth.[185] Lailah also serves as a Guardian Angel throughout a person's life. Upon death, she assists the passage of the soul into the afterlife.[186] These are exactly the attributes of many Egyptian Gods, of which Isis, Horus, Tahuti and Khonsu are to name but very few. In the Christian tradition the idea that an angel is appointed by God to look over every child appears to have been derived from Matthew, 18: 10,

> Take heed that ye despise not one of these little ones; for I say unto you, That in heaven their angels do always behold the face of my Father which is in heaven.

There is a rather charming prayer in the Catholic tradition,

> Angel of God, my guardian dear,
> To whom God's love commits me here,
> Ever this day (or night) be at my side,
> To light, to guard, to rule and guide.
> Amen.

It is worth noting perhaps that the Greek word *mikros* (μικρος) translated in Matthew 18: 10 as 'little ones' does not necessarily refer to children as such, but may refer to every idea of 'least', 'less', 'small' or 'insignificant'. So it might equally refer to 'few in number', as are always those chosen of Nuit. In the Hindu tradition, to be 'as a child' is an advanced yoga state where the person has wholly surrendered their will to the will of God.

---

[182] The name is composed from two words, *melekh* (MLK) and *tzedek* (TzDQ), the 'king' and the 'priest', or one who is concerned with rites of ordination, a holy order.
[183] As prophesied in Psalms, 110: 4 and reaffirmed in Hebrews, 6: 20.
[184] *Tanach with Rashi* [Judaica Press].
[185] Lailah means 'Night'; it is the name given to the night in the book of Genesis.
[186] *Gabriel's Palace: Jewish Mystical Tales*, Howard Schwartz.

The Graeco Egyptian papyrus spell known as the Bornless Ritual is sometimes used as an invocation of the Holy Guardian Angel. The spell is typically Egyptian in form and style and calls upon dozens of names of God, both male and female. Many of these are clearly of ancient Egyptian origin although some are composed from vowel arrangements characteristic of Alexandrian Greek Gnosticism. A comparison can thus be made with the Egyptian Seker Neter, 'Great God encompassing all other Gods', usually winged with the head of a falcon, combining all the forms and attributes of the deities.[187] The word 'angel' in the Coptic form is used in the penultimate part of the invocation, which consists of the ecstatic outburst, Angelos Ton Theon, 'My Angel, my God!'

Throughout the ritual, especially in the identification with the primordial Bornless Spirit, it is clearly the divinity that appears at the level of Tiphereth, the solar centre or world centre, where the individual is able to encounter the immortal realm:

> I am He the Bornless Spirit, having sight in the feet: Strong, and the Immortal Fire! I am He, the Truth. I am He who hate that evil should be wrought in the world. I am He that lighteneth and thundereth. I am He from whom is the shower of the life of earth. I am He whose mouth ever flameth. I am He the begetter and manifester unto the light. I am He the Grace of the World: The Heart Girt with a Serpent is my name.

The Heart Girt with a Serpent is a direct allusion to the *omphalos* symbol found in many cultures and traditions of the world, which we mentioned previously. It is typically an egg-shaped or dome-shaped stone sometimes encircled by the cosmic serpent. This places the Holy Guardian Angel at the centre or 'heart of the world', replacing the individualistic ego-self as basis of all. This is comparable with the symbolic centre of any traditionally constructed temple, shrine or sacred building. It is the place where the four corners and cardinal points meet with the central or world axis that depends from the hub of the universe.[188] All rites and ceremonies capable of preparing the person for initiatic transmission follow such alignments, whether they are physically built into the chamber or location prepared for the rite or not.

---

[187] Seker Neter includes the body of Khephra, the scarab beetle, whose name is usually taken to mean 'Ever-Becoming', although the name might also be understood as conveying a sense of the transforming of the *prima materia*.
[188] Thus eight in all, or nine including the vertical axis.

The spiritual experience of divinity in Tiphereth—a divinity that like Christ or the Hindu Shiva holds the triune key of the past, present and future—constitutes the accomplishment of the royal way or way of kings, sometimes called the 'second birth' or 'birth into spirit'. It is the real beginning of the path, the first effective initiation though not by any means the full spiritual realisation that is the aim of the way of knowledge, the sacerdotal way.[189] It is necessary to realise the royal way, which leads to the centre and soul of the world, before it is possible to realise the final and complete initiation.[190] The first does not lead automatically to the second, which involves full entry into the supra-human realm.

---

[189] In the Vedic schools of the East there is the way of the Raja and the way of Brahmin.
[190] In the book of John, 14: 6: I am the way, the truth, and the life: no man cometh unto the Father, but by me.

Hekate Soteira: Fire of Mind

As we travel deeper into the mystery, the importance of Hekate, the Egyptian Heqt, becomes a constant factor. Hekate was the last of the Old Gods. When Zeus formed the new world order of Olympian Gods, having sent the Titans to the invisible realm, he contrived to give special honour to Hekate—although it seems the honour was hers from the very beginning.[191] The consequence of not doing so would have meant that humanity was prematurely effaced from the world, having no means to contact the divine or supramundane worlds. Something of the importance of Hekate's rôle can be seen in this Orphic Hymn to Hekate.[192]

> Hekate of the Way, we invoke thee, o lovely lady of the triple crossroads, celestial, chthonian and aquatic, lady of the saffron robe.
> Thou of the sepulchre, celebrating the Mysteries among the living souls; Daughter of Perses, lover of solitude, rejoicing in the antelope.
> Nocturnal one, lady of the hounds, invincible and sovereign, who makest the beast to howl! Naked and beautiful in form.
> Tamer of the wild bull, keeper of the keys of the universe, Mistress, way-shower, bride, mentor, mountain-wanderer!
> We pray thee, o Daughter, to be present at our hallowed rites of initiation, always bestowing thy grace upon the Magi.

Hekate is the intermediary, who brings or binds together the soul with deity when the individual turns inward and either needs help, to ask a question or make an offering. She is liminal in all senses of the word, governing sea and sky in the formless, supra-abysmal realms, and earth and all below it in the sub-abysmal worlds of light and darkness. She traverses the planes on behalf of all who come to her, all who come to know her. Hear then, the warning of Hekate from the Chaldean or Zoroastrian scriptures, concerning her dual nature:

---

[191] Jenny Strauss Clay has provided valuable insights into the rôle of Hekate in Hesiod's Theogony, which has been almost entirely misunderstood or overlooked by scholars. *Hecate of Theogony*, Greek, Roman and Byzantine Studies, Vol. 25, No. 1 (Cambridge 1st January 1984).
[192] The new translation is ours.

> Stoop not down to the darkly splendid world wherein Hekate continually hideth in mysterious depth; sinuous and naked, with pleasure alluring, ever espousing the beauty of form, the limitless dimensions of space; numberless, unfigured—concealed forever from the mortal gaze. Arise therefore, with the light-seeing eye of dawn!

Scholars mistakenly assumed from their reading of the Greek that Hekate is the 'one who is willing to serve', whereas in fact she is 'the one who wills'—Thelema.[193] In the Chaldean Oracles and other scriptures collected and preserved, albeit in fragmentary fashion, by the Alexandrian philosophers, the Intelligible is a central idea. The philosophers, who wrote in Greek, also referred to this (Νους) as 'Paternal' or 'Father', and to them this Father was Monadic, the 'One'. From this One, that we call Kether, comes Two, Chokmah, and then Three. Three is personified as Hekate (Binah), the résumé of the Gnostic Trinity.

The Father, Mother and Son trinity has always been somewhat confused. The root of the confusion owes to the fact that the Father Monad was placed first in the scheme of things, which is a natural impossibility. In so far as the great *neters* can be male or female types, there is no Father in heaven and certainly no Monad. The supposition that anything fatherly or paternal can come 'first' and from there a Mother and Son is therefore preposterous. Plutarch wrote, in *Moralia*,

> The race of beetles has no female, but all the males eject their sperm into a round pellet of material which they roll up by pushing it from the opposite side, just as the sun seems to turn the heavens in the direction opposite to its own course, which is from west to east.

This is highly inaccurate, of course—by that time philosophers were not naturalists, whereas the ancient Egyptians most certainly were naturalists. They did not divide and compartmentalise knowledge so that specialists could produce 'learned' hypotheses, independently of all else outside their own narrow field.

---

[193] Beware ye scholars, lest an adjective should turn around and a verb slap you in the face!

Hekate (wood engraving)

This wood graving depicts Hekate in triple form, identified with the Moon as full-faced, in profile (quarter) and unseen (dark phase). The three faces also symbolise the past, present and future. The acorn symbolises strength, endurance, stability and wisdom, and is also the primordial 'height' or North Pole. The rope and dagger are the dual (complementary) principles of binding and cutting or dividing, thus *solve et coagula*, the alchemical action of Sulphur upon Mercury and Salt. The torches are the pillars of dual manifestation and of the Lesser and Greater Mysteries.

Plutarch's fantastical speculation does demonstrate, though, how the Platonists sought evidence in nature of their predisposition to male supremacy and self-sufficiency independent of the female, which they abhorred. Nonetheless, this doctrine formed by reasoning men against nature is now the prevailing mode, where information technology is revered to such an extent that meaningless data and falsehood controls every aspect of our lives. All traditional knowledge is called 'superstition' and is mocked as laughably 'wrong', while the lies and falsehood generated by the manipulation of machines and data streams, which serves no other purpose than to serve the blind worm of plutocracy, are unquestioningly accepted by all.

Hekate's rôle in mysteries such as the Chaldean Oracles is a central one. She occupies the middle ground, as Saviour (Σοτειρα) between Intelligible (divine) and Sensible (corporeal) worlds. At the same time she is outside and beyond, as part of the Trinity. She has a right side that manifests, pouring forth the emanations, and a left side that remains virgin and is ever concealed from mortal gaze. As liminal neter *par excellence* she is on both sides of every side and is truly neither one nor the other. There follows a brief extract from the Gnostic sacred text, *Thunder Perfect Mind*.[194]

> I am the sound that is attainable by all;
> I am the voice beyond reason.
> I am the name of the sound,
> And the sound of the name.
> I am the signature of the letter,
> And the seal of the division.
> And I am the darkness and the light.
> And I am the voice of my listeners,
> And the one who listens to you.
> For I am the Great Power.

Hekate (or Isis-Hathoor) was originally, therefore, the whole Tree of Life, both pillars *and* the middle way. This accords with far more ancient mysteries concerning a sacred tree from which the gods and all life are sprung. The function of Hekate, Isis, or Black Isis—the triune Goddess—provides the key to the reconstruction of the Gnosis.

---

[194] Nag Hammadi Library (contextually retranslated). See *Thunder Perfect Gnosis* for the full translation and a commentary.

Hekate embraces both the Intelligible and the Sensible. Her arms reach upward (in the crescent) to embrace the Intelligible, which is with her from the beginning-less and so endless beginning, the Soul of the Eternal. Below her 'seat'—delta, womb, gate of the eternal—comes forth Cosmos, the Sensible. She embraces it and is at the same time the centre of it, the All. Her Word (Hadit) is her heart and her tongue. As declared in the (Egyptian) Book of the Law, I: 6,

Be thou Hadit, my secret centre, my heart and my tongue!

Occupying the middle world in the Platonic schema, the Goddess Hekate manifests to men as Saviour. To what end then the 'Son' of the mysteries? Originally, this Son called Set or Horus was born from divine parthenogenesis—there is no father in heaven in reality. It is the Initiate that must become the son or king, the Horus. Horus is in one aspect the soul's power of *Discrimination*.[195] The torches that Hekate is frequently depicted bearing are the ultimate symbol of the Intelligible. That is, the Fire of Mind and the End-of-understanding (Νοητον).[196]

---

[195] See the next chapter, 'The Powers of the Soul'.
[196] *The Chaldean Oracles*, translated by G.R.S. Mead [Kessinger Books].

The Powers of the Soul

The Egyptian papyrus spells summarise the doctrine of the living soul. The so-called spells take diverse forms. The spells are 'so-called' because there is a great deal more to them than ordinary magick, and in fact the use of them as funerary texts came at a relatively late time.[197] Through the primary power of the soul called discrimination, which is embodied in Horus as the type of the fully formed Khu, the soul may survive mortal death and all the adverse elements of the underworld, or Sensible world, to achieve immortal life. We give here a part of our translation and comment on Spell 80, the Transformation into the God who giveth Light in the Darkness.[198] The God is Isis, who has power in all three worlds, heaven, earth and the underworld.

> Saith the seer N. _____, I am the girdle of the robe of Nu, radiant and shining, which abides in his presence and sends forth light in the darkness. I have knitted together the two contending serpents that live in my body by the mighty spell of the words I have uttered. I have raised up him that has fallen—oh, he who has fallen! He who now rests in the valley of Abydos.
>
> [Rubric] *I am the girdle of the robe of Nu, radiant and shining, which abides in his presence and sends forth light in the darkness.*

Spell 80 concerns the release of the soul's powers in the underworld, called *duat*. By the power of divine utterance the soul is thereby born as an immortal star or Khabs in the company of heaven. The spell is both poetic and highly technical in its intent. By transmuting the dual power of the *kundalini*, which in the unawakened state enthrals with belief in the appearance of objects, the life force is redirected towards fulfilment of a greater destiny. The Initiate becomes as a god, bearing witness to the unseen. By the power of the all-seeing eye, illumination is shed upon the vastness of the Abyss. By the power of love, truth is never forgotten, as declared in the (Egyptian) Book of the Law, I: 9,

> *Remember all ye that existence is pure joy; that all the sorrows are but as shadows; they pass and are done; but there is that which remains.*

---

[197] The source of many of the papyrus and coffin 'spells' may be found in the Pyramid Texts, which defy all profane attempts at interpretation; the true source is thought to be far older than the Unas Pyramid itself.
[198] *Babalon Unveiled! Thelemic Monographs.*

There is a whole range of what are usually termed 'magical powers' associated with the mirror-world of man's consciousness. It requires the exercise of the powers of the soul, called 'virtues' in traditional lore, to overcome the illusion of the world. Thus it is said that the virtue of Da'ath, Knowledge, is the *Perfection of all Virtues*. There are nine of these virtues, and nine corresponding vices or anti-virtues that come about when the Evil Genius, or the anti-spiritual force in man, refuses to allow the soul to express truth. The powers of the soul are also the powers of Hekate or Isis, the Cosmic Soul and intermediary. Traditionally, the powers correspond to the Qabalistic order of the planets from Saturn (Binah) to the Moon (Yesod), plus Malkuth (Sensible world). In addition, there is a vice and virtue for Da'ath, the eleventh sphere of Knowledge, making nine pairs in all. Our practitioners often neglect these, as at first sight they appear to be ordinary moral precepts. This is not at all the case. As powers of the soul, the virtues must be given free expression or else the ego, deluded in the belief in a separate existence, maintains a deadly grip on the soul, by which she is confined. The birth of her divine 'child', Horus, will never then take place.

Discrimination is the 'first virtue on the path'. Unless this power is exercised and fully realised, there can be no path as such, only delusion, in which the soul suffers immensely. If there are forces of initiation—helpful agencies to guide the soul—then there must be forces of anti-initiation. The forces of anti-initiation have now gained supreme dominance in the world today, as we near the end of a Great Age. Such forces of evil are covered by many masques or disguises. To quote from Guénon,

> It can happen that those who think they have escaped from modern materialism fall a prey to things that, while seemingly opposed to it, are really of the same order; and, in view of the turn of mind of modern Westerners, a special warning needs to be uttered against the attraction that more or less extraordinary phenomena may hold for them; it is this attraction that is to a large extent responsible for all the errors of 'neo-spiritualism', and it is to be foreseen that the dangers it represents will grow even worse, for the forces of darkness, which keep alive the present confusion, find in it one of their most potent instruments.[199]

---

[199] 'Conclusions', *The Crisis of the Modern World* [Sophia Perenis].

The consequence of suppressing the soul's power of discrimination is the vice of *Inertia and Avarice.* Lack of discrimination automatically implies the former, while avarice can take many forms, for example, the acquisition of knowledge for its own sake. In the modern day Information Age (so-called), it is possible to dissipate the mind and will in a sea of confused and meaningless 'facts', narratives, images and icons. Such information is laced with hypnotic commands and subliminal messages intended to first induce acceptance and then reinforce belief in the lie, however improbable.[200]

Independence is given as the power of Yesod, sphere of the Moon and astral tides. These have their counterpart in the dreaming and imaginative worlds. This is really the power of discrimination taken to the psychic level. All thoughts inimical to the goal are harmful. When the individual consciousness has succeeded in overcoming inertia on its own account it comes into contact with external forces inimical to the path—and these may also be masked or disguised. One must maintain independence from all profane organisations, which includes those with political or social aims. Likewise, one must be independent from the influence of those who would subvert all spirituality, whether they are totally opposed to the very existence of the spiritual or whether they are advocates of counterfeit initiation (such as psychologism) or pseudo-spirituality—and this, it must be added, includes nearly all 'non-religious' or doctrinally absent forms of spirituality in modern times.

Idleness comes about as a consequence of failure to allow the soul's independence, failure to protect her from forces inimical to her voice, which would shut her up. There is also the inverse and yet very common independence, which is nothing more than mere egotistical self-assertion for the perpetuation of the state of ignorance. A state of idleness implies the cessation of activity, especially when it is positive activity that is really needed. Activity is very often confused with 'action', which is exclusively physical, whereas intellectual activity is superior. Idleness, in the spiritual sense, naturally comes about when there is overweening dependence on others, even the thoughts of others. Complacency is a near cousin, for it is easy to mistake mere fantasy, induced by a dreaming trance, or a collection of phenomena, for example 'coincidences', as initiation when in fact it is no more than an ordinary function of the mind.

---

[200] Television producers have used subliminal 'flash' messages since at least 2020, without restriction. The words or images are shown too quickly for the viewer to apprehend consciously but they are registered by the mind and then act as hypnotic suggestions. It is essentially a 'brainwashing' technique.

Truthfulness is the soul's power in Hod, sphere of Mercury. The base of the left hand pillar requires equilibration; the concrete mind is a master of deception, for here desire is clothed in form. Any deviation from truth, which is a matter of the heart, not the mind, invokes *Falsehood and Dishonesty*.[201] While the deviation may be a slight one at first, the force behind it may be very powerful for it has an accumulative effect through repetition. The person may even believe in the deception, and in that case the failure is more or less fatal.

Faith and Unselfishness are the powers of Netzach, the sphere of Venus. The totems of Venus include the mirror, which like the Moon, reflects sunlight in ghostly form. Faith, which goes hand in hand with truth, is much misunderstood. Materialists, who do not understand the difference between faith and belief, now compile the dictionaries. This lack of understanding means they do not realise that their belief in scientism is even a belief; they think it to be truth! Faith, according to the Christian doctrine, is a gift from God. That provides a clue to the real meaning of faith, which is adherence to the chosen path realised as a divine gift (providence).

The intellectual intuition must be innate in the person so they can become initiated in the first place. Initiation cannot take place solely from and within the sphere of the person, and so 'self-initiation' is a lie. *Selfishness* is the perpetuation of the lie and is therefore allied to the falsehood of the previous sephira. *Unchastity* means not being faithful to the path.

Devotion to the Great Work is the soul's power in Tiphereth, sphere of the Sun. This naturally arises from the practice of faith on the previous path and is further fortified by sure knowledge. The consequence of avoidance is *Pride and Egotism*—by which the Evil Genius is able to defeat the whole operation of the Great Work. At this level, it is spiritual pride that precipitates a fall into the world of shells, as when self-love is mistaken for spiritual love.[202]

Energy and Courage is the power of Geburah, the sphere of Mars, which we will take as one power, not two. It can now be seen that the idleness and inertia in the lower spheres comes about through fear or lack of courage. From fear too comes forth the vice of *Cruelty and Destruction*.

---

[201] By 'heart' we do not mean 'emotions', or anything of a sentimental or personal nature. It is the higher intuition we are referring to.
[202] The error is sometimes deliberate. See 'Schiller and Self-Love'.

Obedience (to the path) is the power of Gedulah, the sphere of Jupiter. One must have already practiced obedience to the path to come thus far, and it is implied in all the other powers. Therefore, to abandon the path at this stage is to open a Pandora's box and unleash considerable evil. The vices of *Bigotry, Hypocrisy, Gluttony and Tyranny* are the consequences of shouting down the still voice of the soul at this level.

Silence is the virtue of Binah, the sphere of Saturn, the styptic force. It is one of the four powers of the Sphinx, without which the other three can have no meaning. Silence in meditation is necessary to enter into the deeper state, while silence over the mysteries ought to have been practiced at the very beginning—though it seldom is. The consequence of failing to keep silence at this level is *Avarice*. While this appeared in Malkuth in the guise of countless material forms and desires, in Binah the hunger for acquisition amounts to direct denial of the path itself, to the extent of resorting to infernal powers for appeasement. Perhaps Goethe's play of *Faust* provides a useful example.

> I am the Spirit that Denies!
> And justly so: for all things, from the Void
> Called forth, deserve to be destroyed:
> 'Twere better, then, were naught created.
> Thus, all which you as Sin have rated,—
> Destruction,—aught with Evil blent,—
> That is my proper element.[203]

Finally we come to Da'ath, the sphere of Knowledge, which has an intimate relation with Binah, though it is counted as the eleventh (or eighth) and not the third number. *Perfection of all Virtues* is the soul's power here, for we have arrived at the threshold of man's reason, called the Abyss—and which is the inferior aspect of Da'ath. Gedulah or Jupiter, the previous sephira in the order of things, has obedience (to the path) as its virtue. The seven virtues cannot be perfected unless obedience is practiced. This is aptly expressed in the legends of Isis as recounted by Herodotus. For example:

---

[203] *Faust* III, 'The Study'—Mephistopheles introduces himself.

> And in the evening I came forth with my seven scorpions: Tefen and Befen and Mestet and Mestef, Petet and Thetet and Maatet showed forth the way. For as a wise man practices obedience, allowing wisdom to enter into him, so disobedience is the mark of the low man who does not bring forth. Thus did my words enter the ears of the seven scorpions: Ye shall bend down your faces on the way! And downward they bent their faces, to make a way to the hidden places of Khebit.

Failure to exercise any one of the soul's powers bars entry to the Supernal Eden. The consequences of shutting up the soul at this level are *Infantilism* and *Isolationism*. These two are not disconnected. The infantile state usually comes first, and is a form of imbecility when it appears in any culture, for it means the destruction of that culture. The etymology of the noun 'imbecile' is helpful, for it is derived from the Latin *imbecillus*, literally, 'without a supporting staff'. The modern world has turned its face against all traditional knowledge, and mental, moral and physical collapse is the natural consequence. When this condition is very far advanced and there is little or no hope for the patient, so to speak, isolationism is invoked. Isolationism is the equivalent of all the vices or negative powers, and could be termed as the summation of the 'beast' that arises from the pit in the Revelation of St. John. It is of the nature of a machine dedicated to the destruction of the human soul, a type of artificial elementar of vast proportions, with a host of dedicated servitors—these have their counterpart in the mechanistic digital data streams of the technological age.

The powers of the soul are neither moral precepts nor abstract concepts. Developing or allowing the powers of the soul is not about perfecting the personality. The personality, to fulfil its urge for self-preservation, will compartmentalise and divide the truth to serve necessity—as the personality sees fit. If we are Christian, for example, then we must practice it in our whole lives, not pay lip service to the tradition in Sunday church because that suits our need to gain the respect or approval of others. Likewise, yoga is not about perfecting the body or developing physical fitness. All of that derives from ignorance, as does the psychologisation of the mysteries—which has become by now the only accepted approach to finding meaning in ancient traditions.[204]

---

[204] More recently, scholars do not search for meaning in ancient traditions at all. They merely report 'facts' and produce 'evidence' from other scholars and historians, frequently to prove their belief that no such meaning exists beyond necessity, or otherwise political or social convention.

Initiation has become a rare but absolutely imperative matter for those still capable of initiation—those who have intellect, a soul, and the latent capacity to bear supra-human or spiritual influence, and to recognise that for what it is. Practice then the powers of the soul, and hear her voice in the depth of Silence! Vincit Omnia Veritas—*truth is triumphant over all.*

Solar and Lunar Phases

The Cosmic Cycles consist of wheels within wheels, cycles within cycles, as is everywhere evident in nature from the courses of the Sun, Moon and stars. This can be seen even on the relatively small scale of the yearly round. From the winter solstice to the summer solstice there is 'ascent' or increase of the solar power towards full manifestation as the Sun travels ever further towards the zenith of heaven. From the summer solstice to the winter solstice there is a 'descent', as there is a reversal in the declination of the Sun and Ra heads back towards the nadir.

The solstice points are sometimes called the 'two doors', in terms of initiation. The first, at the summer solstice, is called the Gate of Man, for it is where initiation begins for those who seek liberation from the darkness of the fallen world. The second is called the Gate of the Gods, for it is where the Initiate exits altogether from the cosmological sphere, which is called 'deliverance'. This is always, or should be, built into the structure of initiatic rites, and is reflected in such things as the circumambulations about the temple and marking of the cardinal points, or otherwise stellar alignments as the case may be.

The lunar cycle reflects the sun's annual waxing and waning across one month or lunation. The first 15 (or so) days from dark to full Moon see an increase of the lunar or nocturnal light and an 'ascent'. This is reflected on the subtle planes with an increase in activity, which may be likened in alchemical terms to the action of Sulphur (radiance from within) upon Mercury (the astral medium). This brings about 'double Mercury', which is the full manifestation of the Astral Light. The 15th day of the full Moon is thus named 'White Ibis', which is an aspect of Thoth or Tahuti.

As the Moon wanes away towards eventual disappearance, we commence the 'descent', in exactly the same way we commence the initiatic journey of Man (the Neophyte) towards the Gate of the Gods. This is why traditionally the waning period of the Moon is called 'malefic' and the waxing 'benefic'. From the spiritual or initiated point of view, this is reversed: the waxing half is a descent as it passes from spirit towards manifestation, while the waning half is an ascent, as it is passes out of manifestation altogether. The traditional benefic and malefic attribution can then easily be understood. The path of manifestation or reification is easier in terms of the corporeal state of the being, while the path to spirit is much harder.

It may be seen from a thoughtful study of these considerations that in reality, or from the spiritual point of view, the ascent and descent are simultaneous; they only appear to be phasic from the terrestrial or corporeal point of view. This easily gives rise to some confusion with a person that is commencing a spiritual discipline and practice. As soon as the practice is taken up, if it is in any way effective, then the dual current comes into operation. While there will appear to be beneficial outcomes on the side of manifestation, this will seem to be outweighed by the difficulties encountered with the spiritual ascent, which is in material terms a 'descent'. And that is to say, the upward path that leads out of manifestation involves firstly a change of state in the being, which is a type of 'death', and ultimately it involves the dissolution of the ego and of all previous states—for in real initiation it is impossible to return to a previous state of being. Thus, some will burn an incense to Shiva (or the equivalent) on the waxing cycle, and to Parvati (Shiva-Shakti) on the waning cycle. The Shakti is the 'power behind the God', just as Saturn is said to be the 'power behind Venus'.

Both male and female experience a lunar cycle, though the male cycle is nothing like as powerful to cause phenomena as that of the female, which is deeply rooted in the physical body. However, the Lunar Return occurs each month when the Moon reaches the same degree it occupied at the time of birth, and that applies equally to the male or female of the species. The nature of the Moon is such that it is hard to prepare for the 'moment' apart from knowing when it will arrive. Anciently, the Moon was considered to be the mirror to the earth of all other celestial influences. It is declared in the (Egyptian) Book of the Law, I: 15,

> ... in his woman called the Scarlet Woman is all power given.

The possessive pronoun 'his' refers to Hadit (or Set) the Dragon-serpent, the mysterious 'cause' of all phenomena.[205] The bi-monthly cycle is an immensely powerful driving force that does not only change the body of women but also changes their perceptions to a considerable degree. Even through the menopause this continues to be a powerful and sometimes disruptive influence.

---

[205] This is touched on in *Babalon Unveiled*, especially in the section dealing with the various aspects of the Goddess, particularly 'Scarlet Woman or Soul in the Underworld'.

The menstrual cycle in women would not be so disruptive or 'problematical' if it were not for the fact that all our industrialised civilisations, so-called, relentlessly drive the incessant requirements of mundane work and obligations in total ignorance of the meaning and value of what we experience in our bodies, let alone what is suited to our individuality. This is carried through to the extent that profane medicine provides all kinds of artificial means of stifling the natural course or in other ways trying to 'normalise' something that this pseudo-science does not understand and will never understand. Such means are frequently harmful to the being, individually and collectively. Even when no obvious physical damage is caused, there is damage on subtler levels.

In reality there is no 'standard model' for the cycle, though people would very much like that to be the case so they can better adapt themselves to the insane requirements of an industrialised and now a technological 'virtual' world. If the cycle is placed side by side (by counting days) with the monthly cycle of the Moon, which more or less exactly mirrors it (28–30 days in total), we find that sometimes we will get an exact match. At the dark of the Moon (confusingly also called the New Moon) comes the bleeding, and then at the full Moon, the ovulation. But it will not stay like that for long; the cycle is in perpetual motion. It is rather like the tides of the ocean—the times move around constantly with the waxing and waning of the Moon and seasons, or solar cycle, and there is overlap. So we have the cosmic cycles and the personal cycle, dancing around each other, catching up and then moving further away.

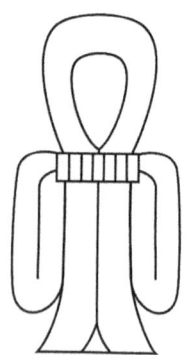

The ancients had a comprehension of spiritual and natural law that dwarfs our own. The Egyptian women wore the 'Knot of Isis' (*tiet*) through the bleeding spell. The Knot of Isis was an amulet fashioned as the Ankh of Life and made of hematite or 'blood-stone', which has magnetic properties—as does blood. Blood carries a great deal of magnetism on a physical level, owing to the iron in it. The magnetic properties are mirrored on subtler planes than the physical. The amulet was tied in linen in a special way. The charm is made in the image of the 'Life' (Ankh) of Isis, the life-giving principle itself. When blood pours forth a considerable weight of vital force goes out with it. In the usual state of affairs this results in depletion of energy. The consequences can even bring about fatal disconnection from the spiritual realm.

With the Knot of Isis, all the vital force and magnetism charges the amulet constantly. Power is not given to the person or to any object or desire of the person. All power is given to the Cosmic Soul, Isis, the principle of life itself. What is given must be returned, which is a natural, not a moral law.

Karma and Sin

The Theosophical Society sowed the seeds of the modern New Age movement, which is an anti-initiatic and anti-spiritual force.[206] It thus successfully subverted elements of the Hindu doctrine, reducing them in an attempt at simplification, and at other times fabricating the meaning. Two particularly subversive and false notions were introduced into mainstream Western culture. The first is reincarnation, which is a misunderstanding and confusion of the doctrine of multitudinous states of being, of which the human is but one very small part. The second, which we intend to deal with here so as to remove the need of further consideration, is that of the Sanskrit word *karma*. Karma actually means 'action', and in the technical sense it means ritual action, for that always includes gestures of the physical body and sometimes symbolic objects, the mantras and yantras or 'words and images'. The meaning of the word *karma* was wrested from its traditional context and a completely artificial and false meaning appended to it, which is akin to 'cause and effect'.

From cause and effect, a chain of consequences, it was a short step to further equate the idea of *karma* with 'sin' or error—the notion that a wrong or evil action would give rise to another and then another. To further compound the fallacy, an even more insidious link was made between *karma* and the false notion of reincarnation, in which a person is thought to be born and reborn 'as themselves', in an endless perpetuation of human (sometimes animal or vegetable) existences. This was eventually taken to the extreme, where 'self-help' books and pseudo-spiritual teachers put it forward that any affliction one might suffer in 'this life' must be due to some wrong committed in a 'previous life'. The notion is incredibly sinister and damaging, and yet countless quite sincere and well-meaning persons have adopted it and sometimes used it unwittingly as a weapon against other people, to attack them under the pretence that they are being helped: 'You have a bad leg in this life because you kicked someone to death in your past life!' Put in this way it might seem infantile and silly—and it is—and yet millions have fallen for it; the corrosive consequences on what is left of our culture are incalculable.

---

[206] See René Guénon, 'Theosophism', *Introduction to the Study of the Hindu Doctrines* [Sophia Perennis]. Also, *The Spiritist Fallacy*, for a more esoteric account of the multitudinous errors involved.

The false notions of reincarnation and *karma*, when added to the widespread use of psychism, where practically anything goes, has meant that the fake witch-doctors of our times have used every means to subvert and destroy all true spirituality and to destroy, for many persons, all hope of initiation. Once such ideas are accepted, the being becomes actually degraded and its intelligence diminished. There then reigns a complete imperviousness to learning anything that contradicts pseudo-religion or New Age non-religion.

Furthermore, the original use of *karma* in Hinduism was that of 'right-action', which is a necessary prerequisite to yoga. As previously mentioned, it can also indicate rites necessary to initiation, at least as a support or preparation. The subversion of the meaning, separating it from its principle, has made *karma* almost exclusively negative, and associated with a kind of distorted or inferior understanding of 'sin' as it is termed in the Judaeo Christian traditions. Sin, in most languages, invariably means 'error', 'deviation', or 'transgression', in the sense of a departure from order. It is 'to miss the mark', and in that sense it may be no more than a 'meditation break'. Apart from when some wilful subversion is being perpetrated, in most cases the idea of deviation from the path is no more than part of learning to exercise the power of the soul called discrimination.[207] And that is to say, notions of chastisement, wrathful vengeance or voluntary self-punishment are very frequently a deviation in themselves and can have no real meaning.

In the present times, most persons are by now accustomed to false disciplines in both education and work. These involve flattery and reward, which is supported by either psychological, emotional or monetary means—or sometimes all of this. The effect of this is insidiously evil. They are so unaccustomed to any spiritual discipline, which does not include any of that, that when confronted with it they imagine they are being made subject to some sort of chastisement. In fact, all that is happening is that a correct procedure or right way of conduct or of doing a practice is being shown them. And thus all of what is now passed off as 'education', and the slavery that is passed off as 'work', carries a wholly negative attitude towards anything either genuinely spiritual or initiatic.

Concerning the practical import of sin or error, there exists an oracular instruction from the Shakti of the Kali Yuga, known by the ancient Egyptians as Sekhet (or Sekhmet). We shall give this next.

---

[207] Cf. 'The Powers of the Soul'.

Oracle of Sekhet

An Instruction to the Devotee concerning Sin, Error, Misdeeds and any fears concerning Impurity or lack of Ability, in this Kali Yuga.

Do not fear for anything. Do not fear for your past, however much evil was in the way of where you trod your feet. Do not even fear of evil that might yet be done, or thought, or willed or spoken of.

You are all of you as children born into a black, poisonous sea in this Age of Iron. Know that I am the Light and the Grace of God, and that I am with you always, and that is all.

Remember it!

It is I that will take you across the waters.

O Soul of the Eternal, let it be thee that I desire!

Then be my serpent flame.

My flame will awaken you.

Sound that is not heard, taste that is not taste.

Fragrance without perfume; flame without light or heat.

Colour that has no colour, and which has no name.

The still voice not uttered—I, without thoughts.

Take away all thought, vision, and voice;

All reflections make still.

Her colour is dark blue, with some violet, and after a while there is a soft golden infusion, which is the promise of the time that will come.

Unicorn of the Stars

The Practicus of the Golden Dawn has the eponymous title of Monokeros de Astris, the 'Unicorn of the Stars'. This is best explained through the name of the Titan, Astris (Αστρις), which means, 'Starry One'. Astris was born from a marriage of the Sun and the ocean (Moon or sea-foam), alchemical types of fire and water. The Practicus degree corresponds to Hod (Mercury), the Water Temple that receives the fiery solar influence from Netzach (Venus).

The Initiate of Hod has first to traverse, at least symbolically, the fiery paths of Shin and Resh before entering Hod, the Water Temple. Hod is thus seen in every way as a sphere of transmutation. Although Hod sometimes symbolises the concrete mind, as 'form-building', it is not the goal of Initiates to become detained by the limits of ordinary reason. In fact Hod, the eighth path or sephira from the Crown or root of the Tree of Life in heaven, is traditionally called the *Stellar Light*, and is also the 'Seat of the Primordial'. This is affirmed by the Greek value of Monokeros de Astris, which is 1,175. What follows is not conventional or traditional Qabalistic *gematria*, but with a little manipulation we can show how numbers can underpin the ideas we want to express.

As 29 x 75, the unicorn's horn corresponds to the 'Divine Pillar of Nuit (or the sky)'. The twenty-ninth path corresponds to the Hebrew letter *qoph*, which is the 'head' or 'pinnacle', while 75 is a number of Nuit (NVIT). While it is true that the letter *qoph* is more frequently referred to as the 'back of the head', the same letter *qoph* (or *quf* in Arabic) is more specifically the skull or cranium. As such it has a special meaning where it is indicative of the gate of egress from the cosmological sphere to the heavenly or primordial sphere. For this reason Christ-Jesus was crucified on a hill called 'Place of the Skull' (Golgotha).

The primordial is variously symbolised as a pillar, mound or mountain—for there is nothing beyond the peak of a mountain except the sky or heaven. The unicorn's horn points straight upward to heaven, and is spiralic. The Arabian white oryx is the original type of the fabled unicorn. The higher end of the ancient Egyptian *hennu* sky-boat of Sokar is fashioned in the shape of the head of an oryx.

The Egyptian God Sokar

The unicorn's singular horn is not descriptive of the beast itself, which has two horns, but is an esoteric assignment for the Primordial Pillar, as well as the upward ascent of consciousness, as in yoga. Sokar, it may further be noted, is frequently depicted as the head of a black hawk, a symbol of the primordial in the very particular sense of the unmanifest or 'dark' state, which necessarily comes first, and is greater than all dual manifestation. Both the unicorn and the yearly ritual of carrying the wooden boat of Sokar around the temple's location symbolise the circumpolar revolution of the 'seven' around the 'eighth' or Pole Star. The Pole Star marks the visible axis of the universe and the height of the visible heavens.[208]

The oryx is reputed to dig a bed out of the desert sand with its hooves, to lie in and keep cool. This explains the attribution of the one horn—the shifting sands of desert dunes have always symbolised the Abyss that defines the limit of human reason. The penetrating horn of mind (reason) must be made concave, so to speak, on the abysmal threshold that closes in upon the limits of human reason.[209]

---

[208] The three-yearly Jubilee of the Pharaoh coincided with the rite of the 'round' of Sokar, proving an identification between Sokar and Set or Saturn, and also the primordial mound.
[209] C.f. 'Dragons and Serpents', the chapter that follows.

Through practice of yoga, contemplation and devotional Tantras, the Flower of Fire (or Mind) is cultivated as the 'fruits' of the flower are rejected in favour of pure receptivity to the intelligence from beyond.[210]

The Gnostic term, 'Flower of Mind' or 'Flower of Fire' is not the mind or intellect in the ordinary sense; it may be likened to an essence that is drawn out and upward. The Egyptian 'flame' hieroglyph, the possible origin of the Hebrew *yod* ('), has both a physical and metaphysical level of interpretation. It carries all the meanings of fire, flame or luminosity, and that of a 'flame of flames' when plural. The latter bears comparison with the yogic realisation of the *tanmatras* or elemental principles, or even that of Atma the supreme principle by upward transposition.[211]

Such knowledge is only attained through yogic concentration of the mind. Veritably, the threshold to the post-abysmal Mind of Minds is fiercely guarded and barred. The rôle of guardians or 'watchers' such as Anubis and other Setian creatures including the crocodile and jackal, as well as the Cherubim in various traditions, is complex. They are guardians of the gates, ferociously attacking or even devouring those who would enter. At the same time, they symbolise the drawing forth of the bolt, which is the means by which the gates are opened.[212]

The action of the bolt symbolises both 'opening' and the image-making or phallic power withdrawn or inverted, which is a reversal of the usual flow of consciousness.[213] The door of the sky or of heaven is not opened by any mortal man but, for example, it was the office of Ankh-af-na-khonsu, the priest and scribe of the Stele of Revealing, to literally 'open the doors to the sky'.

---

[210] See G.R.S. Mead, *The Chaldean Oracles*.
[211] See *Thunder Perfect Gnosis*, Part Two. It is impossible for Egyptologists to construe ancient Egyptian sacred texts, as they cannot admit to the existence or even the possibility of an esoteric level of interpretation. They then produce nonsensical 'translations' of the texts, and say it is nonsense because the ancient Egyptians were themselves confused and irrational!
[212] See John Anthony West, *Serpent in the Sky*, pp. 149–157 (on Spell 316).
[213] Phallus (Greek φαλλος) literally means, 'image' or 'image-making'. The Sanskrit *lingam* has exactly the same meaning. Both words also have the meaning of 'substance', which has a subtler meaning than 'image'.

Ankh-af-na-khonsu performed the ritual of opening the doors to the roof of the temple at certain times of the year so the image of the Goddess, taken from the subterranean vault below, could observe Sirius rising.[214] As declared in the Book of the Law, III: 37,

For me unveils the veilèd sky, the self-slain Ankh-af-na-khonsu whose words are truth.

Sirius, the Star of Egypt, symbolises both Isis (or Hathoor) and her 'son' or divine child, born of the ascent of consciousness arising from the depth. The Greek spelling of the Egyptian name, Sothis (Σθις) or Sopdet, has the value of 419, equal to the Hebrew *teth*, 'serpent'. The word is identical in meaning to the Egyptian *tech* or *djet*, from which the name Tahuti, the Logos or Word, is formed. The serpent symbolises the means of manifestation, by which Nuit is known, or otherwise knowledge itself (as opposed to the knower or the thing that is known). Hathoor was also known as the 'Divine Pillar' at Iunet in Egypt, which implies the ascent and descent of the vertical axis depending from the metaphysical point, of which the North Pole is a symbol.

---

[214] This is explained in detail in 'Star and Snake of Egypt', p. 150 *Babalon Unveiled* in the First Edition, and p. 87 in the Revised Second Edition.

Dragons and Serpents

The Golden Dawn founder, S.L. MacGregor Mathers, provided us with a coherent explanation of the doctrine of the Qliphoth in his translation of *Sepher Dtzenioutha*.[215] The commentary is luminous but it is not composed in a way that is accessible to the modern reader. The Qabalistic doctrine of the Qliphoth or 'Evil Shells of Matter' uses the symbolism of the Dragon or Leviathan. At the base of the Tree of Life, below or otherwise entwined about Malkuth, the shells are 'under the form of a vast serpent extending this way and that'.[216] The implication is that mortal man is under the shadow of what is called 'extreme justice' or severity.[217] This defines the material world, where we are placed under absolute restriction or confinement by our own physical and sensory inclination. Beyond that, extending upward from Malkuth to the Abyss, the human psyche is similarly under a great force of restriction, though it is deemed as less severe than the deep pit of that which is wholly material, and which admits to no spiritual reality whatsoever. That most inferior form of the Beast or Dragon typifies the mentality that shapes today's world, and which is now governed by what we have termed the System of Antichrist.

The psychic force, which has its operation in the subtle domain, and which prevails over the intermediary realms between heaven and earth, or between the spiritual and substantial, is likened to a great sea-serpent, or 'that great dragon which is in the sea'. This dragon is said to have a single nostril (aperture) 'after the manner of whales', so that it is able to receive the influence or *mezla* from the worlds beyond the Abyss.[218] And this is the meaning of Psalms, 74: 13, where it is said,

> Thou hast broken the heads of the dragons upon the waters.

---

[215] Mather's translation of Knorr Von Rosenroth, *Kabbalah Unveiled*, line 25.
[216] Ibid.
[217] This term is used in the Enochian Calls of the Aethyrs.
[218] Mathers [*ibid*].

The subject is unavoidably technical; this dragon (or dragons, for it encompasses two) is a universal symbol that sums up the seven planetary sephiroth or mundane chakras as dependent from Binah. These are seen Qabalistically as inferior or lower *emanations* of that Throne of the Supernal Wisdom. The 'bruised head' of the serpent is Da'ath, the Ogdoad, the highest point that the normal intellectual and moral faculties of man can obtain before the Great Sea of Binah, the wisdom born of the Intelligible Light. The other dragon referred to is that of the lower subtle regions, which form a magnetic belt, as it were, about the earth. This dragon is bound up in Malkuth, and is under the presidency of the Tav or Tau Cross of the thirty-second path that joins Malkuth with the Foundation, also known as the sphere of the Moon. The path is attributed to Saturn, Lord of Time. Human consciousness is bound fast to the time process in the normal state of affairs, even as Malkuth, the world, is symbolically cut off from the rest of the Tree by the coils of the dragon. Thus, there is an abyss of height and an abyss of depth; naturally these reflect one another. For example, the sephira Binah (Intelligible) and non-sephira Da'ath (Knowledge)—which is secreted within her—are attributed to the mundane chakra of Saturn, as is the path of Tav (ת). However, they exist on different planes, above and below, of heaven and the earth, and should not be confused.[219]

Comparison may be made with the dismemberment of Osiris by Set or Saturn. Osiris, as a consequence of the trick played on him by Set, had to undergo death, being bereft of the immortal principle as symbolised by the phallus of Osiris or 'lost word'. He was then made subject to time. The phallus or rejected immortal principle of Osiris was cast, it was said, into the Nile where it was swallowed by a fish, or otherwise lost at sea. This obtains on more than one level, as we shall explain. According to the Hindu doctrine of the Cosmic Cycles, Vishnu assumed the form of a fish at the end of the last great Manvantara. He told Manu, Lord of the Manvantara, that he would carry the seeds of the great cycle over to form the new Manvantara cycle after the great deluge.[220] Thus on the microcosmic scale, the mind of man may resurrect as Horus, the divine 'child' of Isis so the immortal principle may be restored through the power of love.

---

[219] A simple presentation of the Tree of Life, the sephiroth and paths, is given in our book *Hermetic Qabalah Foundation—Complete Course*.
[220] See 'Cosmic Cycles', *Nu Hermetica*.

In the concave head of the Dragon then, the phallic power is withdrawn so that the feminine principle can obtain. To use the Taoist terminology, the sage must become *yin* to the *yang* of the primordial principle, so that earth and heaven may be reunited. The soul is able to 'give birth to herself', or in other terms, accomplish the miracle of resurrection. It is the rôle and function of Isis to give life, for she is life itself, and the breath of life, the *ankh*, seat, throne or foundation of all that can exist.

The Qliphoth, 'shells' or so-called demons, are therefore no more than inverse and distorted forms of the sephiroth of the Tree of Life. The sephiroth hold the dual function of transmitting and receiving, for they receive higher influence and transmit it to the emanations below. The 'nostril' of the dragon is its receptivity as opposed to its horn or crest, which is active and penetrative. When the dragon's head is broken upon the waters and the crest is made receptive or concave then all conceptual thoughts, numbers or emanations, are seen to emerge from and fall back into the mind that produced them. This is no different than Raja Yoga, where it corresponds to the stage where the concentration of mind shuts down all mental processes to be fixed on the unity of the mind of God (or Shakti) and the goal, or at least the primary one, is reached, which is called Samadhi.

The nature of Saturn (or Set) is concentration. The translation of the penetrative horn of the dragon into a receptive vessel allows the possibility of a miraculous Flower of Mind, from which may emerge the divine 'child', Horus. The dual modes or functions of expansion and contraction are therefore both necessary for the realisation of spiritual consciousness. However, if one over-uses the concentration faculty of the dragon or becomes bound up by it, the result is a hardening, the forming of a shell-like exterior; in other words, the mind is not then capable of receptivity to the spiritual influence.

This is why it is said that some persons are suitable for initiation while others are not, for when the shells have tightened their grip so as to completely seal off the doors to heaven, so to speak, that person is impervious to initiation. It is impossible for them to understand even the outer mysteries of symbol and allegory. Profane scholarship, philosophy and science alike do not only encourage such hardening, but also positively exalt it and, by its easy domination of the lower worlds and the minds of the ignorant, it is used to gain power and influence through total denial of spiritual realities.

One of the clearest doctrinal fragments of Liber AL vel Legis sums up the dual nature of the Serpent or Dragon, whose power can bring wisdom to the wise and ignorance to the foolish. This Serpent Power is identical to that force linked with the Shakti power in the Hindu Tantras, and spells out the dangers of all such practices:

> *I am the secret Serpent coiled about to spring: in my coiling there is joy. If I lift up my head, I and my Nuit are one. If I droop down mine head, and shoot forth venom, then is rapture of the earth, and I and the earth are one.*
>
> *There is a great danger in me; for who doth not understand these runes shall make a great miss. He shall fall down into the pit called Because, and there he shall perish with the dogs of Reason.*[221]

The soul whose desire to bond for completion is not informed by the True Will but is mislead by her reason or controlling ego, perishes in the Abyss, the 'pit called Because'. In the Hindu tradition, no person would attempt to practice Kundalini Yoga, or any form of yoga, without first obtaining a guru willing to help them. As for magick, which consists of various applications of traditional sciences, only in modern times, and particularly in the West, would it become possible that so many persons, believing in the illogicality of 'self-initiation' would lead themselves and others into total self-delusion.

Without the power of concentration there can be no ascent, no elevation of consciousness. Having arisen, one must not presume oneself Lord of All, as do the tyrants of the world.[222] One must be receptive to spiritual influence. Dissolution of the egoistic counterfeit of reality is here implied, for man's reason cannot penetrate beyond the objects created by his own mind. The premature use of the receptive mode, on the other hand, results in a gradual wasting away and dispersion of the soul for there can then be no involvement with spiritual or initiatic transmission.[223]

---

[221] II: 26–27.
[222] Such tyrants climb an inverse hierarchy, of which the 'pinnacle' is the pit of Satan—the 'top' is therefore the bottom, regarded spiritually.
[223] See Guénon, *Perspectives on Initiation*, Chapters 21 and 22, where the magical powers are explained very thoroughly [Sophia Perennis].

By 'premature', we refer to the excessive use of the receptive mode before sufficient knowledge and experience has been built into the structure of the individuality, making the mind flexible and thereby capable of operating according to both modes of function at will. The consequence of such an error, which is sadly very common among those who seek something vaguely spiritual but refuse to take up the discipline and work of an initiatic Order (assuming they can find one), is much the same in the end result as that of the Saturnian contraction. The person is ultimately bound to the planes of illusion, captivated by the magnetic force called variously Leviathan or Beast. It must be said also that this is frequently the case with 'psychics', and those who would, as a matter of habit or preference, place far too high a value on the magical powers (so-called). And although there are many of these who would not think of themselves as psychics as such, and may not even believe that the subtle plane exists in its own degree of reality, these have nonetheless over-developed certain very particular magical or otherwise purely imaginative functions. The latter are more dangerous than the psychics for they retain an active will that is invariably turned towards evil, if they know it or not.

There is a further symbolic aspect of the dragon to consider. The serpent holding its tail in its mouth forms a circle—the serpent of Saturn, *ouroboros*. In his action upon Malkuth, the material world, he is not only the executor of judgment but he is also the Destroyer. His power is therefore that of destruction as opposed to creation, death as opposed to life. Furthermore, this dragon is concealed. He is only known through irregularity or disequilibrium. In that case, his appearance is as the accuser, or the executor of judgment, and it is for this reason he is known as the Destroyer. Spiritual realisation nonetheless requires destruction of the previous state, and that is why many seekers of that which they think of as initiation baulk no sooner they come anywhere near contacting the spiritual forces that would undo them. The slightest degree of contact is only perceived in their minds as an overwhelming accusatory force. In self-protection, they turn against those who would help them if they were brave enough to attempt to master the acquisitive force in them. The human ego (*ahankara*) becomes destructive or separative when it mistakes sensorial impressions for the true Self. According to Advaita, the senses are 'the slayers of the Real'. The power is turned against itself, so to speak, for reality to be known.

A priest makes a 'sacrifice' so that he becomes a word made perfect, a truth-speaker such as Ankh-af-na-khonsu. The sacrifice is only a preparation for real initiation that involves irreversible change in the state of the being. The translation of the *Stele of Revealing*, given in Liber AL, III: 37, is questionable:

For me unveils the veiléd sky, the self-slain Ankh-af-na-khonsu.

The office and real function of Ankh-af-na-khonsu as the 'opener of the doors of heaven' means he had not only made the priestly sacrifice but was also an intermediary between Heaven and Earth, the principle and the manifested state. He was as one who ascends and descends the ladder of the stars or worlds. The Egyptian words *ma'a kheru* mean, 'Whose word is true (before the Gods)'. The 'self-slain' notion derives from a misunderstanding of the hieroglyph *kheru*. It is thought to be a sacrificial block, but is used in this context as a phonetic, not a determinative. Also, whether it really does symbolise a 'sacrificial block' is open to question. Comparison with other hieroglyphs suggests it may symbolise the door to a shrine—which more accurately reflects the priestly rôle and function.

The ass, a Setian creature, must be prepared to carry the ark, which is to say we must be prepared to submit egoistic pride to that which is above and beyond us. Set, a strange creature-symbol that was carried over to Egypt from the Atlantean tradition, is usually depicted as having truncated ears.[224] However, on the two pillars of the festival hieroglyph for the king's thirty or (subsequently) three-year Jubilee, Set is shown at the head of the right-hand pillar with unusually elongated (thus receptive) ears.[225] At the head of the left-hand pillar, Set is depicted wearing the symbol of Ma'at, 'Truth'—for he is here fully justified. Likewise, the name of IAI, the Ass god, is spelled with the plumes of Ma'at. This is a subject we will return to later.[226]

---

[224] The Atlantean tradition preceded the present Great Year commencing with the precessional Age of Leo. The 'sinking of Atlantis', whether a fact of history or a symbolic allusion to the ending of a complete world and the start of a new one, coincided more or less with the melting of the glaciers that brough the last Ice Age to a premature conclusion.
[225] Both 30 and 3 correspond to Saturn, the formative principle. Thirty is an approximation of the number of years it takes Saturn to complete a round of the zodiacal circle. Binah is the third emanation and the Mother of Form.
[226] See 'The Ass of God'. Also our *Egyptian Tarot* trump XXI.

The Sorrows of Isis

It has been said that the dragon's head is broken upon the waters of the great sea, which is wisdom. It is by this great sea (Binah) that the power of the shells to do harm is restricted in itself, for Malkuth (the world) is the reflection of her. It has also been said that there are two dragons, and in the commentaries it is explained that one is male and one is female, but the female Leviathan is sacrificed, as it were, so that the begetting power of the dragon is thwarted lest they produce further judgments or severities. Here we must depart altogether from the erudite though somewhat exoteric explanation of MacGregor Mathers. The meaning of the sorrows or lamentations of Isis is expressed in the word for 'dragons', ThNINIM, for it has a common root with ThANH, which can mean either the fig-tree or the fruit of the fig-tree. ThNH (*tannah*) is usually an expression of woe or lamentation.[227] The verb also has the meaning, 'to give presents' or 'distribute'.[228] It generally has the meaning of conveying honour, to commemorate or remember and also (therefore) to rehearse.[229] Thus ritual, or sacred rites, especially in the commemorative (or seasonal) sense is implied. The 'giving forth' has the nature of a sacrifice.

The weeping of the fruit of the fig-tree combines lament and sorrowing (Binah) with virginity, sweetness or ripeness. This is well illustrated in the somewhat ambiguous account of the tale of Seila ('petition', 'sent out') or Iphis ('beautiful'), the daughter of Jephthah, in Judges, 11: 40. Seila laments her virginity with her companions on the mountain for two months before being offered for sacrifice, thanks to a bargain made by her father with the Demiurge in return for defeating the Ammonites. The oracle had demanded of Jephthah that, 'Upon returning, you shall offer up the first thing that comes out of your house'. This turns out to be Seila, dancing and playing upon a tambourine.

There are some that dispute the outcome or meaning, however, for the elements of the story do not tally. Firstly, it was customary in those times for the first-born son to be sacrificed, though in this case Jephthah did not have a son. Secondly, why would Seila lament her virginity if she were about to be sacrificed? And thirdly, who are these companions, and why would she be allowed to go up into the mountains with a band or troupe of friends?

---

[227] Judges, 11: 40.
[228] Hosea, 8: 10.
[229] Judges 5: 11.

It has therefore been suggested that Seila actually went into exile and was not sacrificed. While her sacrifice is implied by the biblical narrative, it is not explicitly stated or recorded. We can look at this another way. Seila was an only daughter, which is a special attribute of Hekate and other female Saviour divinities. Such female divinities have the precise rôle of occupying the 'middle ground', which is the domain of the sea dragon between heaven and earth. They thus act as intermediaries between the heavenly and earthly worlds, both the spiritual and the substantial.[230]

Seila is distinguished by the fact that she is a dancer. Dancing in ancient times was always sacred and was associated with temple priestesses and virgins. This is reinforced by the presence of her mysterious companions. The departure for the mountains signifies initiatic rites even older than those that were done in caves, for the mountain peak is the 'opening to the sky', the door on the roof of heaven. The lamentation of Seila is thus the trial of her initiation; for she mourns the sacrifice of the worldly life, in which she would be expected to bear sons, keep a household.

According to the book of Judges, the lamentations of Seila became a custom, so that the daughters of Israel would lament for Seila four days out of every year. The 'four days out of every year' of the rite of commemoration is the difference between the symbolic solar round of 360 days and the lunar year of 364 days. The solar round symbolises the full reach or circumference of the visible or outer world while the lunar year symbolises the interior path of the priestess. As one short of 365, the number 364 is the 'breaker of the circle' and a symbol of Set, showing the very ancient nature of the rite referred to originally.

It is stated more than once that Jephthah had opened his mouth before the Lord, and had thus committed an irrevocable act. The root of the name Seila is ShLCh (*shelah*), a temurah of ChLSh, 'a whisper', and an amulet worn by women. The name Jephthah is cognate with that of the Egyptian creator god Ptah, and the meaning, 'opener' or 'engraver', is identical in both the Egyptian and Semitic languages.[231]

---

[230] The 'spiritual' and 'substantial' equate to *purusha* and *prakriti* in Sanskrit. 'Substantial' is here used, and not 'material', for matter is really a human construct and owes to a level of sub-manifestation—it is not the true complement of the essence or *purusha*.

[231] Budge, *The Gods of the Egyptians Vol. I* p. 500.

In this context, Jephthah is one who has opened his mouth before the Lord of Judgements and has thereby carved out his fate, which is to be subject to the forces of time and death, as was Osiris.[232] ShLCh has the meaning of an arrow or dart, flying forth, extending or stretching. It also refers to the falling of leaves from a tree and is thus associated with the account of the 'fall' in the book of Genesis. This involves a multiple play on words, for ShLCh also has the meaning of undressing or disrobing—and so nudity. At the same time the word carries the meaning of 'casting down' or 'casting out'. The poison of the Qliphoth is the antithesis of the elixir of life or immortality, the fruit of the Tree of Death as opposed to the fruit of the Tree of Life. To be 'unclothed' is to undergo the dissolution of ego. This is the necessary condition for the unveiling of the true nature of Nuit-Isis.

The tale is undoubtedly much older than the time in which it is set in the Bible, where the sacrifice of first-born children had been introduced for the pacification of an angry, jealous and bloodthirsty Demiurge. As such, the meaning is esoteric, and so it baffles profane scholarship. The sacrifice of the female dragon is synonymous with the Sorrows of Isis.[233] The weeping of the fig-tree is her lamentation for having brought souls into the world to suffer death. It is also the lamentation of Isis for the slaying of Osiris, which is the rejection of the chance of immortality by the profane. A further meaning, and a quite opposite one, is that tears (or dew-drops) can be a metaphor for the *mezla*, or spiritual influence beyond the realm of the abysmal outer threshold of man's reason.[234]

In the Age of Kali Yuga it was the vital function of the priestess that was 'lost' or forgotten, and not the phallus of Osiris—although the former effectively brings about the latter in real terms, in so far as the phallus symbolises the immortal principal. It was necessary that the ritual of lamentation or of the Sorrows of Isis be performed once per year high up in the mountains so that the dragon's head could be 'broken upon the waters'. If not, then Seila's father, as Osiris slain, would remain shut up in his ego, bound to the forces of time and death, and subject to the extreme judgments of Leviathan—or of a vengeful Demiurge.

---

[232] Ptah of Memphis is a very ancient and mysterious *neter*; in later dynastic times he was identified with Osiris and Sokar.
[233] The Sorrows of Isis may be found in the legend as described by Plutarch.
[234] Mezla (MZLA, 78) is the 'starry influence'. Mazloth, 'Zodiac', is derived from the same root.

Nu and the Number Eleven

The number 11 has some considerable weight as a numerical and geometric symbol, and so it seems to be well worthwhile explaining some of it here. We can count 44 right-angles in the figure of the Triple Precinct of the Druids, which was previously explained.[235] As a multiple of 11, this is a number of Nuit, who declares in the (Egyptian) Book of the Law, I: 24,

> I am Nuit, and my word is six and fifty.

The number 56 is that of 'Nu', which is the hieroglyphic name of Nuit as shown by the pot or vessel, the container of all, which she wears upon her head. In the Book of the Law, I: 60, Nuit declares,

> My number is 11, as all their numbers who are of us.

The addition of the numbers 5 and 6 results in 11. The 'five' is the symbol of man or the microcosm while the 'six' symbolises the macrocosm or Universal Man. In 'Celestial and Terrestrial Numbers', René Guénon has given us some very useful considerations on the number 11.[236] He is there concerned particularly with the Chinese *yang* and *yin* Heaven and Earth symbolism though, as always, he demonstrates the universality of the knowledge across all traditions. He shows the complexity of the relations between the Heaven and Earth as metaphysical reality, and of numbers as being analogous to that reality. The numbers 5 and 6 relate geometrically to the square and circle, Earth and Heaven.[237] According to Guénon, the number 11 symbolises,

> ... the central union of Heaven and Earth. The importance of the number 11 as well as its multiples is yet another common element in the most diverse traditional doctrines, as we have already noted ... although for reasons that are not very clear it goes largely unnoticed by those moderns who claim to study the symbolism of numbers.

According to the oracle of Nuit, the Book of the Law, I: 21,

> I am Heaven, and there is no other God than me, and my lord Hadit.

---

[235] See 'Return to the Holy City'.
[236] *The Great Triad* [Sophia Perennis].
[237] The reasons why this appears to reverse the usual *yin* as even numbers and *yang* as odd numbers in the I-Ching are too complex to go into here. The reader must refer to *The Great Triad* [ibid].

Nuit says of herself that she is 'Heaven', and as we have seen previously, that her name is Nu or 56, and that the numbers of all her followers are 11. Although it is heterodox to use the Hebrew Qabalah to calculate English words, it is difficult not to notice that 'us' adds to 66, a multiple of 11. The principle of Earth is contained within that of Heaven, which is the greater. It cannot be otherwise, although it may appear to be so from the terrestrial point of view.[238] From all of the above considerations, the following passage from the oracle of Nuit, I: 53 will become clear.

> *This shall regenerate the world, the little world my sister, my heart and my tongue, unto whom I send this kiss.*

The 'regeneration of the world' has already been explained in the oracle as having to do with devotional practices dedicated to Nuit. This begins in I: 9,

> *Worship then the Khabs, and behold my light shed over you!*

Here again is the symbolism of the microcosm, as the 'star of man', which contains the seeds or roots of the five senses and elements, and the macrocosm, as Nuit, who in this case is the intermediary between Heaven and Earth. The number 11 as the union of the pentagram and the hexagram is the 'central union of Heaven and Earth'. The significance of 11 as of those who follow Nuit is then explained. The central union is the means by which the square is turned back to the circle; the Earth is reunited with Heaven.[239] Thus the unification is inclusive of both dissolution of the previous state and manifestation of the new. The Tiphereth or 'world centre' is vital to the Great Work of 'creating a new heaven and a new earth' because by that alone man may realise a destiny as the 'Son of Heaven and Earth'.[240] According to John, 15: 6,

> I am the way, the truth, and the life: no man cometh unto the Father, but by me.

The Greek word for 'eleven', *endeka*, has the value of 85, which is that of 'life' (ζοη). It is not life in the biological sense of the word (βιος) but in the true metaphysical sense, the principle. The number 85 is also equal to the Greek words for 'knowledge' and 'to know'. According to the oracle of Nuit, I: 57,

---

[238] See 'The Star of the Order' regarding the Khabs in the Khu.
[239] It is also thus with the Cosmic Cyces. See 'Cosmic Cycles' and 'Return to the Holy City'.
[240] 'See *The Great Triad* [ibid].

> *Invoke me under my stars! Love is the law, love under will. Nor let the fools mistake love; for there are love and love. There is the dove, and there is the serpent. Choose ye well!*

Nuit-Isis is life, therefore her knowledge, symbolised here as the love of the dove, is the knowledge of life. She is the Soul of the Eternal, hidden or unmanifest in the principle, but who is able to manifest or appear by virtue of the power of Hadit as the Serpent of Knowledge. The knowledge of the Serpent is the knowledge of death, however:

> *I am the flame that burns in every heart of man, and in the core of every star. I am Life, and the giver of Life, yet therefore is the knowledge of me the knowledge of death.*

Thus Hadit reveals his dual nature. As the unmanifest principle, he is unknowable, but his manifestation as the Serpent seeks only the appearances of things, which is the knowledge of death. The love of the serpent can only lead to death as finality.[241]

If we return to those words of John, 15: 6, it is Christ-Jesus that says, 'I am the way, the truth and the life', which can by now be seen as a statement of irrefutable spiritual fact. To 'cometh unto the Father' indicates the final deliverance. In all the traditions since the Alexandrians—in so far as it was written in Greek but also centuries before that—the 'sky' or Heaven principle, also called the First Principle, is always attributed to the Father. In the Chinese or Far-Eastern tradition, it is the *yang*, which is masculine as opposed to the feminine *yin*; in all these traditions the feminine principle is the soul, which can only be reflective of the primordial centre considered as the First.

As has been said previously, the rôle of the intermediary between Heaven and Earth, the Saviour, was originally the domain of Hekate or other female divinities, often regarded now as 'chthonic' although that description could only come about at a time when the knowledge of previous cycles was completely forgotten.[242]

It is worth repeating what was said about the association of the Goddess with will:

> Scholars mistakenly assumed from their reading of the Greek that Hekate is the 'one who is willing to serve', whereas in fact she is 'the one who wills'—Thelema.

---

[241] This is continued and explained more fully later in 'The Sons of God'.
[242] See 'Hekate Soteira: Fire of Mind' and 'The Holy Guardian Angel'.

The will called 'Thelema' in Greek (Θελημα) has nothing at all to do with 'will' understood in any psychological sense, or in the sense of self-determinism. It is the 'will from the centre', the primordial, and is thus ordinance but not determinism. Determinism can only ever involve peripheral modifications of the being or, as in the case of magick, which is an application of knowledge, modifications of the environment that is contingent to the being in the corporeal state. We can then see what might appear to be a contradiction between the relatively modern 'Father in heaven' superimposition and the much older supremacy of the Mother-Typhon.

γ

The Greek letter *gamma* in the lower case form is identical with the symbol, hieroglyph or mudra of Typhon. The upper case form is the 'set square' (Γ). This is why Typhon, or Set-Typhon, has been quite correctly identified with the Mother, though this also includes her Son:

> *With the God and the Adorer I am nothing: they do not see me. They are as upon the earth; I am Heaven, and there is no other God than me, and my lord Hadit.*

The words here delivered in the voicing of Nuit, I: 21 reaffirm a science of metaphysics owing to a time far more ancient than that of Plato or Pythagoras. This is natural, because the knowledge already existed. Nuit asserts unequivocally that she is 'Heaven'. And furthermore, there is no other God than she and her Son, Hadit or Set, who is able to 'cause' her appearance.[243]

We must return to what was said concerning Advaita Vedanta, and that Shankara, as according to Guénon, must have known that Brahma has a dual nature but would not say it.[244] Nuit is more or less the equivalent of Brahma, in which case Hadit is the Atma. However, there is no 'Father in heaven' in the most ancient doctrines, there is only Nuit and her Son-star—and these two are in no way to be considered as separate.

---

[243] This has been misconstrued—by those who will always seek a Monad—as Hadit being a causative and Nuit as merely a secondary 'appearance'. Some followers of Crowley even thought that Nuit is no more than an 'elemental God' for this reason.
[244] See Return to the Holy City' and 'The Star of the Order'.

There is a difficulty that arises with Hadit, in that his nature is also dual. While he represents the unmanifest principle, which includes the metaphysical 'point', he may also appear as the Serpent of Knowledge. The confusion of these dual aspects is very dangerous, for as the Serpent or 'animator' of life, he is at the same time the Adversary, Satan, that will trick or delude the person into placing his self, as subject to modifications and determinations, at the centre. The reason is a powerful and persuasive force; it persuaded those who came after Plato to confuse man's reason with the supreme principle Itself, seeing as how all was seen to depend from the Mind of God.

The final deliverance is impossible without going by way of the Saviour. Thus the words of John quoted previously, where there is no way to the Father (or Mother) but by the way of the Son of God. Both 'salvation' and the 'final deliverance' (*moksha*) are available to the followers of Nuit, those who love the dove. The dove symbolises both descent (as in the case of an avatar) and ascent, or reascent. This can only take place on the vertical axis of the world tree or cross.

It remains to look once more at the *gamma*, which is always considered to be a feminine symbol, while at the same time it is the symbol of Set-Typhon. The same symbol was placed by the Egyptians at the very centre of the cosmic wheel of heavens, as the 'hub'. It was afforded a strange creature that looks like a hippo with a crocodile's tail. While this was always identified with the Great Mother, the same terrible beast was also the 'Devourer' that would consume the soul that failed in the judgement or weighing of the heart. This can be looked at two ways. The devourer of the soul that sends the soul to destruction is, from another point of view, the agent of the positive dissolution that the initiate must pass through on the way to final deliverance or *moksha* (also called 'liberation' sometimes).

While all really effective initiation takes place on the central pillar (or trunk) of the Tree of Life, there are intermediate degrees (or 'branches') that are placed on the two side pillars to the left and the right of the central column. The 'second birth' equivalent to the 5=6 degree (Tiphereth at the centre of all) is in nearly all cases only symbolic or virtual upon admission to the degree. It is not until later that this is in any way accomplished or fulfilled and even then, owing to the dual nature of the pillars of the Tree, there is disequilibrium until the true Self is realised as Atma.[245]

---

[245] One should bear in mind that the two pillars are also 'eleven'.

The completion of the primary initiation, when considered as truly effective and not merely symbolic, can only take place through a departure from equilibrium and then a return to the central column. This is often misunderstood by those who imagine that one must somehow 'leap' or find a way across the Abysmal threshold of Da'ath.

There is a certain symbolism where the initiate is called a 'Babe in the Egg of Blue', or 'Babe of the Abyss', which is likened to the aspect of Horus in his Silence, called Hoor-paar-kraat. This is certainly not wrong, in so far as the initiate—who may well think of himself as 'adept' by that time, however rightly or wrongly—must 'sacrifice' his self to the Mother Isis to realise the 'other side' of Da'ath, which is hidden in the secret places of Binah. However, the symbol of Typhon (Y) has its base in Yesod—and we should at all times remember that Da'ath is not in any way a sephira; it is not a 'place' or location in any sense of that. To arrive, so to speak, at the juncture where the two arms reach out to Chokmah, Wisdom, and Binah, Understanding, Tiphereth must be entered—or *re-entered*. There is a correspondence here with the two faces of Janus, of which the third is not seen, for it is the 'eye' that if opened, dissolves a whole world or universe. And this may in some ways be equated with Da'ath. It might also be remembered that both Christ and Shiva are traditionally understood as the bearers of this triune principle.

The two arms of Typhon, or of *gamma*, also symbolise the 'two ways', which are that of the Lesser Mystery and the Greater Mystery. Continuing with the Tree of Life symbolism, we can consider that the paths of Zain, the seventeenth, and Hé, the fifteenth, represent these. The path of Zain is the Lesser Mystery, for although the path contains the 'two ways', they are depicted in the sign of Gemini by a horizontal and not a vertical polarity. Thus, there can be a division in the self that arises from incomplete initiation. One cannot return to a previous state and yet, if for some reason the being is unable or unwilling to sacrifice all, then a 'fall' may occur, in which case a degradation takes place in the being.

The path of Hé, on the other hand, is symbolised by the vertical polarity of the sign of Aquarius, which is also the path of Nuit in a certain respect. This path is the fulfilment (and so completion) of the Lesser Mystery, which can only take place when the way is opened to the Greater. Hekate, mentioned previously, also embodies the two faces of Janus and the third or supreme awakening. Sometimes this was shown by her bearing two blazing torches, one in each hand, and with the pinecone, symbol of the primordial tradition, as a crown.

The legends concerning Sekhet the Egyptian lioness Goddess are pertinent here, for she is the Eye of Ra, the fire, the flame and the light itself. On being sent out into the world to destroy the enemies of Ra, Sekhet became bloodthirsty; she would not stop the slaughter until she had completely wiped out humanity. Tahuti then changed the blood into wine (or red beer), so that Sekhet became drunk and was pacified, returning peacefully home to Ra. The destruction of all previous states is here symbolised, but with the transformation of the blood into wine, the essence of the soul is drawn out and taken up to a higher plane as it were—thus Sekhet 'returns' to Ra, the principial state of being.

There is a secondary meaning to this: the changing of blood into wine is sometimes thought to indicate the departure from animal or even human sacrifice, and the substitution of red wine, as for example in the Christian Mass. However, this explanation rests on confusion or even a type of inversion. There is no substitution involved at all in this, for the changing of blood into wine symbolises the passing out of the corporeal state and into the supra-human state. Thus, to think of it in terms of a substitution is, however unwittingly, to exchange the lower for the higher and not the other way round. And certainly the confusion born of ignorance has been used as a weapon against Christianity or any rite that involves wine as a sacrament.

It is fitting to look again now at the oracle of Nuit, I: 21, already quoted above. Nuit says that she is nothing with the God and the Adorer and that they do not see her, for they are as upon the earth. This refers to those that remain in the corporeal state, and are subject only to a distorted reflection of the supreme reality, without which nonetheless they would have no existence. Those that would have the sacrament of wine as a mere substitute for a blood sacrifice reveal something of their own nature, but nothing of the mysteries they pretend knowledge of. To them, there is no spiritual meaning in such symbolism; it is as nothing, as they cannot see it; even if it should be written down or told them they will hate it and not even try to comprehend it.

This qualification regarding the corporeal state and the supra-human state is followed in I: 21 with the powerful assertion from Nuit that 'I am Heaven, and there is no other God than me, and my lord Hadit'. Hadit, we should remember, is the lord that reigns over all the lower worlds—he is not the creator of Nuit, only that which is able to cause her appearance through cognition; as such he is the 'knower', and there is still a dualism of subject and object.

It remains to be said, though it is implicit in what has been discussed, that the letter *gamma* is not only the 'G' used by Masons in their symbolism but is also the equivalent of the Hebrew *gimel* (ג). The letter *gimel* corresponds to the thirteenth path on the middle pillar of the Tree, connecting Tiphereth with Kether, and is called the 'Uniting Intelligence'. The Tarot trump placed here is that of *The Priestess II*. Here is Nuit-Isis in her central position as intermediary between the upper worlds and the lower worlds that correspond in turn to the more limited range of the individuality. The thirteenth path of Gimel can be viewed as a continuation of the twenty-fifth path of Sagittarius the Arrow and the Tav (or Tau) that links Malkuth the Kingdom with the rest of the Tree. The Arrow symbolism has a dual function, for while it is usually seen as being fired upward towards the goal, Nuit may also send this Arrow downward, which is the descending ray of force or *mezla*.[246] Returning to the 'Y' or *gamma* symbol of Typhon, this can equally be seen as marking a downward trajectory. The ascent and descent, in terms of an initiatic force, takes place simultaneously in reality.

---

[246] It might be worth repeating here what was said earlier, that the Hebrew word *mezla* is related to Mazloth, the name of the Zodiac, and is sometimes likened to a 'celestial dew'.

The Rejection of Religion

It follows from all these considerations of the numbers 5 and 6, central to the Way of Initiation, that there is a need to recollect the fact that the Adeptus Minor grade of 5 = 6 marks an entry to the Order of the Rosy Cross. While there is nothing particularly 'Rosicrucian' about any initiatic organisation that exists today, and there has not been for many centuries, the power of the Symbol endures. The 'Rose blooming on the Cross of Gold' is an indication of the 'five' of the Rose emerging from the 'six' of the Cube of Space, these two things finding their unity both in the number 11 and in the primordial centre of all. It is the fulfilment, in symbolic terms if not in actual or real terms, of the Lesser Mysteries, by which man is able to become the 'Son of Heaven and Earth'. Thus, on the reverse side of the Rose Cross Lamen on the top arm it is written,

MAGISTER IESUS CHRISTOS DEUS ET HOMO

'The master Jesus Christ, God and Man.' This is inscribed between four Maltese crosses. In the centre, written in Latin,

BENEDICTUS DOMINUS DEUS NOSTER QUI DEDIT NOBIS SIGNUM

'Blessed be the Lord our God who hath given us the Symbol Signum.' Additionally, though it is not integral to the meaning of the whole, the alchemical symbols for Sulphur, Mercury and Salt are inscribed on the left arm, and Salt, Mercury and Sulphur on the right arm (as though mirroring). The fraternal name of the Initiate is placed on the lowest bar.

Now while an initiatic Order needs not at all to be concerned in any way with religion or exotericism, it is nonetheless sometimes said that a prior affiliation with exotericism is necessary for any real initiation to take place.[247] This does not mean that a person attends 'Sunday church', a mosque or other place of worship; but the normal rites of affiliation such as baptism, as according to each tradition, supplies the horizontal bar of the Cross, which is the link to tradition in time. It is the vertical bar that represents initiatic transmission, but one cannot exist without the other or the lines go nowhere.

---

[247] Guénon has frequently stated this across his works.

This brings us to the question of the rejection of religion, which is very common among occultists, although each one usually imagines that he is the special case. It is one thing to dislike Buddhism, for example, especially if it is the Westernised, denatured or otherwise diluted versions of Buddhism that one has in mind. It is quite another thing to reject the Buddha, which is the symbol of that religion—a word we use here for convenience, as it is not really any more correct to call Buddhism a religion than it is to call Hinduism a religion, or that which was practiced by the ancient Egyptians. And likewise, it is one thing to dislike Christianity, especially in some its modern forms, but quite another to reject Christ, which as we shall explain in a moment poses a real spiritual danger to the person.

Even worse, it has become popular among those who dislike or even hate Christianity to then embrace Buddhism, nominally at least, as a kind of 'healthy alternative', while at the same never being ordained as a monk or even following any true Buddhist rites or practices. Such a person is no better than the 'Sunday Christian', who attends merely because it is the respectable thing to do, or because it is an entrance to certain elements of the community deemed as favourable to that person.

The person who dislikes a particular religion or even all religions is expressing an opinion, often formed through some unpleasant experiences or sometimes through sheer ignorance and prejudice. But whatever the case should be, and whatever justifications there might be, their likes and dislikes exist completely in the personal domain and so have nothing whatsoever to do with initiation and spiritual realisation. If such prejudices or opinions become extreme, they may even act as a permanent bar to real initiation.

There is an even worse danger than this, however, which was alluded to previously. If a person goes so far as to not only reject Christianity, for example, but also to reject Christ as a matter of fact, then they place themselves on the side of the Antichrist. While many might suppose that the Antichrist is peculiar only to Christianity, or certain fanatical factions of it such as fundamentalism, or worse still the 'psychobabble' of modern media platforms, they are very wrong in that assumption. The Antichrist—a term that was not actually used in St. John's Revelation but is frequently associated with it—is purely and simply the anti-spiritual force in man. The anti-spiritual force necessarily reaches its apotheosis towards the end of a great age of time or Manvantara, immediately before the final dissolution and withdrawal to the primordial.

The anti-spiritual force is a movement that is fully supported by humanism, psychology, the education system that is meted out in our schools and universities, 'media campaigns', and indeed all of our governmental and corporate institutions. To be on the side of that means having no chance whatsoever of real initiation. Even the salvation afforded by exoteric religions will be denied, and the final deliverance (*moksha*) will be an absolute impossibility. The person that imagines they are the exception to the rule is merely adding hubris to hypocrisy.

It is easily possible, though, that a person may enter with that attitude; pass through various degrees of virtual (symbolic) initiation and then at some point experience *metanoia*.[248] With this comes not only a change of mind, as indicated by the etymological meaning of the word, but also a change of heart. The absurdity of the posture previously assumed becomes all too painfully clear. The ways to real initiation are then opened.

---

[248] Our use of the term here has nothing to do with 'religious conversion', which is a description afforded to it by the profane writers of modern dictionaries, and has absolutely nothing to do with initiation.

The Sons of Gods

Here are two fragments of very ancient knowledge texts, and a commentary on both. The first text, *Sons of Seth-Hermes*, is attributed to Josephus and the second, *The Sethian Gnosis*, is attributed to Hippolytus.[249] The legends concern the followers of the way of Set, the first among the Egyptians. The Sethians were the builders of the great ancient monuments, the wonders of the world. 'Monument' is the word that is used in the text, though it is hardly descriptive of sacred architecture, which symbolises that which lives and is eternally true, and is not to commemorate the dead. As we have stated earlier, there is an association between the Sethians, the Kings of Edom and the so-called 'race of giants' called the Nephilim. However, the surviving narratives concerning this are corrupt. This owes to the onset of the Age of Kali Yuga or Age of Iron from about 6000 years ago, in which the knowledge of all previous times was either forgotten or erased. What little remained was demonised. The Hermetic fragments contain a brief but possibly the only true and reliable account of the Sons of Seth-Hermes. The first section, 'Sons of Set-Hermes', is certainly a testament to historical events that refer at least as far back as the last great Ice Age.

The second section, 'The Sethian Gnosis', conveys the fragments of a very potent metaphysics that clearly, in its original form, must have vastly predated Pythagoras and Plato.[250] This begins with pure metaphysics and considerations of the unmanifest state, comparable in some ways to Brahma of Advaita Vedanta and the Ain Soph Aur of the Qabalah—though again, as it predates these, its value is beyond measure, not only in its agreement with all traditional knowledge but also in its unique difference. There is development from the triune metaphysical reality, which is the basis, to a cosmology, and in that are the seeds of what would later be fleshed out in the narratives of the Gnostics, for example the personification of the principles in the divine personages of Christ-Jesus and Mary Magdalene. The doctrine of the death and resurrection and final return to the supreme state is contained therein.

---

[249] Josephus (37—100 AD) was a Jewish historian, while Hippolytus (170—235 AD) was an early Christian that wrote against the Gnostics as heretics. The Gnostic scriptures as translated by G.R.S. Mead are given in *Thrice Greatest Hermes* [Kessinger Books].
[250] There are lacunae in the original manuscript.

The Sons of Seth-Hermes

0. The Sons of Seth were all of fair temperament. They dwelt happily together in the same country, free from quarrels. They encountered no misfortune even to the end of their long lives. They were learned in the wisdom of the stars and the orderly arrangement of the celestial bodies. Adam had foretold of the world destroyed by fire and after that, by the strength and mass of water. Therefore, to ensure the knowledge would not be lost before it was even known, the Sethians made two monuments, one of brick and the other of stone. On each of these they engraved their knowledge. Then, if the monument of brick should be swept away by the heavy downpour, the stone monument might survive and let men know what was inscribed upon it, at the same time informing them that a brick one had also been made by them. And the stone monument survives even to the present day in the land of Egypt.

Comment

It is possible that the monument of stone and the monument of brick refer to the Great Pyramid and the Sphinx of Giza respectively. The Sphinx vanished beneath the desert sand many times over the course of history, and was restored again and again. So it is very possible that at the time this text was written down, the Sphinx was no longer visible while the Great Pyramid of course was. It is possible, though speculative, that the prophecy of the destruction of the world by fire and then water was fulfilled when a very large meteor impacted North America, a matter that is by now well documented. This is thought to have brought the Ice Age to a premature end, and a great deluge. This great flood, which took place approximately 12,000 years ago, is the same that, according to all accounts, sunk Atlantis. Atlantis was the secondary centre of the primordial tradition after that of the Hyperboreans.

The Sethian Gnosis

1. The Sethians profess three universal principles. These possess particular qualities yet at the same time unlimited possibilities. Light and darkness are their essence and in the midst of these is pure spirit. The spirit is set in the midst of the darkness below and the light above. It is not a spirit or breath like a blast of wind or some light breeze that can be felt. It is more akin to the delicate scent of unguent or of incense compounded and prepared.

It is a force of fragrance that travels with a motion so rapid as to be quite inconceivable. It is far beyond the power of words to express. Now since light is above and darkness below, and spirit is in some way, as I have said, between them, then the nature of the light is to shine forth from above. The light shines forth like a ray of the sun, into the darkness beneath. The fragrance of the spirit, which is between the light and the dark, is contrary wise in that it extends itself and is carried in every direction. As when incense is thrown upon a fire, we see the fragrance of spirit carried in every direction.

Comment

The three principles are here arranged vertically, which is suggestive of the primordial pillar of height and depth. Light is placed at the top, darkness at the bottom, and spirit or fragrance radiates outward from the centre. To the Sethians, the light and dark were not seen as opposed to each other but on the contrary were seen as intermingling with spirit or fragrance in order to create the womb of existence. This womb or cave—identified with darkness though not thought to be evil in itself—is the key not only to generation and incarnation but also to freedom from the illusion of the material world that arises from ignorance, as it is put in Advaita Vedanta. One of the earliest forms of the Tree of Life, existing long ages before Plato, was the tree of fragrance, the Tree of Eternity from which gods (such as Horus) were born from the primal mother. The Great Work is to build the image of such a fragrant Tree as a terrestrial Eden, reflective of the primordial or supernal Garden of Eden. The purpose of such a centre is to nourish forever the soul-essence of those drawn to it.

However, it must first be understood that in this section the three principles of light, darkness and spirit do not have any place in the worlds of manifestation at all; these exist in the unmanifest state. It is for this reason that there is no contention between them. In fact, even at the unmanifest level, there is an order to things in that the light is deemed to be 'above' and the darkness 'below', while the spirit or essence freely intermingles with both. Now by 'above' we mean the higher principle. From that we can glean that 'light' in this context has little if anything to do with light as that is commonly understood. In theology and ancient philosophy, the light and spirit are often interchangeable terms, yet here they are posited as unique and different. According to Advaita, the Atma shines but does not radiate light until it is reflected 'below', in the worlds of manifestation. Thus it is said that the yogin may perceive the 'light of Atma shining upon the universe', which is not the supreme realisation, though it is quite advanced on the path.

The spirit and the darkness then are equivalent to *purusha* and *prakriti*, the 'essence' and the ground 'substance' of the universe—though neither of these are part of the manifest state. There is here a hint of the dual nature of Brahma, which is only known in any direct way in the supreme realisation, of which Shankara would not speak.[251]

Whenever there are three principles, there must be a two joined or united by a third. And as the darkness, in the sense it is used here as the unmanifest ground, must contain all possibilities, and in a sense comes 'first', then we can see that the principles are three in one, and that what is called spirit is the unitive and combining force.

2. This is the power of the triune principles: that spirit and light combine and descend into the darkness that is set beneath them. And the darkness is an awesome water into which the light together with the spirit is drawn down and transferred. The darkness, however, is not without understanding. It is quite intelligent, and knows that if the light were taken from it, then the darkness would remain isolated, unmanifest and without splendour. The darkness would be powerless, weak, ineffectual. The darkness is constrained therefore with all its intelligence and understanding to hold down to itself the lustre and spark of the light together with the fragrance of the spirit.

Comment

While this may appear to contradict the previous, the subject has moved on to the *power* of the principles, and not the principles themselves. In the Hindu doctrine, the triune Brahma, Vishnu and Shiva each have their Shakti, these being named Laxmi, Sarasvati and Parvati respectively—'Shakti', as with the Egyptian Sekhet and Hebrew Shekinah, means 'power' or 'presence'. Comparison may be made here with the 'darkness' attributed to Binah in the Qabalah, which means 'understanding' or 'intelligence'. Binah does not stand alone and separate, but is within the union of the triune principles—and in fact in many ways, she binds them together, or as it is put here, she receives the combining of the light and the spirit, and holds them to herself, as it were.

---

[251] See 'The Star of the Order'.

3. One can see this nature reflected in the image of a man's face, namely, the pupil of the eye. The pupil of the eye is dark because of the waters underlying it, yet illumined by spirit. As the darkness contends for the splendour in order that it may make a slave of the light-spark and see, so also the light and the spirit contend for their own power. They strive to raise and bring back to themselves those powers mingled with the dark and awesome water beneath.

Comment

The pupil of the eye is used analogously across many traditions. It is the centre, and so like the primordial centre itself; yet it is also a void or opening, which is the receptive power, for by that the eye is able to observe. The 'image of a man's face' is also used in the Qabalah to symbolise the primordial light reflected in the waters of space. This is shown geometrically by the Creator holding an upward-pointing triangle that shines its light onto a downward-pointing triangle, and an image of the Creator is shown forth there, though it is an inverse one.

4. Now all the powers of the three principles are infinitely infinite in number. They are sagacious and intelligent—each according to its own essence. They are countless in multitude yet being sagacious and intelligent they are always at peace—so long as they remain by themselves. If, however, one power is brought into contact with another power, the dissimilarity in their juxtaposition brings about a certain energetic motion. This takes its shape from the simultaneous stirring of the juxtaposition of the contacting powers. This is somewhat like the impression of a seal struck off by concussion. The seal resembles the die that makes its impression upon the substance of the seal. As the powers of the three principles are infinite in number, and from the infinite powers are infinite concurrences, then images of infinite seals are necessarily produced. These images are the forms of the different kinds of living creatures.

Comment

Herein is described how the sum total of all manifestation comes forth from the powers of the triune principle. It is here explained how dissension, disturbance or conflict appears in the world, and yet this is inevitable as it derives from the manifesting power itself. While resting in the principle, there is difference but no separation. As manifestation must naturally lead outwards and away from the principle, then the further away that it travels the more increased are the possibilities for disorder and conflict.

This mirrors the Cosmic Cycles, explained previously, where at the beginning of a great Manvantara, manifestation is closest to the primordial centre.[252] Towards the end of the Manvantara there is an increase of darkness in the inferior sense of that word, which is ignorance. The first Yuga is the Age of Gold, the second the Age of Silver, the third the Age of Bronze and the fourth and last the Kali Yuga or Age of Iron. The 'seals' or impressions referred to, which are stamped or carved out, as it were, upon the *prakriti* or ground substance through the action of the multitudinous powers, bear a great likeness to what is described much later in the Qabalistic tradition, where receptacles or vessels are hollowed out, each being receptive or passive to that above, and transmissive or active to that below.

5. Now from the first mighty concurrences of the three principles there comes forth a mighty type of seal, Heaven and Earth. Heaven and Earth have a configuration resembling a womb, with the embryo in the middle. In the gravid womb of every living creature can thus be seen the perfect model of Heaven and Earth and of all things between them. And this is all as according to the first concourse of the three principles. In the midst of Heaven and Earth infinite concourses of powers occur again and again. Each effects and expresses the image of nothing else but the seal of Heaven and Earth, which is alike unto a womb. In the Earth itself there develops from the infinite seals of every kind of living creature the fragrance of the spirit together with the light. And it is as sown and distributed therein.

Comment

This section is a recapitulation concerning the perfection of the first triune principle, which is beyond manifestation. The mighty type of seal of Heaven and Earth that Hippolytus describes as coming forth from the three Sethian principles may be compared to the Taoist I-Ching, the *yang* Heaven and *yin* Earth principles. These are the basis of manifestation but are not part of the manifest world or states of existence. The seal is likened to a womb archetype for all created life, containing an embryo. The Greek word used for 'embryo' is literally 'navel', standing for any nucleus or centre such as the hub of a wheel, which is as the primordial centre reflected in the Cosmos, usually symbolised as the Pole Star.

---

[252] Cf. 'Cosmic Cycles'.

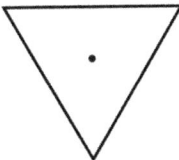

Comment: The Yantra or 'womb' with *bindu*, or the mighty seal of Heaven and Earth.

6. Accordingly, there arises out of the awesome water a first-born source—a wind-vehement and boisterous genesis. For by making a seething ferment in the waters, this wind raises up waves from the waters. The genesis of the waves, being as it were a certain pregnant impulse, is the source of the production of man or mind whenever it is quickened by the impulse of the spirit. Whenever this wave, raised from the water by the wind and rendering nature pregnant, receives the female power of production then it keeps down the light that has been sown into it together with the fragrance of the spirit. That is to say, mind that takes forms in the various types is a perfect God, brought down from the ingenerable light and spirit into a human nature, as into a temple. Such a God is brought down by the course of nature and motion of the wind, generated from water, commingled and blended from bodies as though it were the salt of existing things. The light of the darkness then struggles to be freed from bodies, to find liberation from itself.

Comment

Hippolytus ascribes the earliest form of the Christian Gospel writings to the Sethians, and it is very clear from the above, and what follows, that it was a great influence on the Egyptian Valentinus, reckoned to be the first Christian theologian. This is the foundation of all Gnostic scriptures that followed, including matters essential to the Christian doctrine.

The section begins with a further stage on the descent towards corporeal manifestation, which may be likened to the ninth sephira Yesod, the Foundation of the Tree of Life. The divine name afforded this is Shaddai El Chai, affirming that all life owes to the living Spirit of God. And yet, in the 'fall' into the densest or most material level of manifestation, man is imprisoned and seeks liberation, which can only be attained through knowledge—by which is not meant here knowledge in any ordinary or conventional sense, but that which is more akin to the *ynana* of the Advaitans.

7. Every thought and care of the light above, therefore, is how and in what way mind may be liberated from the death of the evil and dark body, from the Father below, who is the wind that in ferment and turmoil raised up the waves and brought to birth perfect mind, son of himself, and yet not his own in essence. For He was a ray from above, from that perfect light, over-powered in the sinuous and awesome and bitter and blood-stained water; and that light is the Spirit of Light borne upon the water.

Comment

The 'Father below' is clearly the Demiurge, whom some Gnostics called Ialdaboath, abortive child of the divine Sophia. Thus Christ, or any true avatar, is born into the earth but is not 'of the earth', being of spirit. Thus we are told of the descent of the avatar to be born into the flesh as a terrestrial man, so as to open the ways for salvation and deliverance. This cannot be accomplished by the self-alone, which is in itself a condition of ignorance that binds the soul to ignorance, and keeps her confined in the lower worlds. Malkuth abuts on to the world of shells or Qliphoth, these being essentially the intrusions from the outer darkness that seek the annihilation of the soul. One must constantly turn the mind towards the light, which is above and beyond the personal domain. So long as the person remains fixed on himself, he is enslaved by the power of a vengeful God who exacts judgements upon him.

8. But the wind, being both boisterous and vehement in its rush, is in its whistling like unto a serpent—a winged one. From the wind, that is from the serpent, the source of generation arose in the way that has previously been said—all things receiving together the beginning of generation. When then the light and the spirit have been received down into the impure and disorderly womb of manifold suffering, the serpent—the wind of the darkness, the first-born of the waters— entering in generated man, and the impure womb neither loves nor recognises any other forms other than that of the Serpent. And so the Perfect Logos of the Light from above having made Himself like unto the Beast, the Serpent, then entered into the impure womb, having deceived it through His similitude to the Beast; in order that he may loose the bonds that are laid upon the perfect mind that is generated in the impurity of the womb by the first-born of the water—Snake, Wind, Beast. This is the Servant's Form; and this is the necessity of the descent of the Logos of God into the womb of the virgin.

But it is not sufficient that the perfect man, the Logos, has entered into the womb of the virgin and loosed the pains that are in that darkness; nay, but after entering into the foul mysteries in the womb, He washed Himself and drank the cup of living water bubbling-forth—a thing that everyone must do who is about to strip off the Servant-form and put on the Celestial Garment.

Comment

The word used for the hissing sound made by the wind of spirit may also suggest the fluting pipes of Pan, the All-begetter. The hiss of the serpent is the primal vibration that animates all things, while the flute was the wind instrument played by Greek shepherds who brought the divine child to the Rites of Eleusis. However, here, the Serpent of Generation, which is the inferior aspect of Hadit—for in him is also man's reason, which is the knowledge that brings only death—is here named as the 'first-born of the waters', and also the 'Beast', and that is to say, he is an inverse reflection of God, no different really than Satan.

The practice itself, or one of its primary aims, is called 'stripping off the Servant-form', which is to discard the enslavement to the Beast or Leviathan, the Dragon of Time and Death. This is the task of the 'perfected' or Universal Man, of which the pharaohs and Christ, or other avatars, are the type. To liberate oneself, the body of flesh must be transformed into a Celestial Garment. The Celestial Garment equates to the incorruptible soul, which the ancient Egyptians called the Sahu. The body of the King—the human ego or *ahankara* in Tiphereth—dissolves as aromatic essences that return to the heart of Nuit in her infinite or principial aspect.

The above text is a key to the Valentinian Gnostic 'Thirty Aeons', in which Christ and Mary Magdalene, or Sophia (in fleshly form) is the means of liberation from the magnetic restriction of the coils of the dragon that encircles the world, as it is symbolised in the Qabalah. Here, the Light disguises Himself, through being born in the flesh, as the Beast or Serpent of Death so as to pass upwards through the Aeons and return Magdalene, who must follow him, to the primordial or Supernal Garden of Eden. Mary Magdalene is absolutely essential to this initiatic return, which is the means of return for all men and women that are capable of it. She must receive the seed of Light, as a virgin, which is to say she must receive the pure consciousness of Atma in her womb, so to speak—for that womb is a reflection of the primordial principle. Thus she is the Soul and Christ is Logos, her Word.

While it is not always wise to correspond every trinity with every other trinity, as these can have very different meanings and context, it seems not without some justification to equate the triune principle of the Sethian Gnosis with that of the alchemical tradition. In this case, light is the equivalent of Mercury, darkness is Salt, and spirit or fragrance corresponds to Sulphur. The latter is the radiating force, always transmitting its rays outward from the centre, from within. It has a correspondence with the will, so long as that is understood in the sense of Thelema, which is a Divine Will or ordinance. As we have frequently stated, this has nothing to do with any psychological or personal will-determination. Alchemical Mercury is as *yin* to the *yang* of Sulphur; it is nearly always regarded as a reflective feminine or aqueous principle—this is particularly emphasised in the Tarot, where the Priestess II is the 'higher moon', alchemical Mercury and also the letter *gimel*. Salt is 'body' and is fixative or stabilising.

When we arrange these principles vertically, in accordance with how they are described in the Sethian Gnosis, then a very interesting and useful symbol emerges. Sulphur as 'spirit-fragrance' is placed centrally, and we must remember it acts on the other two—none of the principles are separate in nature. Mercury (☿) is then placed at the top and Salt (⊖) at the bottom. We can place with this the square or cube. The symbol of Sulphur (🜍) is sometimes represented by a square or cube surmounted by a triangle or pyramid. In the early stages of the work, the active Sulphur works on Salt to overcome inertia. But in the later stages, once the first Mercury has appeared, then Sulphur works on Mercury and creates the 'double Mercury', which is also likened to the universal solvent or agent, the Astral Light. The final stage is then to 'fix the volatile', which brings Salt into play once more. This produces the philosophic stone and simultaneously there is a return to the principial state, which is the goal of the Great Work.

Now it can be seen, as we have placed the principles here in a vertical column, that Mercury works *inwards* as a centripetal force, as opposed to Sulphur working *outward* from within. The combined action creates a movement. This can be posited by a wheel or circle around the three principles that is very much like the Wheel of Force, called 'Fortune' or sometimes 'Destiny' in the Tarot. Whichever way we see the direction of motion, there will always be an ascent of the circle on one side and a descent on the other. This is the ascending and descending force, which also equates to the two doors of the Lesser and the Greater Mysteries.

In terms of the round of the year, the ascent is from the winter solstice of Capricorn, and the birth of the light into the darkness of the world, towards the summer solstice of Cancer. From the summer solstice to winter solstice is the descent, which is also the initiatory path—for man enters at the summer solstice, and makes his exit from the corporeal world at the winter solstice, and these are called the 'door of man' and the 'door of the Gods'. Once the being has passed through the door of the Gods, and departed from the cosmological sphere, the departure is final, as is all initiation in the real sense as opposed to the symbolic or virtual. This situation is only reversed in the case of an avatar, who ascends and then *re-descends*, is 'born into the earth' so to speak, to fulfil a special mission to help others make the ascent.

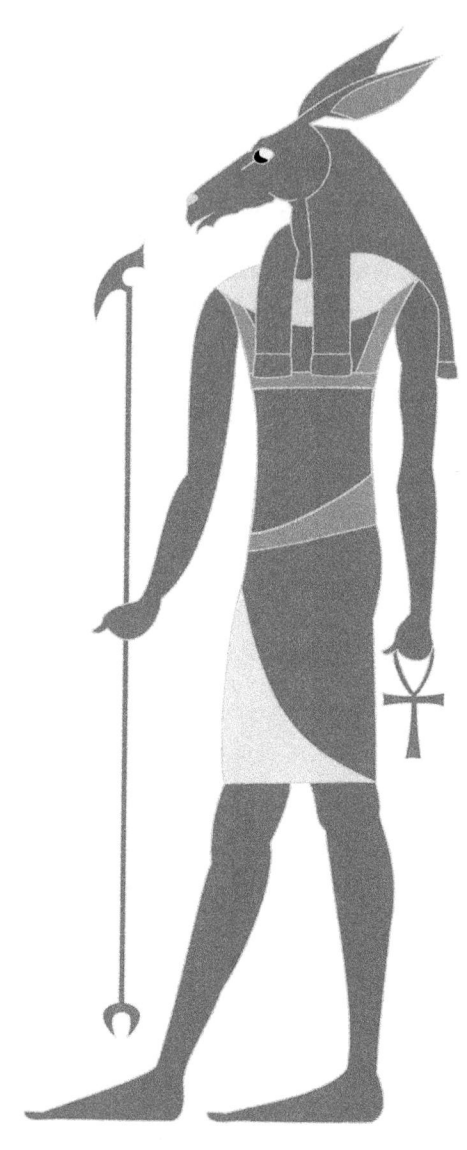

IAI (from Egyptian Tarot)

The Ass of God

There are further aspects to consider concerning the Sethian Gnosis. In the Valentinian schema of Thirty Aeons, as was previously stated, the Master Emmanuel casts off the 'Servant-form' and puts on the 'Celestial Garment'. To receive the five words that were hidden in the seamless robe he had to re-ascend, after having redescended from full and complete spiritual realisation. While an avatar can descend the worlds, having already made the full ascent he does not revert to a previous state; he remains what he is forever. In that way he adopts a 'garment', which is a modality, while remaining unchanged. In another sense, as he remains what he is, he only appears in the modality that those in the lower worlds can see. A person strictly limited to the corporeal state cannot see him at all; to them he does not exist. Or if they see him then they see only what corresponds to the individuality, which is a very small fraction of the total being. This difficulty was emphasised in the Gospel narratives, where, even after the transfiguration of Jesus on Mount Hermon, the disciples still struggled to see beyond the 'person' even to the end—the fact that they were present and saw the transfiguration did not change their state of being as such.

In the Sethian Gnosis it is said that the perfect Logos of the Light is only born into a semblance of the womb of necessity, which owes to the foul Serpent born of the lower waters—the inferior aspect of Hadit. That is the mystery of Christ Jesus being born into the womb of a virgin. He only appears to be of the world and like the Serpent or Beast below; he is disguised by the appearance or semblance but in reality is born purely of the Light. The 'casting off of the Servant-form' is not only what an avatar does:

> He washed Himself and drank the cup of living water bubbling-forth—a thing that everyone must do who is about to strip off the Servant-form and put on the Celestial Garment.

The cup of living water is mentioned in the Orphic mysteries: 'I am a child of earth and stars but my race is of the heavenly order'. Ascent, descent, redescent and reascent are only possible from the centre, which is on the axis where the horizontal meets the vertical. That is evident from the sephirotic Tree of Life but is expressed more simply as a cross, where the horizontal bar is 'time' and also the human state, among all other possibilities.[253]

---

[253] Cf. 'Metaphysical Basis of Thelema'.

The vertical bar is the pillar of the primordial, which has its source at the 'top' (*purusha*) and its complete manifestation at the 'bottom' (*prakriti*). It is only from the centre where any of this can be known by the human. The vertical axis is Will and the horizontal bar (or circumference) is Love. Our commentary on the Sethian Gnosis says,

> To liberate oneself, the body of flesh must be transformed into a Celestial Garment. The Celestial Garment equates to the incorruptible soul, which the ancient Egyptians called the Sahu.

If it is a seamless garment, then it belongs beyond the cosmological sphere. But in time and space all the individual possibilities are to be fully realised. Unless this is so, there can be no real and lasting departure from the individual state. The individuality is by definition the separate self, the human ego and psyche. There is an integral individuality where all the possibilities are realised but that is still in the domain of human possibilities, even if these are extended.

The 'Celestial Garment' at once brings to mind the figure formed by the natal horoscope, for it is a 'map of the heavens'. As a terrestrial view of the heavens at the birth 'moment', the natal horoscope indicates particular possibilities as limited and defined in time. It is the 'child of earth and stars' but not the 'heavenly race', for that is concerned with universal possibilities—'universal' here must not be taken to imply 'cosmological'. By casting away the Servant-form, the being is liberated from all terrestrial limitations and enters into the metaphysical Heaven, of which Earth is the reflection at the lowest polar extreme.

The avatar assumes a Celestial Garment on the reascent, which is a way of saying that he assimilates the celestial influence to transmit it to the worlds below. As the mediator he is 'in the middle', at the centre of a cross where the vertical and horizontal bars meet. To avoid confusion, it should be restated that there is a primary centre at the top of the axis and a secondary centre in the middle, equivalent to Tiphereth. And to be quite clear, the natal horoscope can only be a type of the Servant-form as it is what defines the human.

There are two distinct degrees along the vertical will-column. The first is the 'perfected man', the ancient Egyptian truth-speaker or *ma'a kheru*, in the middle between Heaven and Earth. The second is the Universal Man, beyond the cosmological sphere altogether. These terms are a little bit unsatisfactory but at least they distinguish the second and third birth.[254]

A further clarification is necessary. The Greek word *eidolen* is sometimes defined as 'image'. While this is better than what is said in conventional dictionaries, which degrade this to the level of 'idealised person or thing', the more exact meaning is 'essence', which has nothing to do with images as such. The essence is the *purusha* that has its abode in the heart of Brahma but pervades the whole axis, of which the lower half translates into *prakriti*, 'substance'. But neither *purusha* nor *prakriti* is in the world of manifestation. And so, when it is said in certain Egyptian translations, 'I am the eidolon of my father', which refers to the principle itself, and which is a quality of the Son (or Hermes-Thoth) as he appears on the Middle Way, the term 'image' is misleading. In the same way the biblical translation of God as making man 'in His own image' is far from exact.[255] It is more 'of the essence', which is *purusha*.

A further confusion comes about when the word 'idol', from whence 'idolaters', is not understood as having anything to do with the divine essence but is only thought to be the appearance of a thing. The accusation of idolatory against the 'worshippers of pagan gods' then owes to the ignorant state of those who make it.

The horizontal bar of the axial cross is then Love, and the vertical axis is Will. Love and will, in the metaphysical sense, are not separate in reality; they only appear to be separate from the point of view of the divided self. It is at the centre of the horizontal bar, where the axis and horizontal meet, that these are no longer perceived as separate—both Will and Love rest with the principle. And for the human, it is only from the point of view in that central position that anything can be known at all about what is beyond it. Love and Will are the first duality that emerges from the indivisible principle. They are also like *purusha* and *prakriti*, essence and substance—two poles of one axis. Also, they are comparable to the alchemical Sulphur radiating outward and the Mercury closing inward.

---

[254] This matter is explained by Guénon, *The Great Triad* [Sophia Perennis].
[255] To confound matters further, the word translated as 'God' in English is actually Elohim, 'Gods male and female'—for it is only by a combining of the 'essence' that man could be 'created'.

From the point of view of the axis, manifest principles could be this or that; some definitions are a matter of pure expediency. It might not seem to make any difference—one could take this view or that for there is no contradiction at the centre of all. The Will is not even a part of manifestation in that respect, as is also the case with *purusha* 'essence'. From the point of view of the horizontal and also the human, definitions can seem to make a good deal of difference because what moves, or appears to move in time, makes definition, it delimits in the same way that what is 'past' has become defined. Or at least it appears to be the case until the centre is reached. If this centre is part of the individual possibility, then one may be in it at any moment and then perhaps not in it the next moment. It is the moment of the centre that is the real 'moment', in which all things occur simultaneously. Furthermore, any horizontal axis is at the same time an axis of its own kind, especially as it must cross the vertical axis at the central point. It is a radius in respect to the centre and circumference. And in this case, then from the terrestrial point of view the primordial polar source exists far back in time, at least as far as the formation of some particular cosmic cycle.

The Middle Way always gives rise to the idea of priestly sacrifice, which in the Egyptian tradition is depicted usually in the form of Set, or of Ra in the form of the Ass God—which in some respects amount to being the same thing, for the Ass is a Setian animal. Those who have accepted into their self the humanistic prejudice conveyed by what passes for 'education' will hate any kind of sacrifice whatsoever. They will even dislike any discipline so long as it appears to them to be external to themselves—a view that is both true and false in itself, for the self does not exist without the higher principle. These cannot admit to a higher principle; to them it does not exist. The humanists reduced everything to the lowest and most degraded level possible and for those who accept rationalism, there is no escape.

The sacrifice of love, as a matter of the heart, or out of what is known in the heart, is made out of love—and that does not involve 'subservience' or even any kind of pain, whether inflicted externally or through self-admonition, for as it derives from love it is from the centre of all. In that way it is perfectly natural, because it is true. The Devil finds it easy to lie. For the Son of Light, a lie is an impossibility.

The hieroglyphic spelling of the Egyptian Ass God IAI consists of three flowering reeds and the vulture—which is sounded as 'A' and is comparable to the Hebrew *aleph* and Arabic *alef*. Both hieroglyphs have associations with Ma'at, Mut and 'truth'. It is sometimes said that the first or 'secret' name of God, before EL, was 'I'.[256] The letter 'I', like the Hebrew *yod*, is the symbol of the metaphysical 'point' or principal and its extension into the pillar or world axis. The 'I Am' of AHIH, the word that was given to Moses on Mount Sinai, indicates the principle, and the word adds to 21.

Strangely, IAI also adds to 21 (by Hebrew values). It is an expressive symbol as we have the '11' or two pillars and between them the 'A', which is also the primordial (as *aleph* is equal to 1), and can be figured as a pentagram.

I	A	I
A	A	A
I	A	I

IAI can form a Saturn Kamea of nine squares with either the centre square left empty or an 'A' put there, in which case the sum total is 45, the correct number of Saturn and a number of the Moon by the extension of Σ (1–9) = 45. This emphasises the special relation between Saturn and the Moon, the rulers of the two solstices of the year. It also depicts an equal cross composed of five A's, and there is a principial figure 'I' on all four corners—the cornerstone reflects the capstone.

---

[256] See Guénon, 'The City of Willows', *The Great Triad* [ibid].

The letter 'A' in the centre could also be reversed, to indicate that from the supra-cosmic point of view the world tree depends from the principle, where it has its root, and not the other way around. If the centre is left empty then the square adds to 44, which is a multiple of 11 expressive of the 'manifestion of perfect harmony'.

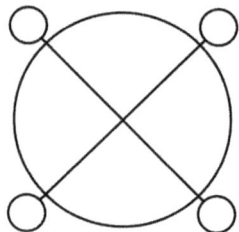

If we draw a circle around the A's and then connect the four I's in the corners with two lines then the Seal of Jupiter is formed, as though Jupiter were contained within Saturn, which it actually is, as Saturn is the higher principle.[257]

The Ass is both Ra, the principle, especially in his aspect as burning heat (Sulphur) and the 'resistance' (Mercury), which is also the 'Servant-form'—the 'stubborn Ass', or otherwise the 'rebellious Ass'.[258] It is said that the Ass carries the Ark, for it carried Jesus into Jerusalem. In Egypt, the Ass God was the opposer of Apep, who threatens to stop the Sun Boat of Ra every evening with his hypnotic stare—to overcome Apep, the Ass is (apparently) 'sacrificed'. In some other accounts, the companions of the Ass (IAIU) defeated Apep by using their power of enchantment![259] Furthermore, the companions are the 'Old Gods', which would place the Ass with Set as of Atlantean origin at the very least.[260] Finally, the hieroglyphic symbol for the Egyptian King's Jubilee, which was worked out on a 30-year and 3-year basis corresponding to the motion of Saturn, has two pillars (11), each surmounted by a head of Set. One wears a plume of Ma'at and one has the ears of an Ass.[261]

---

[257] Jupiter is exalted in Cancer, sign of the summer solstice. There is also in this something of the mystery of 7 as the invisible part of the Sun, the axis or 'seventh ray', and also of the addition of the numbers 3 and 4 to make 7.
[258] See Bika Reed, *Rebel in the Soul* [Wildwood House Ltd.].
[259] See Budge, *An Egyptian Hieroglyphic Dictionary* Vol. 1 p. 17.
[260] *The Egyptian Tarot* has the Ass in place of the 'Magician' of the older Tarot decks.
[261] See the illustration p. 154.

Monas Hieroglyphica

There is a small book written as long ago as 1564 that, through the use of alchemical and Pythagorean numerical and geometrical analogy, is a remarkable accomplishment in its ability to convey the 'secret' of true metaphysics. The language of symbolism is the most direct way to convey metaphysical reality—that which encompasses all beyond the physical, which is the etymological meaning of 'metaphysics'. Ancient languages, with their subtlety of etymology, roots of words and phonetics, are perfectly well equipped to symbolise metaphysics, which is solely concerned with principles. The earliest forms of the written word, for example the Egyptian hieroglyphs, are in truth a language of symbolism. The difficulty with all modern languages is that they are incapable of supporting that which is conveyed through the ancient languages.

Before metaphysics can be explained discursively in a modern language, the terms used must be in some cases redefined, lest there be error. Metaphysics, in the sense we use it in this book, is not a branch of philosophy or of any other science.[262] Philosophy and other modern sciences were derived from metaphysics and not vice versa. René Guénon coined the use of the term 'metaphysics' that we have adopted, as there is no word in a modern language for that which he wanted to explain. This particular use of the word owes to its etymological meaning and has nothing to do with 'abstraction', as is falsely put in modern dictionaries. Metaphysics is concerned with the principles that amount to pure knowledge and are most adequately set down in the Hindu Vedas and Vedanta. Inevitably, Sanskrit terms are sometimes used; there are no words in modern languages to describe Atma or Brahma, let alone the vast array of technical terms.

The book referred to above is the *Monas Hieroglyphica*, written by John Dee, the Elizabethan astrologer, alchemist and scientist. His book was dedicated to the King of Bohemia, as a gift, for reasons perhaps best known to himself. Before going further, we should say that the reading of a book will not convey any 'secret' at all to anyone that does not already know that secret. Metaphysical reality can only be known metaphysically. At the beginning of the book, Dee explains in the first two theorems that,

---

[262] See Guénon's first book (1921), *Introduction to the Study of the Hindu Doctrines*, 'Essential Characteristics of Metaphysics' [Sophia Perennis].

It is by the straight line and the circle that the first and most simple example and representation of all things may be demonstrated, whether such things be either non-existent or merely hidden under Nature's veils. Neither the circle without the line, nor the line without the point, can be artificially produced. It is, therefore, by virtue of the point and the Monad that all things commence to emerge in principle. That which is affected at the periphery, however large it may be, cannot in any way lack the support of the central point.

The *Monas Hieroglyphica* is an exposition on what John Dee called the 'Monad', a composite glyph of alchemical Mercury. Through the exactitude of the geometric numbers and proportion, and through the symbolism of the solstices and equinoxes of the year, the pure metaphysical reality is conveyed. The equinoxes are symbolised through their astrological rulers, Mars and Venus, while Aries is emphasised as the Sun's exaltation at the base of the figure. The Sun, which has the same symbol as the metaphysical point in the circle, which is an analogy for the principle itself, is bisected by the arc of the Moon at the precise midpoint between the centre and the circumference. This forms a *vesica piscis*.

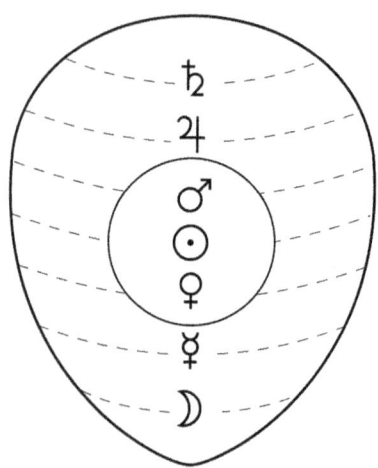

The same principles are shown forth in the 'Celestial Egg' as are contained within the 'Monad' symbol, though after a different fashion. The order of the planets is that of the Qabalah and other traditional knowledge, so that each has its proper numerical value and place in the cosmos. From the top to the bottom, the astrological principles are given the numbers 3, 4, 5, 6, 7, 8 and 9. The Sun, Mars and Venus, depicted within the circled centre of the egg, symbolise the solar ray passing through the twin gates of the equinoxes of the year. It is the metaphysical 'child' or Flower of Mind that it is the object of alchemy to realise. While the centre is placed within the cosmos here, it is in reality beyond the cosmological sphere altogether.

The shape of the egg is more or less identical to that of the human skull and of the symbol used in many traditions of the world for the primordial centre, including the Egyptian *ab* or 'heart' vessel. The Sun, Moon and Venus, which strike a diagonal across the centre of the Tree of Life in the Qabalah, form the number 657, a number that has some remarkable properties. The number has the same value as that of Zelbarachith.[263] The name is probably a corruption of the Arabic Al-barq, a word that nonetheless can be found in both Hebrew and Arabic languages.[264] It is commonly translated as 'blessing' but means more specifically initiatic transmission, a heavenly influence. It may also be likened to the celestial 'arrow of fire' sent down the vertical axis of a cross, as was previously explained.[265] In Hebrew, the word also has derivations that denote 'thunder' and 'lightning', which further affirms the influence from heaven to earth. The horizontal bar of time and space meets the vertical bar or will-column at the exact centre, which is in turn a reflection in the human individuality of the primary or universal centre and source of all. There is both ascending and descending spiritual realisation, for an avatar or other mediator is able to reach down to the secondary centre (Tiphereth of the Qabalah) to initiate the human, without suffering any 'fall'.

By multiplication of the integers, 657 is equal to 210, which has a great many relevant equivalents, not least of which is NOX or 'Night', symbolic of Supreme Reality containing all possibilities—including the totality of manifestation itself.[266] The Night Sky, as in the case of the Egyptian Nuit, is a symbol of the unmanifest state. The supreme principle of Advaita includes the possibilities of both manifestation and unmanifestation. Herein is what appears to be a contradiction: Brahma has a dual nature, but even Shankara would not speak of it. Now it can be seen that if Venus and Mars, the 7 and the 5, are Nuit and her 'star', then the Sun (6) may symbolise the spiritual principle that contains and transcends the two—yet none of these are separate.

---

263 The value is derived from its Hebrew spelling: זלברחית. It is traditionally given as the nocturnal Angel of Leo the Lion. This may be found in our *Flaming Sword Sepher Sephiroth*.
264 In Hebrew the word, or one form of it, is BRQ.
265 See 'Metaphysical Basis of Thelema'.
266 Spelled in Hebrew letters: נעצ = 210. It is curious to note that 210 results from 70 (*a'ain* the 'eye') multiplied by 3 (*gimel* or *gamma*). The Archangel said to preside over the third sephiroth or emanation is Tzaphkiel, the 'Eye' or 'Watcher' of God, for example.

The two principles, which manifest as the primary duality, are not opposite but complementary.[267] Both are contained as possibilities within the supreme principle, which is neither the 'one' of Monism or the 'two' of Dualism. It can only be expressed verbally by Advaita, 'Non-dual'.[268] That happens to be a negative statement, which is best understood as a 'positively negative statement'.[269]

It hardly needs to be explained that the Monas Hieroglyphica and the Celestial Egg of Dee are representations, among other things, of Hiranyagarbha, the 'world egg' as found in the Hindu tradition and all other traditions in various forms. This is not, as is frequently supposed, a symbol of the cosmos. It is the principle from which the cosmological sphere is able to manifest. The arrangement of Sun, Mars and Venus (657) in the centre conveys the impression of the pupil of an eye. This symbolism is also found in all other traditions, as representing the 'cavity' or 'void' (in a manner of speaking) that is the entrance to the 'world centre' or 'heart lotus', the seat of Brahma or otherwise *purusha*, his divine 'essence'. The symbolism of the holy city or palace, called Briah in the Qabalah, will now be looked into.

---

[267] For example, Chokmah and Binah.
[268] When in the first edition of *Babalon Unveiled* we said, in 'Lapis Philosophorum', that Advaita is really Monism and that Buddhism is a rational doctrine, of course this is true of the corrupt versions of these traditions. [268] It happens to be the case that the degraded forms of these traditions are thought by all commentators to be 'authentic', while those carrying real initiatic possibilities are dismissed. And this is even more the case with all Westernised adaptations of these so-called philosophies. What we said of those traditions is true in so far as how they are understood in the West. So there should be no error, we have corrected and qualified this in the Second Edition of the book, so as to reflect the real Advaitan tradition.
[269] See, in particular, pp. 103–4 Guénon, *Introduction to the Study of the Hindu Doctrines* [Sophia Perennis].

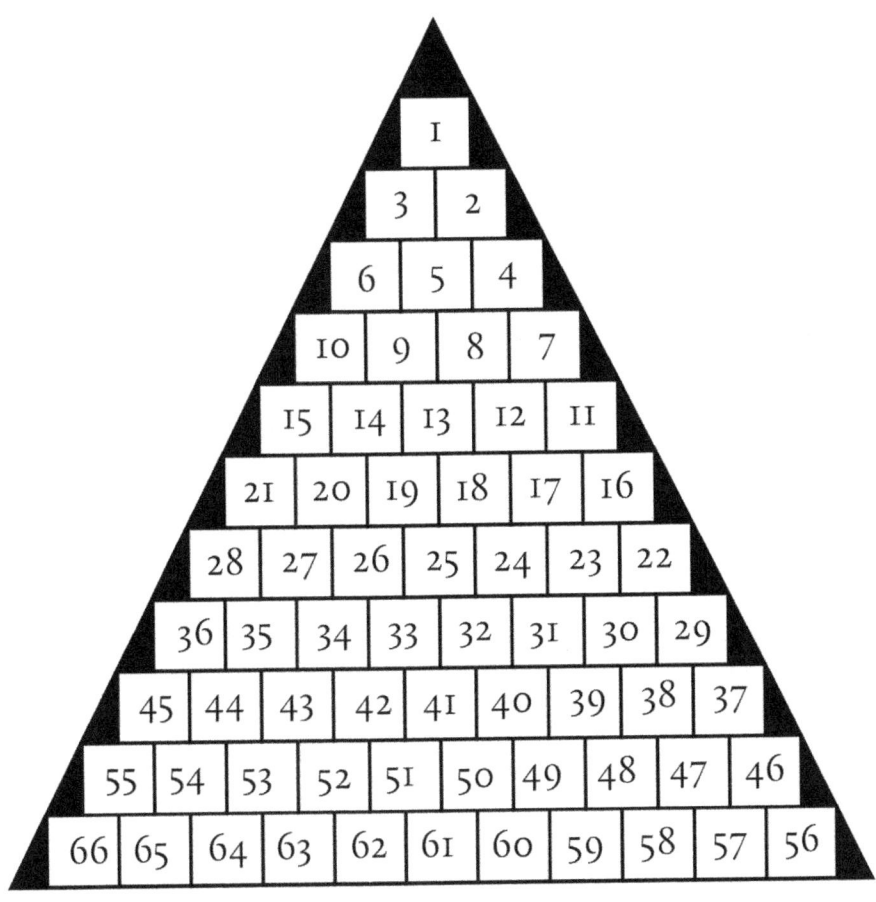

'Paste the sheets from right to left and from top to bottom: then behold!'

Pyramid formed from the triangular number 66 or $\sum$ (1—11), as according to the instruction of the (Egyptian) Book of the Law, III: 73.

The Honeybee

The art of Gematria is a branch of the Qabalah and a traditional science. Sometimes it is confused with Qabalah itself, though the word Qabalah means 'transmission' (and so reception) and refers to the initiatic tradition as a whole, not any particular practical application of that knowledge. Gematria is also frequently confused with numerology. Numerology, however, is not a traditional science. It is merely an arbitrary and invented system of attributions based on numbers, not words, and we will not go further into it here.

Gematria means 'equal to', which is similar in meaning to that of a mathematical equation, where the symbol of Libra (♎) represents the same idea. Words are said to have related meaning if they share the same numerical value. Only the old languages, Hebrew, Arabic and Greek, have number values for letters. Numerical equations are secondary in importance to etymology and phonetics. Words in an old language can have many meanings depending on how they are pronounced, the contextual frame of reference and most importantly, the level of understanding or initiation of the interpreter.

Practicing the art of Gematria then requires that one study the etymological roots of words in the original language; comparisons may also be made thereby with the same or a similar word in another language. The scriptures in the old languages are always unpointed, so that a word is never determined and thereby limited exclusively to one meaning. A determined, specific meaning cannot be universal or metaphysical. When scriptures or sacred texts are translated into modern languages, the traditional meaning and knowledge is lost, unless it is 'amplified' and an initiated commentary supplied.

With the example that follows, it will be seen that when words have the same number in Hebrew, especially old words, they very often share etymological roots and are sometimes what is called a 'permutation' (*temurah*), which means that the letters of a word are the same as another word but appear in a different order. These will frequently have phonetic similarities.

The Qabalistic World called Briah (BRIH) has the value of 217. It is said that a number is known by its factor. The number 217 is equal to 7×31. We could turn this round and say that 217 divided by 31 equals 7, or that 217 divided by 7 is 31. Either way, both 31 and 7 are factors of 217. The arithmetic of the equation $7 \times 31 = 217$ means '7 of 31 is equal to 217'.

Now the number 7 is the centre of the Cube of Space or three-dimensional cross, which produces six directions formed from three lines—the form of this symbol known as the Chi-Ro is depicted to the left. The number 31 is that of EL, one of the oldest names for 'God'. So we can say that 'the centre of space is the centre of God and that is also equal to 217'. Words that are equal to 217 are then worthwhile looking into, as 217 expresses the totality of manifestation.

Briah is most often translated as 'creation', though that has led to some absurd notions, such as that a God brought forth the universe from 'out of nothing', as though from outside of Himself, whereas in fact nothing can be created that does not already exist within. The Latin root, *creat*, means 'produced', which does not have these strange connotations. Another meaning of the word Briah is 'food', or 'produce', which serves to demonstrate how the so-called 'creation myth' of the biblical book of Genesis has undergone confusion and distortion, for Briah is the root of the first word of the first verse of the first book of Genesis, 'In the beginning...' This has suffered distortion through language translations, for even in the Latin, *In principio*, means 'in (or from) the principle', which has nothing at all to do with a linear sequence in time. The principle, which we will mention again later, is symbolised as the metaphysical point in the circle.

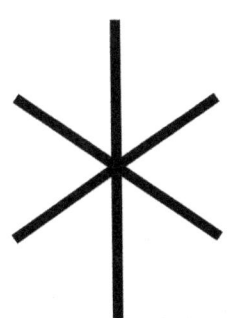
Birah (BIRH), 217, is a natural permutation of Briah, and means 'temple or palace'. What we want to know is, what is the relation of Birah with the principle or the metaphysical point? How can we know something that has no dimension, which does not occupy space, unless there is some 'housing' or space surrounding it? It is through the point's radiations or emanations that the point is known. Space, as we referred to earlier, can be formed into a 'world' by merely three lines. We take a vertical line (or extension of the point) and then bisect it with a horizontal line, forming a cross. A third line is then passed through the centre of these at right angles to both, forming instantly the Cube of Space of six directions: above, below, north, south, east and west.

While this is called the 'Cube', for it naturally forms the six-faced solid, the three-dimensional cross can also be placed in a wheel or sphere. Now it becomes clear why in our *Flaming Sword*, Volume 1, it is said of Briah that it is 'the palace of light that sustains all', for it encloses, as it were, the principle of 'unity' itself, the incommunicable mystery. This is no different from the Egyptian name of Hathoor, Het-hor, 'the House of Horus'. Horus is the principle that abides eternally with a bride and consort that also happens to be his mother, and the Mother of All. As the 'abode' and the 'dwelling' she is Shakti (or Shekinah). The Tree of Life belonged with her since before there was a beginning of things, as it is put in Egyptian sacred texts, and this is once again an allusion to the metaphysical point.

The 'palace of light' is further supported by the word *bohir* (BHIR), which is another permutation of Briah and correspondent of the number 217. Bohir means 'bright, clear or brilliant' and also 'transparency', for it carries an idea that can only be conveyed otherwise in the Sanskrit *darshana*, 'a window or point of view'. The same word is used to describe the 12th path of the Tree of Life, the Intelligence of Transparency, associated with the first numbered Tarot trump, the Magus of Power. Bohir has a shared root with words meaning 'whiteness' and 'spot'; thus it is analogous with the idea of 'seeing the white (or pure) spot', or the metaphysical point in the circle. Bohir has the same root as *bohu* (BOHU). This is usually translated as 'void' but the original meaning includes an 'opening' or 'entrance'; metaphysically it is the door that opens to the inner palace or temple of formless light and is at the same time the 'window' or point of view by which the principle is known.

It has been said that Briah is a 'palace of light that sustains all', for which there can be no better symbol than the honeybee, *deborah* (DBVRH), which is also found under the number 217. The bee is associated naturally with the hexagon or 'six', the solar principle, space, vibration and immortality. The word *deborah* is also a girl's name, as is the Greek word *melissa*, which also means 'honeybee'. 'Honeybee' was an eponymous name for the women that served as priestesses of Hathoor, or of Sekhet, or other equivalent goddesses. The 'honey' is the root of the Greek name for the Elysian Fields (the Egyptian Sekhet-Arat), and through the association with flowers is 'fragrance', or spirit-emanation. Deborah is related to *d'vir* (DBIR), 'vibration' or the medium for vibration, variously called 'ether' or 'space'. Light and sound, at the metaphysical level as well as the physical one, are not separate. They are depicted in conventional physics and in Egyptian hieroglyphs as waveforms.

The Egyptian Ba, often interpreted as 'soul', is synonymous with the bee through the identification with honey as divine 'food' (Briah) of the soul and of the Gods. The intoxication or 'drunkenness' of the lion Goddess Sekhet, as recounted in Egyptian texts, is a metaphor for spiritual exaltation, as is the wine of Dionysus or Bacchus.

Space or ether is needed for light and sound, terms synonymous with the divine Word or Logos. Avir (AVIR), 'ether, space or air' is comparable with the Greek *aer*, 'air', the Latin *avis*, 'bird', and according to René Guénon, Avir concerns the Inward Palace (Briah) by which the metaphysical point is made comprehensible:

> It is that 'point' of the ungraspable ether (*Avir*), in which is produced the concentration whence light (*Aur*) emanates.[270]

According to the Sepher Yetzirah, when the *yod* (left) or 'I', the jot, mark or flame is removed from Avir then what is left is Aur, 'light'. The *yod* is itself a symbol of the metaphysical point, and the 22 letters of the Hebrew alphabet are formed by *yods*, the extensions of light.

Auri (AVRI) is a permutation of Avir and has the meaning of 'fiery, shining or lustrous, of light'.[271] The root of Auri is *Aur*, the light that when woven or coagulated (to use the alchemical term) provides the basis for spiritual transformation. Auri is also a name of the star Sothis or Sirius, the home of the Gods. Sirius has an analogous correspondence with the Nile floodwaters, and is then identical with Avir (above)—for the metaphysical point only occupies space in so far as its radiations or emanations carry it to extension. Furthermore, the 'unity' of the point is only made comprehensible when space is occupied, in which case the point is at the centre.

Iaur (IAVR), a name of the Egyptian Nile, also has the number 217. This is a permutation of Avir, 'ether' and Avri, 'Sirius'. The Nile is an analogous natural symbol, for on the cosmic level it mirrored the glittering Milky Way in now long-distant precessional ages, and on the metaphysical level is the light radiation or first emanation from the principal that is Isis or Hathoor, the 'House of Horus', the divine personification of the principal. Thus the name is cognate with all the terms previously discussed.

---

[270] *The Symbolism of the Cross*, p. 24.
[271] A related Egyptian name, 'Hoori', was the first transmission heard by Rose Edith Kelly in Cairo, prior to the reception of the Book of the Law. A variant on the name of Horus, it means 'sky', 'light' and 'countenance' or 'face', and has every idea of a 'view', 'eye' or 'window' into infinity.

Finally, V-IRA, 217, 'to see, behold', or in its biblical context, 'to see the light' (Genesis 1: 4), is the *darshana* or 'window' by which the principal may be known. These permutations of words all sharing the number 217, concerning the formless light, thus indicate the esoteric or metaphysical means of perceiving the incomprehensible reality.

The House of the Net

An article by Sir Peter Le Page Renouf, 'Neïth of Sàis', was an influence on the orientalist Kenneth Grant, who took the Egyptological confusions of Renouf and then added many more from his fanciful imagining.[272] Egyptologists and historians have looked for meaning in ancient Egyptian words by searching for etymological associations in Greek and Latin. This is, to say the least, mistaken. The Egyptian language is far more ancient than Greek and Latin. The etymology of Egyptian words is in the Egyptian language itself. This is the earliest and most subtle Gematria, for number values are not required.[273] There are thousands of hieroglyphs, and countless ways of spelling and arranging each word and name. One word can have dozens of meanings, depending on how it is pronounced, spelled, and which determinatives are used. This opens an infinite vista of related meanings, literal, metaphorical and metaphysical.

Renouf took the beginning of a Saitic inscription found on a statue of Neïth and then went to considerable lengths to try and prove what was no more than speculative fantasy.[274] Renouf proposes that the bee hieroglyph, which he thinks is a 'wasp', has a phonetic value, and is part of the name of Neïth.[275] He then produces an argument to demonstrate it must be the 'n' in the name 'Net' (Greek Neïth), and not any other sound. In fact, the bee hieroglyph is an ideograph and does not have a phonetic value. The sound and contextual meaning depends on the accompanying hieroglyphs.

---

[272] The article is from *Proceedings of The Society of Biblical Archaeology*, April 1890.
[273] Gematria is a branch or particular application of the Qabalah. See 'The Honeybee'.
[274] The inscription was found on an exhibit at Florence (No. 1522). This is presumably now in the Egyptian rooms, presently located within the Archaeological Museum of Florence.
[275] The Egyptian bee is much smaller than the British variety and has a smaller body, proportionately. This is explained in a wry and very amusing tale by Algernon Blackwood, 'The Egyptian Hornet'.

The honeybee is generally *khebit* or sometimes *af abat*. The honeybee does indeed have a very ancient symbolic relation with the Temple of Neïth or 'House of the Net' in the Egyptian Delta region. The Net, the abode of the Goddess, has a correspondence with the 'Inward Palace' of Briah in the Qabalah, as previously mentioned.[276] The bee makes honey, the food of immortal life, and carries the sting, the poison of death. The bee also symbolises the land of the North generally, Lower Egypt, the swampy Delta region and birthplace of the Gods. This is located in many traditions to the north of their homeland, as symbolising the seat of the primordial.

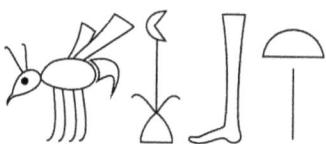

The bee is a royal emblem. It is not a phonetic, *ant*, or *net*, as according to the theories of Renouf. For example, here it is used as the determinative for *khebit*, which means literally, 'little creature that dances on the flowers and makes sweet honey':[277] The word is etymologically associated with the flowering lotus (the *chakra*), and 'honey', its secretion and product. The lotus is Kether as 'Keeper of Treasure' (honey), the equivalent of the *sahasrara* chakra in the Tantras.[278] Beehives were kept at the great temple complex of Sàis (Egyptian Sait) and there was a part of the temple called the 'House of the Bee' (*het-khebit*).[279] The bee is the immortal principle as active, sonic vibration.

When the bee hieroglyph has the definite article (or 't') placed below, then it has the specific meaning of 'to see'. In the context of the inscription, it actually means 'she who is not seen', as it refers to Neïth.[280] While Neïth has many aspects and attributes, the most important of these is that she is the unmanifest principle itself. To continue the comparison with the Hindu Tantras, she is the principle hidden in the triangle in the centre of the *sahasrara* chakra, the ultimate Abode of the Shakti.

---

[276] See 'The Honeybee'.
[277] Reading from left to right, after the bee determinative: 'Lotus in flower', *kha*. 'Small thing', *bit*. Also, without the 't' termination (definite article), we obtain the verb *kheb*, 'To dance, to fly through the air'
[278] The lotus (*kha*) is also used for the number 1000, equal to Kether and Malkuth, 000 or ∞.
[279] Budge, 'Net or Neith', *The Gods of the Egyptians Vol. 1* [Dover].
[280] Budge, *An Egyptian Hieroglyphic Dictionary Vol 1*, p. cxxii, line 33.

Cosmologically speaking, Neïth is the 'other side of the sky', the half of the heavens that is never seen. This brings to mind the fact that one of the images for Kether in the Qabalah is of a face in profile, for while one side looks upon manifestation the other side always gazes on eternity and is not seen.

We can now look at the rest of the inscription and determine its meaning. The first two letters spell Neïth's name phonetically (N-T), while the third carries the meaning of 'hidden', or better still, 'half hidden', as for example when the Sun is still below the horizon but the first ray appears, as a flame or an arrow of light. In context, while Neïth is not seen by any man, she may be known by her appearance, by her 'arrow of light' or her flame. The pyramid with an inset conveys this in another sense, as the indicator of the sky or heavens that carries a secret within.

The 'cross' hieroglyph also means, 'who is in', or 'within' and is sometimes spelled by a simple four-petalled flower. This conveys a rather profound metaphysics. The point where the horizontal plane meets the vertical axis denotes the 'centre'. When the three-dimensional cross is depicted as a wheel of six spokes, the centre of the wheel or 'seventh ray' is the 'mover that does not move', the principle itself, which cannot be modified or determined. The cross as a whole is then the unmanifest principle within manifestation. When the horizontal axis symbolises man, then the centre is the place where he is conscious of the higher and the lower worlds, symbolised by the vertical axis.[281]

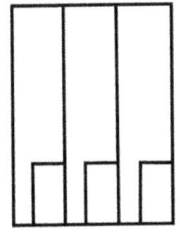

The last part of the opening phrase is the ideograph for 'many shrines' or 'many gods'. The thrones of gods such as Sekhet, often associated with both Neïth and the honeybee, were made of granite. This is an extremely hard, heavy, enduring stone, and includes as many tiny glittering crystals as there are stars in the sky. The Throne or Seat is a symbol of the primordial centre, the Supreme Principal itself, and is found in many other traditions as well as that of Egypt. The opening of the invocation may thus be construed,

Neïth, who is not seen by any man, to whom are many shrines.

The hieroglyphs, as can be seen by the above commentary, convey far more meaning to the Initiate than the translation.

---

[281] Cf. *The Symbolism of the Cross*, René Guénon [Sophia Perennis].

Renouf and later, Kenneth Grant, made much of the arrow and crossed arrows symbol of Neïth, but used imaginative invention to cover their incomprehension. There is quite a lot more to the crossed arrows symbol than the simple notion of shooting an arrow from a bow. Furthermore, a notion of a 'poisoned arrow' was concocted, which was derived from the confusion of the honeybee with the wasp. A further confusion was then made through identifying the 'sting' and the 'arrow'. The arrow hieroglyph is indeed used to indicate 'shooting forth', however, and for example, four goddesses, Isis, Nephthys, Neïth and Selket are said to 'shoot forth flame'.[282]

The Egyptians depicted the pouring forth of light and life as a cascade of small arrow-like *ankhs*. When a flame of fire is specifically intended, then the flame hieroglyph is used, and with the 'shooting forth of flame', the arrow and flame hieroglyphs are used together.

When the arrows of Neïth are in the form of a cross, then the 'centre' or metaphysical point is at the junction of the two shafts. The barbs of the arrows shown here indicate upward movement, towards the primordial source of manifestation. If the crossed arrows are shown pointing downwards, especially in combination with 'house' or 'shrine', then they indicate the place itself as reflective of the higher principle.

When the crossed arrows denote upward or downward trajectory, then ascent and descent of the vertical axis of the world tree or Tree of Life is indicated. It is on the vertical axis that the totality of being is realised. The first crossing on the upward path is that of ritual death or crucifixion, Qabalistically Tiphereth. When this is 'symbolic' only, then it constitutes virtual initiation. For initiation to become effective the renunciation of the personal will or ego wish-desire is a practical necessity, otherwise the way is barred permanently through incomprehension. The second crossing involves the dissolution and reformation in the post-abysmal realisation of the true nature of the Self as continuous with Nuit's 'company of heaven'. In this, there is difference but there is no separation. It is neither the atomistic 'one' of Monism nor any homogenous collection of separate entities.

---

[282] Budge [*ibid*]. The four mentioned were associated with the Canopic Gods and thus served as guardians of the sarcophagus. They were often shown winged and at the corners, equivalent of the cornerstones in architecture.

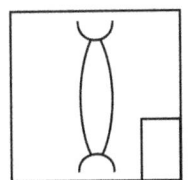
The arrow, whether single or dual, is a complement to another very important symbol of Neïth, the weaving shuttle. When the shuttle symbol is placed within the 'house' or 'shrine' (left) it declares 'House of the Net'. The Sanskrit word *tantra* means literally 'weave' or 'thread', and is also indicative of fabric. The cross-cross pattern made by the warp and weft on a loom was used by the Egyptians to symbolise the subtle 'network' or thread of all life that provides the basis for gross or subtle manifestation and the totality of the indefinite modalities of being. The points of the intersections symbolise both the totality of being and the individual being. The arrow is then similar to the needle, by which thread is passed through the weave of the fabric or 'substance'. Unlike the harpoon hieroglyph, which can mean 'one', the arrow is pure will. The warp and the weft can be likened to the Sanskrit *purusha* and *prakriti*, the vertical and horizontal axes.

The pattern of the warp and weft is called the Web of Wyrd by the Druids, and the 'hair of Shiva' in the Hindu tradition. The 'hair' symbolism is also used in Qabalistic source texts as descriptive of the primordial emanations. It is frequently shown on garments worn by deities, such as dresses, tunics and the nemmys. It is shown on the walls and ceilings of temples, in which case five-point stars may also be incorporated. According to the Book of the Law, I: 3 and I: 59, where the 'hair' is of Nuit:

Every man and every woman is a star.

My incense is of resinous woods and gums; and there is no blood therein: because of my hair the trees of Eternity.

The point of intersection of any two lines symbolises a fifth element amidst the four directions of the arms of the cross. Thus the point in any 'world' or microcosm is the summation of the individuality, while the point in a macrocosm is the universal being. One may also posit a two-dimensional cross and then pass a third line through the centre at right angles to the vertical and horizontal axes, forming the Cube of Space or three-dimensional cross.

The End is with the Beginning

There is a direct allusion to the dual nature of the Supreme Reality in the (Egyptian) Book of the Law, III: 72. This, as with much else in the book, has given rise to speculation and is sometimes used as a justification for merely personal invention or notion. In the light of what has previously been said concerning the Non-dual metaphysics of the Advaitans, the verse is not as abstruse as it appears. Furthermore, while the meaning cannot be discovered through manipulation of the numbering of the verse, for example, in this case that can act as a support.

> *I am the Lord of the Double Wand of Power; the wand of the Force of Coph Nia—but my left hand is empty, for I have crushed an Universe; and nought remains.*

This firstly needs to be looked at in context. Who is this? In the Book of the Law, III: 70, this is made quite clear:

> *I am the Hawk-Headed Lord of Silence and of Strength; my nemyss shrouds the night-blue sky.*

It has already been said, in III: 34, that at the end of time, or the 'fall of the Great Equinox', Horus ceases to appear as the 'mystical God' or otherwise as the object of worship. All religion is exoteric, but the exotericism or outward form must agree with or complement the esoteric or more profound meaning—the exoteric and esoteric are as two sides of one door, where one side is viewed from the outside and the other viewed from the inside. When the esoteric or metaphysical truth is entirely withdrawn from the 'centre', which is symbolised by any church or place of worship, then the exoteric religion effectively ceases to exist, or only continues as a kind of semblance of what it once was. Such a withdrawal of force is here implied. Horus is then transformed into Hrumachis, or the Sphinx, the 'Lord of the Two Horizons', also called the 'double-wanded one' in III: 34. This is identical in meaning to what comes later with the verse in question, where Horus declares himself as the 'Lord of the Double Wand of Power'. The double wand or sceptre was in fact the *nome* centre symbol of Aunnu (Heliopolis), where Horus ascends to the sky or heaven at the end of time or at the end (literally) of the Nile. In ancient times the Milky Way coincided visually with the Nile as seen from Giza, so that the great river appeared to continue on into the night sky as a glittering veil of stars. The phenomenon is no longer there in modern times, owing to the precessional rotation at the Pole.

The 'Hawk-Headed Lord of Silence and of Strength', whose dark blue nemyss covers the whole of the night sky, is descriptive of the same God, though here it is not really a 'God' as such that is being alluded to but the metaphysical principle itself, which has both a manifest and an unmanifest aspect. The 'night', as we have said, is used as an analogy for the unmanifest aspect. We are looking here at a symbol that can be understood in two ways. Firstly, there is the matter of time and the Cosmic Cycles, for we are presently drawing near to the end of a Great Year and of a Manvantara.[283] Then there is the initiatic view, where there is ascent and descent of the vertical axis of a cross, while the horizontal bar is where the will-column is intersected in time and space. The first view is of the withdrawal of the entire manifestation of 'our world' at the end of time. The second is that of the completion of the way or path by those who are able to accomplish the 'third birth' or possibly the 'fourth state' of entering the Supreme Reality.

The words 'Coph Nia' do not comprise any conventional term and must be taken as symbol. The most obvious is as a permutation of the Qabalistic Ain Soph, the second veil of the infinite that precedes manifestation. That, in itself, gives us quite enough, but it is hard to resist some of the numerical analogies that are enclosed within both Coph Nia and the number of the verse.

Coph Nia may be taken as equal, by either Greek or Hebrew values, to 231. This happens to be the Pythagorean Number of the 22 scales of the Serpent of Wisdom, equivalent to both the Tarot trumps and letters of the Hebrew alphabet, which form the connecting paths of the Tree of Life symbol: $\sum (0-21) = 231$. The number is the 'full extension of the Serpent of Wisdom' (or the branches of the Tree of Life). It is then a symbol of the totality of manifestation. As it is also a veiled form of the Ain Soph, then it is the unmanifested principle that contains all possibilities. This is sometimes figured, as we have previously mentioned, by Nox, Night or Nuit.[284]

The reduction of verse numbers to whole numbers is something of an arbitrary assignment but in this case there seems to be some justification for it, as 372 is the number of OQRB, the Scorpion and the name of the 8th astrological sign of the Zodiac. Scorpio is always associated with 'power', which is a dual force in manifestation.

---

[283] See 'Cosmic Cycles'.
[284] See the previous chapter, 'The House of the Net'.

The Western or modern convention is to take one side only of a dual symbol, so commentators associate the scorpion exclusively with death. The ancient Egyptians, on the other hand, were able to understand the scorpion as a symbol of life and of 'breath', the life-giving power. The Egyptian name of the scorpion, *selke*, means 'breath' (also *hedjet*) and this is the equivalent of the Sanskrit *prana*. There is no equivalent in modern languages for *prana*, which is the subtle force, not the physical breath. Without *prana*, however, no creature can live, for it is that which sustains existence of the being.

While the scorpion symbolised the death by 'poisoning' of the mortal soul, as in the legends of Isis and Horus, it was always seen as essential to the resurrection of the immortal soul and was associated with the number seven, which figures greatly in the metaphysical doctrines of all world traditions. From the point of view of the terrestrial human, everything beyond its reach, or which pertains to the non-physical realm, is seen as a mystery as much as is death itself. From the point of view of the initiate, the mortal life is akin to a death-like existence, a mere semblance of the Real.

Lucie Lamy has mentioned that the scorpion feeds her young by what appears to be osmosis, and that is to say, there is no visible means by which she manages to pass sustenance through her hard exterior shell.[285] So long as the baby scorpions cling to the mother, they are nonetheless given life from the mother. This is a perfect analogy for the practice of faith and obedience to the path that is the theme of the legend of Isis and Horus as recorded by Plutarch. The seven scorpions bend down their heads to show the way through the Delta region, for they are obedient to the command of Isis. In the corporeal state, it is impossible to know anything of that which lies wholly beyond the physical domain. Isis is the Mother of Faith, and so long as faith and obedience are practiced at the very outset, life is given to the disciple. This is not of course life in any biological sense (Greek *bios*) but is life in the real sense (Greek *zoe*), which is not separate from knowledge of the immortal principle. The foolish man, as recounted in the narrative, will not hear the word of Isis; he will not 'bend' to a higher truth. But the wise man practices obedience, because he is then able to hear the 'word', which is identical to the root vibration of Aum.

---

[285] Lucie Lamy, *Egyptian Mysteries* [Thames and Hudson 1989].

The etymology of the scorpion OQRB reveals still more. The root QRB contains several Qabalistic 'permutations' (*temurah*). Firstly, the root itself means 'interior' or 'within', also 'to draw near to', which is identical with the Latin-derived 'attain', 'to touch upon'. The interior is the esoteric doctrine and, at its ultimate, the realm of pure metaphysical reality.

BQR means 'dawn', and also 'discrimination', which immediately symbolises the way of supreme knowledge, called the way of Ynana in Sanskrit. In the Egyptian language, Beka is the gate of the future and Manu is the gate of the past as symbolised by the two horizons of east and west, the dawn and the evening.

QBR is 'to protect' and also a 'womb or enclosure', which is the sacred 'cave' or centre, and the 'heart of the world' in all traditions. Curiously, the same word also means 'grave or sepulchre', for some initiatic forms require entry into a tomb—something that is often misunderstoosd, for the exit from the tomb is on the 'other side'. This is symbolised in the Christian tradition, for example, by Mary going to the sepulchre of the crucified Emmanuel.[286] She is alarmed to find no corpse there, for Christ was in the midst of the transformation, having cast off the 'Servant-form' in order to assume the 'Celestial Garment'.[287]

RQB means 'to putrefy', a term used in alchemy to denote the corruptible 'first matter' (*prima materia*) that is worked upon by the radiations of Sulphur; this is a seasonal attribute of Scorpio and the month of October, which is followed in the year by the resurrection or ascent of the Arrow of Sagittarius. The month of Scorpio is said to be the only time when iron may be transmuted into gold—which also marks the end of a Manvantara and beginning of a new cycle from the primordial font.

Finally, BRQ is 'lightning', a flash of brilliant light, and this forms part of the name Zelbarachith that was explained in the previous chapter, the blessing of spirit or initiatic transmission.

We can now look further into the meaning of Coph Nia. There are three 'veils of negativity' in the Qabalah, usually shown as preceding Kether the Crown or first number. These are called Ain, Ain Soph and Ain Soph Aur respectively. They are only termed as negative because what they symbolise cannot be conveyed in language, which must always be positive and determinative. Thus the Advaitan Non-dualism is really a 'negative-positive' assignation.

---

[286] Emmanuel is a name of Christ Jesus and means 'God be with us'.
[287] Cf. 'The Sons of Gods'.

These three principles, very aptly called 'veils', are necessarily contained within the unmanifest principle. Ain is usually translated as 'Negativity', which obscures or takes no account of the fact that the word Ain (אין) is etymologically and phonetically related to A'ain (עין), the 'eye'. The eye receives light through its opening or 'void', the pupil, a symbol of the principle itself—especially as the dark pupil is surrounded by the light or aurora of the iris. It is possible that from this came forth the peculiar Judaic notion of God the Creator, or Demiurge, making the universe 'begin' an existence from nothing, or as outside himself. Whereas of course nothing can be created that does not already exist within. This is further confounded through the simplification that takes place when ancient languages are translated into modern ones. For example, in the same creation myth it is said that the universe was 'formless and void', as derived from the Hebrew Tohu and Bohu. Sometimes this duality is even described as 'chaos and night'.

תוהו ו-בהו

Tohu and Bohu

Multiple confusions arise through translation across more than one language. The Greek 'chaos' (καος) in its original meaning bears no relation to the modern conventionality of 'disorder', 'confusion'. Its meaning is much alike that of Ain as an opening, eye, mouth or aperture.

The related word A'ain, 'eye', is close etymologically and phonetically to the Sanskrit AUM, which conveys a purely metaphysical idea, of which the most outer meaning is that of the universal root vibration. Sound is here used as an analogy for its equivalence in the physical world to the *akasha* or spirit element in nature. Metaphysically, there is no difference at all between hearing a word and speaking it—hence the power of words. The word A'ain is very close, phonetically, to the Sanskrit *ajna*, and has the same meaning, for *ajna* is the chakra of 'knowledge', and AUM is the symbol placed there in the Tantras.

Likewise, the void or 'emptiness' of Bohu conveys no idea of its etymological root as 'the entrance', *baha* (בהא). Any door, gate or entrance is dual. It can be either an entrance, a place of ingress, or an exit, a place of egress—yet it is one door. It all depends on the point of view, or 'window', which is a further relative of Tohu and Bohu and all these root terms, HA, AH, HU.

We might also consider the Arabic letter *ha*, which has the same meaning:

ح

The letter *ha*, in its closed form, resembles an eye. In the Arabic language it is called a 'moon letter' as opposed to a 'sun letter', for it has no phonetic impact on a definite article as does a sun letter. In that sense, the letter may symbolise the 'formless', or better still, something that cannot be limited or determinate in itself. This line of thought could be extended almost indefinitely but by now we can see that 'negativity', let alone 'naught' or 'nothing', conveys nothing of the real nature of Ain, the first veil on the Supreme Reality.

The second veil, Ain Soph, is usually described as 'the limitless', which is not inaccurate but nonetheless conveys a sense of space, whereas the three veils are not within manifestation and are therefore completely beyond time and space. The equivalent Greek word, *apeiros*, 'unlimited', has the value of 767, which is also the number of *ta tekmar*, 'the end'. The end is with the beginning.

The third veil, Ain Soph Aur, is thought of as 'limitless light in extension', although in fact it is not extended at all as we are still in the realm of the primordial unmanifest. The 'infinite light within the hollow of night' might communicate this better, though anything we say will place some kind of limitation on that which is unlimited.

Kether, the first number, the product of the incommunicable, nonetheless has a dual image, which is that of a king in profile. The title Lux Occulta, 'Hidden Light', is aptly applied to Kether as the 'light in extension' is only the side of the face that can be seen. The other side gazes always into infinity. The number three is considered to be the most perfect expression of the unity of the 'one', so there is no need here to go into an explanation of the other nine numbers that form the sephiroth; they can be seen as three triads from which depend Malkuth, the 'end' or manifest.[288] It is no accident, though, that there are nine letters in the Hebrew Ain Soph Aur.

---

[288] See 'Until the Stars be Numbered'.

אין סוף אור

Ain Soph Aur

Comparison may readily be made with the Sethian Gnosis.[289] There, the unmanifested trinity consists of light, darkness and 'fragrance' or spirit, but no exact equivalent may be made as these derive from different traditions, the one Hebrew and the other Egyptian. There is also the dual nature of Brahma, as previously dicussed, and Nuit and Hadit of the Egyptian cult of Mentu at Thebes or Waset. What is essential to all these traditions is that the Supreme Reality contains the sum total of all possibilities for manifestation while at the same time remaining unchanged in itself by any of the infinite possibilities. It cannot be otherwise, for neither the unmanifest nor the supreme principial state can be the product of any other thing whatsoever.

---

[289] Cf. p. 170.

APPENDICES

i
Schiller and Self Love

Information on the letters and biographies of Beethoven owes to an article, 'Nietzsche and Beethoven, Tracing Beethoven's Relationship to Literature and Philosophy'. The article is uncredited but seems to owe to the research of Ingrid Schwaegermann.

The original text from Schiller in German is as follows:

Die Epopten erkannten eine einzige höchste Ursache aller Dinge, eine Urkraft der Natur, das Wesen aller Wesen, welches einerlei nur mit dem Demiurgos der griechischen Weisen. Nichts ist erhabener als die einfache Größe, mit der sie von dem Weltschöpfer sprachen. Um ihn auf eine recht entscheidende Art auszuzeichnen, geben sie ihm gar keinen Namen. Ein Name, sagten sie, ist bloss ein Bedürfnis der Unterscheidung; wer allein ist, hat keinen Namen nötig, denn es ist keiner da, mit dem er verwechselt werden könnte. Unter einer alten Bildsäule der Isis las man die Worte: 'Ich bin, was da ist', und auf einer Pyramide zu Sais fand man die uralte merkwürdige Inschrift:

'Ich bin alles, was ist, was war und was sein wird: kein sterblicher Mensch hat meinen Schleier aufgehoben.'

Keiner durfte den Tempel des Serapis betreten, der nicht den Namen Iao oder I-ha-ho—ein Name, der mit dem hebräischen Jeovah fast gleichlautend, auch vermutlich von dem nämlichen Inhalt ist—an der Brust oder Stirn trug; und kein Name wurde in Ägypten mit mehr Ehrfurcht ausgesprochen, als der Name Iao. In dem Hymnus, den der Hierophant oder Vorsteher des Heiligtums dem Einzuweihenden vorsang, war dies der erste Aufschluss, der über die Natur der Gottheit gegeben wurde. 'Er ist einzig und von ihm selbst, und diesem einzigen sind alle Dinge ihr Dasein schuldig.'

Friedrich Schiller, Gesamtausgabe, Band 6/2: 270-27.

Complete Works, Volume 6/2: 270-27.

ii
Gold Tablet Orphic Inscription

The Petelia Gold Tablet or Petelia Tablet is an orphic inscription inscribed on a gold charm that was found near the ancient city of Petelia, southern Italy in the early nineteenth century. Since 1843, the original has been kept in the British Museum. The translation:

Thou shalt find in the halls of Hades a well-spring on the left,
and by the side thereof, a white cypress tree stands;
Do not approach this well-spring at all.
But thou shalt find another, from the lake of Memory,
With refreshing water flowing forth. And there are Guardians before it.
Say: 'I am a child of the earth and stars;
But my race is of the heavenly order; and this you know yourselves.
And lo, I am parched with thirst and I perish. Give me quickly refreshing water flowing forth from the Lake of Memory.'
And they will give of thee to drink from the holy fount,
And thou shalt enter into the Mystery in the company of the blessèd.
[You must recollect this, upon death.
In right margin: When the shadow falls over all.]

Translation Notes

The inscription on gold (rather like a charm or amulet) was found in Italy, which shows how far and wide the popular cult of Orpheus went. Orpheus, as according to legend, was a brilliant musician. The Orphic rites were essentially a means to enter eternity and so enjoy everlasting bliss forever. The meaning of 'bliss' is better conveyed by the Sanskrit word *ananda*.

'I am a child of the earth and stars' was originally translated as 'earth and the Starry Heaven'. 'But my race is of the heavenly order' was originally translated 'my race is of Ouranos'.

Note that the 'Lake of Memory' is Mnemosyne in the Greek, which is also the name of a goddess.

'And thou shalt enter into the Mystery in the company of the blessèd' was originally translated as the company of 'heroes', in the ancient Greek sense of that, which is a corruption.

We have retranslated and completed the lucanae in the last lines and margin.

The Gold Tablet Inscription

ΕΥΡΗΣΣΕΙΣ Δ' ΑΙΔΑΟ ΔΟΜΩΝ ΕΠ' ΑΡΣΤΕΡΑ ΚΡΗΝΗΝ,
ΠΑΡ Δ' ΑΥΤΗΙ ΛΕΥΚΗΝ ΕΣΤΗΚΥΙΑΝ ΚΥΠΑΡΙΣΣΟΝ.
ΤΑΥΤΗΣ ΤΗΣ ΚΡΗΝΗΣ ΜΗΔΕ ΣΧΕΔΟΝ ΕΜΠΕΛΑΣΕΙΑΣ.
ΕΥΡΗΣΕΙΣ Δ' ΕΤΕΡΑΝ ΤΗΣ ΜΝΗΜΟΣΥΝΗΣ ΑΠΟ ΛΙΜΝΗΣ
ΨΥΧΡΟΝ ΥΔΩΡ ΠΡΟΡΕΟΝ, ΦΥΛΑΚΕΣ Δ' ΕΠΙΠΡΟΣΘΕΝ ΕΑΣΙΝ.
ΕΙΠΕΙΝ· ΓΗΣ ΠΑΙΣ ΕΙΜΙ ΚΑΙ ΟΥΡΑΝΟΥ ΑΣΤΕΡΟΕΝΤΟΣ,
ΑΥΤΑΡ ΕΜΟΙ ΓΕΝΟΣ ΟΥΡΑΝΙΟΝ· ΤΟΔΕ Δ' ΙΣΤΕ ΚΑΙ ΑΥΤΟΙ·
ΔΙΨΗΙ Δ' ΕΙΜΙ ΓΕΝΟΣ ΟΥΡΑΝΙΟΝ· ΤΟΔΕ Δ' ΙΣΤΕ ΚΑΙ ΑΥΤΟΙ·
ΨΥΧΡΟΝ ΥΔΩΡ ΠΡΟΡΕΟΝ ΤΗΣ ΜΝΗΜΟΣΥΝΗΣ ΑΠΟ ΑΙΜΝΗΣ.
ΚΑΥΤ(ΟΙ ΣΟ)Ι ΔΩΣΟΥΣΙ ΠΙΕΙΝ ΘΕΙΗΣ ΑΠ(Ο ΛΙΜΝ)ΗΣ
ΚΑΙ ΤΟΤ' ΕΠΕΙΤ' Α(ΛΛΟΙΣΙ ΜΕΘ') ΗΡΩΕΣΣΙΝ ΑΝΑΞΕΙΣ
⋯ ΙΗΣ ΤΟΔΕ ⋯ ΘΑΝΕΙΣΘ ⋯
⋯ ΤΟΔΕΓΡΑΨ ⋯
In right margin: ⋯ ΓΛΩΣΕΙΠΑ ⋯ ΣΚΟΤΟΣ ΑΜΦΙΚΑΛΥΨΑΣ

iii
Biblical References to the Nephilim

In Genesis, 6: 4: There were giants in the earth in those days; and also after that, when the sons of God came in unto the daughters of men, and they bare children to them, the same became mighty men which were of old, men of renown.

—The Sons of Anak are first mentioned in Numbers, 13: 22, as dwelling in Hebron. In 13: 28 it is said they lived in walled cities.

In Numbers 13: 33: And there we saw the giants, the sons of Anak, which come of the giants: and we were in our own sight as grasshoppers, and so we were in their sight.

Deuternomy 2: 11: Which also were accounted giants, as the Anakims; but the Moabites call them Emims ['terrible men'].

Deuteronomy 2: 20: That also was accounted a land of giants: giants dwelt therein in old time; and the Ammonites call them Zamzummims.

Deuteronomy 3: 11: For only Og king of Bashan remained of the remnant of giants; behold, his bedstead was a bedstead of iron; is it not in Rabbath of the children of Ammon? nine cubits was the length thereof, and four cubits the breadth of it, after the cubit of a man.

Deuteronomy 3: 13: And the rest of Gilead, and all Bashan, being the kingdom of Og, gave I unto the half tribe of Manasseh; all the region of Argob, with all Bashan, which was called the land of giants.

In Deuteronomy 9: 2 it is said: A people great and tall, the children of the Anakims, whom thou knowest, and of whom thou hast heard say, Who can stand before the children of Anak!

Jos 12: 4: And the coast of Og king of Bashan, which was of the remnant of the giants, that dwelt at Ashtaroth and at Edrei.

Jos 13: 12: All the kingdom of Og in Bashan, which reigned in Ashtaroth and in Edrei, who remained of the remnant of the giants: for these did Moses smite, and cast them out.

Jos 15: 8: And the border went up by the valley of the son of Hinnom unto the south side of the Jebusite; the same is Jerusalem: and the border went up to the top of the mountain that lieth before the valley of Hinnom westward, which is at the end of the valley of the giants northward.

In Joshua 15: 13: And unto Caleb the son of Jephunneh he gave a part among the children of Judah, according to the commandment of the LORD to Joshua, even the city of Arba the father of Anak, which city is Hebron.

Jos 15: 14: And Caleb drove thence the three sons of Anak, Sheshai, and Ahiman, and Talmai, the children of Anak.

Jos 17: 15: And Joshua answered them, If thou be a great people, then get thee up to the wood country, and cut down for thyself there in the land of the Perizzites and of the giants, if mount Ephraim be too narrow for thee.

Jos 18: 16: And the border came down to the end of the mountain that lieth before the valley of the son of Hinnom, and which is in the valley of the giants on the north, and descended to the valley of Hinnom, to the side of Jebusi on the south, and descended to Enrogel.

Jos 21: 11: And they gave them the city of Arba the father of Anak, which city is Hebron, in the hill country of Judah, with the suburbs thereof round about it.

And finally in Judges, 1: 20: And they gave Hebron unto Caleb, as Moses said: and he expelled thence the three sons of Anak.

iv
Notes on the Khabs Hieroglyphs

The verb *kheb* (from whence *khebit*, the honeybee), is related to the noun, Khabs, often translated as 'star', although a star, when the literal meaning is intended, is *seba*. Khabs means 'to shine like a star', and has many spellings to show a flame, a light, illumination and so forth.

The Khabs is personified in the name of a goddess, Khabset (above). Khabset is the jewel in the lotus, the goddess who is 'shining or sparkling like a star'.

When the word Khabs has the meaning of 'illumination', or esoteric knowledge, it is spelled with the rolled up and sealed papyrus scroll determinative.

As a living soul or intelligence (Khu), Khabs is spelled with a bird (probably water foul) determinative.

A living star is a flame of fire; the censor determinative is sometimes used therefore.

Selected Works of Oliver St. John

Hermetic Astrology (2015)
Magical Theurgy (2015)
The Enterer of the Threshold (2016)
Liber 373 Astrum Draconis (2017)
Hermetic Qabalah Foundation—Complete Course (2018)
Babalon Unveiled! Thelemic Monographs (2019)
Ritual Magick—Initiation of the Star and Snake (2019)
The Way of Knowledge in the Reign of Antichrist (2022)
Thirty-two paths of Wisdom (2023)
Thunder Perfect Gnosis—Intellectual Flower of Mind (2023)
The Law of Thelema—Hidden Alchemy (2024)
Metamorphosis—Hermetic Science and Yoga Power (2024)
Dreaming Thelema and Magical Art (2024)
Advaita Vedanta—Question of the Real (2025)
Egyptian Tarot and Guide Book (2025 Crossed Crow Books, Chicago)

The dates given are of first publication. All works published prior to 2021 have since been extensively revised and new editions produced.

Contact the O∴A∴
Contact details and information is posted on our website:
www.ordoastri.org

www.ingramcontent.com/pod-product-compliance
Lightning Source LLC
Chambersburg PA
CBHW051047160426
43193CB00010B/1094